MIDDLE EASTERN COOKING

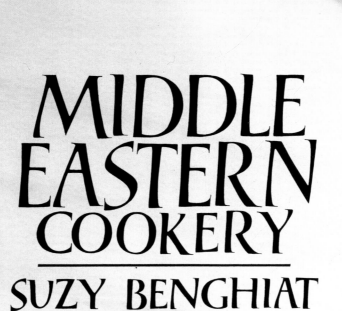

MIDDLE EASTERN COOKERY

SUZY BENGHIAT

SMITHBOOKS

NOTE

1 All recipes serve four unless otherwise stated.
2 All spoon and cup measurements are level.
3 Preparation times given have been calculated from recipe testing and indicate the average time a cook might expect to spend; adjust the time accordingly if you are a beginner or an experienced cook.
4 Cooking times may vary slightly depending on the individual oven. Dishes should be placed in the center of the oven unless otherwise specified.
5 Always preheat the oven, broiler or grill to the specified temperature.
6 If a certain dish can be prepared in advance to a certain point, this has been indicated in the recipe with an asterisk (*).

THIS PAGE Apricot Petits Fours, Konafa and Baklava
(*recipes on pages 128 and 130–1*),
traditionally served with tiny cups of strong black coffee
PREVIOUS PAGE Filo Pastry Borek with Spinach Filling
and Spiced Carrots (*recipes on pages 35 and 88*),
served as *mezze*, with bread rings, *crudités*, olives and feta cheese.

To Pa, Monique and especially Fred for their loving and sustained support

Copyright © 1984 by Suzy Benghiat

Published by Smithbooks Canada,
113 Merton Street, Toronto, Canada M45 1A8

Originally published in Great Britain by George Weidenfeld & Nicolson Limited.

Library of Congress Cataloging in Publication Data
Benghiat, Suzy.
Middle Eastern cooking.

Bibliography: p.
1. Cookery, Near Eastern, I. Title.
TX 25.N36B46 1985   641.5956   84–10916

Reprinted 1993
Printed in Italy

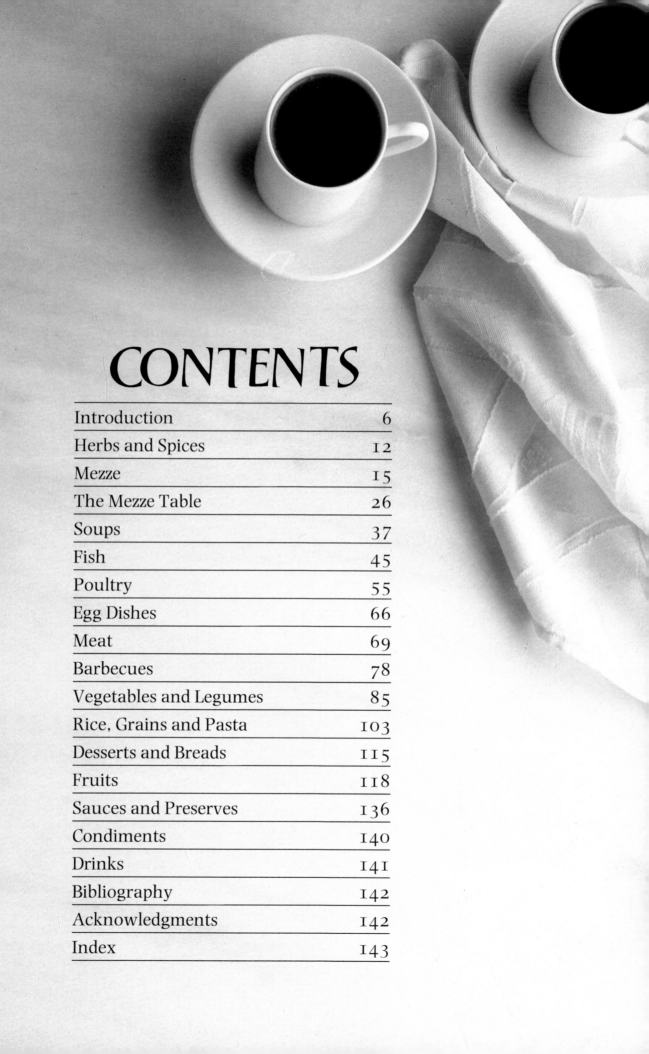

CONTENTS

INTRODUCTION

The choice of dishes in this book is the fruit of over thirty years' cooking experience and constant research and innovation. My experience began long before I myself learned to cook. It is rooted in Cairo, where I was born and spent all my early years before I went to settle in London with my parents and brother.

In fact, Egypt, especially the Egypt of my childhood, is a very good starting point for learning about the cooking of the vast, amorphous area loosely described as the Middle East. Throughout history, the country has been a crossroads of many civilizations, a fact reflected in the composition of its population in the 1930s and 1940s. In the large cities, people of various origins, religions and nationalities had been living side by side for generations, forming an integral part of Egyptian society, yet keeping their own cultural identity and customs. This complex mosaic of groups was loosely defined not only by nationality – native Egyptian, Italian, British, Greek or French – but also by religious tradition and language. Moslem, Jewish and Christian communities embraced the different nationalities, and everybody spoke the local Arabic dialect, French and any of several other languages. Only the British community stood rather stiffly aside. A strong Turkish influence also lingered from the time of the Ottoman occupation, though without much actual Turkish presence. I myself went to the French school, the Lycée, while my brother went to the English school, and we enjoyed a multitude of national and religious holidays.

Cooking is as much a means of expression as language, and of course each nationality kept its own way of cooking. Yet, just as language is alive and changing, so eating habits and tastes were also exchanged and shared. Food in Egypt therefore included elements from the whole range of what is thought of as Middle Eastern fare. There were charcoal-grilled kebabs, *koftas* (meat

Melons on sale by the Caspian Sea, the world's largest landlocked body of water, bordered by Iran and Russia. The Caspian is the world's richest source of the finest gray-black caviar, tiny sturgeons' roe which are treated by salting. Each year, Iran harvests more than 200 tons of caviar, a delicious – and expensive – delicacy, usually eaten as an appetizer.

balls) and fish, with various accompanying dips; savory pastries of different kinds filled with cheese, meats and vegetables, either fried or baked; stuffed vegetables, poultry and fish; rice, couscous and other grain dishes; stews combining meats with fresh vegetables or pulses; candies, desserts and pastries with nuts and dried fruits flavored with rose or orange flower water, or sometimes with mastic, which itself was used as a chewing gum. The *mezze* tradition was important: meals were generally composed of a large assortment of dishes from which one chose, rather than a rigid number of courses served western-style. My mother made dishes mainly of an Italian type. Both she and my paternal grandmother provided Spanish Sephardic specialties and we also had food of Syrian and Lebanese origin – all of these strongly influenced by Turkish cooking – as well as North African and Greek dishes and ones peculiar to the Jews of Egypt. Most important of all was the strong sense of hospitality and generosity that is a feature of the whole region.

Like most children, I had limited tastes, and avoided most soups, cooked vegetables and all sweet things other than ice cream. Even so, I had an enormous range from which to choose. Within Cairo's small Jewish community much diversity had resulted from the migration of peoples. What I liked best of all, however, was the real Egyptian Arabic food of the people: *foul* (beans), falafel and fried fish bought from street vendors, or cooked by the servants for themselves on days when the menu was too western for their taste. In the afternoons I used to slip away from my homework and visit the kitchen to sample their leftovers – which perhaps explains my preference for cold food!

One of my fondest childhood memories is of the time of Ramadan, when Moslems are forbidden to eat or drink during the hours of daylight. I didn't fast during the day, of course (nor did I on the Jewish fast day of Yom Kippur), but I would sit with the servants, cross-legged in front of a huge tray of food, impatiently waiting for the *muezzin* to announce that night had fallen. As this exciting moment approached, groups of servants from the apartment block where we lived would gather on the terrace, each bringing some succulent and fragrant dish. There was always enough to feed unemployed relatives, friends and gate-crashers like myself. There would be Melokheya (page 42), the national soup; *bamia* (okra); rice and lentils; stews; the ever-present *foul* and falafel; salads and a profusion of raw vegetables – lettuces, cucumbers, long white radishes with their peppery green leaves. It was inexpensive fare, but delicious.

Years later, I began cooking under the guidance of my mother in London. My nostalgia for Egypt led me to try, with the naïveté of a beginner, to reproduce what I hoped would be the exact flavor of the tahina dip of a famous popular restaurant or of the kofta in tomato sauce made by our old cook Fatima. Eventually I did achieve some measure of success, and some dishes here are hardly altered from those I ate as a child.

But my choice of recipes for this book is also governed by the way my own cooking has evolved. With increasing experience I have learned both to be more adventurous in my tastes, and to develop my own style. I have also gained a more realistic view of what a regional or national specialty is, in part as a result of my traveling and meeting people from different parts of the world, and in part because American and European interest in ethnic foods has generated a plethora of books – some excellent, some not – which have revealed often quite unexpected similarities. Thus, I have come to realize that a dish we considered typically Egyptian might well be of Turkish origin and eaten in countries as far apart as Yugoslavia and Tunisia. Likewise, I have also discovered many genuinely Egyptian dishes that were unknown to my family. In any one country – particularly one where transport and communications were undeveloped – there is often great diversity between the cooking of the big cities and that of different rural regions where traditions are handed down from mother to daughter, and each family evolves its own style.

Let me give one example of what I mean. A few years ago a young Egyptian friend in London cooked for me what she considered a well-known and typical Egyptian dish: Chicken Kishk (see page 60). She was astonished to learn that it was quite new to me. I later returned to Egypt after twenty-seven years' absence and mentioned the incident to an old schoolmate. Not only had she always known about the dish, but she was even more surprised that I did not, for she had always considered me to have more 'Egyptian' tastes than herself. This brought home to me how limited one person's experience must be.

On the same visit to Egypt I interviewed a nutritionist interested in the food of ancient Egypt, much of which has survived in the countryside remote from foreign influences. As an example, she spoke of *kishk*, and the bewildered expression on my face made her laugh. She explained that the *kishk* I knew was a bastardized metropolitan version. *Kishk* is really a traditional peasant way of preserving milk: wheat is boiled in sour milk and dried in the sun, then crushed.

This description further reminded me of something I had read, and when I got home I looked through my cookbooks and found the explanation in Amaranth Sitas' delightful book on Cypriot customs and cuisine, *Kopiaste*. Exactly the same process is used in Cyprus to make what they call *trahanas*, and there, too, the children eat it like candy. In fact, you can find *trahanas* in Cypriot food stores, and a similar product is used by Iranians and Lebanese.

There are dishes here that I have gradually adapted, sometimes under the influence of other national cuisines. For instance, I do vegetables by the traditional method of cooking them in a simmering sauce; but the example of Chinese food has taught me to cook them very lightly so that they are still crisp. I have made certain changes, such as reducing the amount of fat in a dish, or replacing butter with vegetable oil, for dietary or health reasons. One prevailing myth that I would like to dispel here is the notion that a diet of Middle Eastern food is some kind of key to good health. It is healthy enough, but only insofar as it uses fresh ingredients, freshly prepared, instead of manufactured convenience foods, and because it is well balanced, with plenty of vegetables (often raw), pulses, nuts, fruit and rather limited amounts of meat. If people in the Middle East escape many of the ailments of industrialized society, it is principally because they live simply and cannot avoid at least some strenuous exertion. Those who overindulge in butter, oil and sugar, whatever the cuisine, are prone to exactly the same cardiovascular diseases as westerners.

I am presenting here dishes as I cook them, taking advantage of today's wealth of ingredients from all over the world and of modern kitchen equipment, especially the food processor. Some dishes I have cooked on vacation, perhaps in a trailer or a beach hut, using a single frying pan. Some call for careful planning, others can be improvised in minutes. In a deliberate effort to avoid any mystique about 'authentic' ways of cooking, presenting or eating Middle Eastern food, the presentation of the dishes in the photographs has been left as it might be seen through western eyes.

These recipes represent different aspects of Middle Eastern cooking, but I have deliberately avoided an academic, comprehensive survey of the food of individual countries. With only a few exceptions I have not ascribed a particular location to a dish.

The names, too, of the dishes and ingredients have been chosen in a very arbitrary manner, since each dish is known under many names in the diverse languages of the Middle East. Anyway, the exotic-sounding names of a given dish used in different regions often all translate to some prosaic term such as 'stew'.

Often it is the vessel in which food is cooked that gives it its name, as with the *tajine*. This word for the typical North African earthenware pot with the conical lid has an Egyptian equivalent, *tagen*, which, however, means a wide metal saucepan. The well-known Moroccan and Algerian *tajines* are essentially stews; but those of Tunisia are more like rich omelettes, a kind of cross between an omelette and a soufflé similar to the *eggah* of Egypt, the *kuku* of Iran, the 'Spanish omelette' or the Italian *frittata*.

To confuse things more, different names may be used in one country for the same dish: what is called 'falafel' in Cairo is known in Alexandria as '*ta'meya*'; *melokheya* in Egypt means a leafy plant used for a green soup, while in Algeria and Tunisia the word is used to mean okra pods, which only a botanist would recognize as a distant member of the same plant family. Their relationship is shown only by the fact that both have a slightly glutinous texture – and, incidentally, both have long been favorites of mine! In this book, I have used names either because they are the ones most commonly used in English; or because they refer to a specific dish in one country; or, where neither of these reasons applies, I have generally used the dish's name in colloquial Egyptian Arabic.

Following the recipes

Real cooks do not cook in the ideal way most cookbooks are written, and it is hard to reduce to mere words an activity which relies on taste, smell, sight, skill, judgment and common sense, not to mention creativity – especially when writing for a generation of readers who are accustomed to following a recipe word for word as though it were a knitting pattern. I have tried to come to a satisfactory compromise by giving quantities according to current conventions in the ingredients lists, while at the same time often making it clear in the instructions that the cook has quite some leeway. The ingredients list will be a good guide for the first time you use a recipe, particularly for the inexperienced cook; but my step-by-step instructions also tell you how the food should look or smell, or how flavors develop, to give you confidence to use your initiative. Terms like 'a pinch', 'a touch of', or 'walnut-sized' are accurate enough, and intended to encourage you to rely on your own senses and judgment rather than precise measurements.

Total quantities should also be taken only as a rough guideline, not only because people's appetites vary, but also because the amount one needs of each dish depends on the number of dishes offered. Both with *mezze* or 'appetizers' and in the substantial part of a Middle Eastern meal there are usually a number of dishes to choose from. The recipes here are, unless otherwise stated, for four portions when served in a conventional way; but obviously if you have two meat and two vegetable dishes, served with rice and a salad, there should be enough for more people.

As to the time it takes to prepare a dish, the average preparation time given for each recipe is approximate. The actual amount of time required will depend on how you go about cooking, how well done you like your food and external factors, such as altitude and the freshness or size of your ingredients. You will notice that cooking times are generally given as part of the

Weighing out olives at the Athenian Grocery in London. In recent years, Middle Eastern food stores have become a familiar sight in towns and cities all over the world, offering a wealth of ingredients – from vine leaves to *melokheya*, filo and konafa pastries to ready-spiced coffee – and a source of inspiration to cooks.

total preparation time. This, and the instructions for preparing each dish, reflects the way I teach cooking and the way I cook myself. For example, when making a stew, sauce or soup which requires chopping onions, other vegetables and meat, I do not chop and measure all the ingredients before beginning to cook. It is far less time-consuming to begin cooking the onions in butter or oil over low heat while simultaneously trimming the meat and preparing the other vegetables, starting with those that take longer to cook and adding them to the pot as they are ready. Remember, too, that preparation time depends on your skill and experience. Though I can stuff two dozen vine leaves in less than an hour without hurrying, the first time you try this it will take you much longer.

This leads me to more general advice on how this book, or indeed any cookbook, should be used. Read it first, leaf through the recipes, including the chapter introductions and other notes. In addition to providing step-by-step instructions for preparing individual dishes, my recipes also include general tips of interest to any cook who aims to achieve good flavor. Use this cookbook as a sourcebook not only for new recipes, but also for ways to enliven and improve your everyday cooking.

If Middle Eastern cooking is unfamiliar to you, don't attempt to prepare a whole meal of dishes you have never cooked before for an exotic dinner party to impress your guests. It is much better to start by making simpler dishes, using only one or two new ingredients, and to try them out on your family before you move on to more complicated things. A good example of this would be Persian Chicken with Rice (see page 63), which includes an unusual garnish of caramelized orange peel. First master the method for Persian Rice with a Crust (see page 106), and perhaps also try out the caramelized peel as a garnish for something else. After that, this spectacular dish is very easy to make.

I realize that much of the advice given above and in the cooking tips throughout the book – for example, on choosing the right size saucepan, or on making soft breadcrumbs, or on frying or grilling – are superfluous for experienced cooks. But their inclusion has been prompted by my experience as a teacher, where they have proved useful to a number of my students – and not only to the least experienced among them.

Utensils and appliances, traditional and modern

Most of the cooking described in this book is done on top of the stove, mainly because this is how I have always done it myself. Many of the dishes can be cooked in the oven if you prefer, but I find it easier to control the speed of cooking and in particular the amount of liquid by using a saucepan. Because many of the dishes need simmering and long, slow cooking, it is very important to use a heavy-based pan. The shape of the pan also matters: it is generally better to use a wide pan, except, of course, for making soups.

No utensil does everything. Thus, for example, I like to use a pressure cooker only for certain specific purposes, as one part of the whole cooking process. The cooking of foods that require a very long time can be speeded up in this way – but only to a point. When cooking *foul* (beans), for example, I cook them for about 25 minutes under pressure, but then release the pressure and simmer them half covered for some time afterwards. Only in this way can the full flavor develop.

For indoor grilling, I find using a broiler less effective than grilling on a hot burner. Dry foods, such as sweet bell peppers, eggplant or corn-on-the-cob, can be grilled on a wire mesh heat diffuser – the type normally used under saucepans, and which has replaced the old, dangerous asbestos mats. Meat, poultry and fish can be grilled on a heavy, ridged cast-iron griddle, some of which have a non-stick coating. The griddle must be extremely hot before beginning to cook, and if the food to be grilled is without fat and has not been marinated in oil, the griddle should first be heated, then lightly brushed with oil immediately before putting the food on. Grill the first side of the food just long enough to sear it, then turn it over and treat the other side the same way. If the food then needs more cooking (which will depend on its size and how well done you like it), lower the heat to medium. When you have finished grilling, remove the food and deglaze the griddle by pouring a little marinating liquid, wine or water onto it. The liquid will sizzle, loosening and dissolving the scraps and juices on the griddle as you stir, and will soon reduce to make a tasty sauce.

I began using a steamer for food that is traditionally cooked this way, such as couscous and some Chinese dishes – and since

The most popular desserts of the Middle East, Baklava and Konafa, may be purchased ready-made from specialist pastry shops and grocery stores. Here sweet and savory pastries are traditionally baked in vast round trays, then cut into pieces.

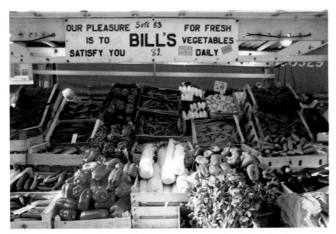

Many local street markets now supply much of the produce needed for Middle Eastern and Indian cooking. At this stall, vegetables which are common to a number of classic cuisines – zucchini, peppers, green beans, chicory, artichokes, snow peas and eggplant – jostle with small 'Cyprus' cucumbers and cilantro – two essentials of Middle Eastern cooking.

then I have found it invaluable as a way of reheating many foods without drying them out. Most Middle Eastern dishes can be reheated very successfully in a steamer, to the extent that it is often worth while making more than you need at the time, and storing some in the refrigerator or freezer.

I also like to use a Chinese wok for deep-fat or semi-deep frying. It uses much less oil than conventional pans or a deep-fat fryer.

A blender or, even better, a food processor is a real boon. Without my food processor I should never have started making some of the traditional Middle Eastern dishes that require much tedious and exhausting work, such as Kibbeh (see page 110) and minced fish dishes (see page 52). It is also useful for chopping large amounts of parsley or cilantro (fresh coriander), and for making *do'a* (see page 140).

Freezers and microwave ovens

You can store Middle Eastern dishes in the freezer just the same as any other food. Stews, soups and pastries all freeze excellently. Where any dish in this book is best frozen at a particular stage, or needs any other special treatment, I have added a note to the recipe. Otherwise, follow the freezer manufacturer's instructions.

A microwave oven is not often suitable for this kind of food. Certain types of dishes can be cooked in a microwave – again, follow the manufacturer's instructions – but not those whose flavor depends on browning the ingredients, or on slow cooking, or those which feature a crunchy texture. However, a microwave is useful for quickly thawing bulky frozen dishes such as stews and soups.

Special flavorings and ingredients

The speed at which new and exotic ingredients are now being introduced and becoming widely available makes a list like this very quickly obsolete. Anyone who lives in a city or large town with a cosmopolitan population is well placed to find almost anything. If you can't find what you need in the international section of your supermarket, look at local markets, health food shops, specialty food stores and especially check out ethnic grocery stores of all varieties – not only Greek, Middle Eastern or Asian, but also try your local Chinese or Mexican-American grocers. However great the variety available, it would be

mistaken to assume that you must have a large number of exotic ingredients to cook in a Middle Eastern style. In fact, unless you are already familiar with this style of cooking, I would advise you to start using ingredients, herbs and spices that you already know. You may well have met them in Indian or Mexican-American cooking.

Herbs and spices for Middle Eastern cooking are illustrated and their use described on pages 12–13. Chili peppers, either fresh, dried, powdered or in the form of hot pepper sauces, would be a good place to start – but avoid 'chili powder', which is a mix of spices specifically blended for Mexican-American cooking. After that you might try cardamom, ginger and perhaps fenugreek (though personally I don't like this, and you won't find it recommended in this book).

Other characteristic flavorings include sesame seeds and roasted almonds, which give a crunchy texture and nutty flavor to many dishes and are a very good way for vegetarians to supplement their diet.

Acid fruits Another distinctive flavor in Middle Eastern food comes from lemons and other sour fruit. To my taste, limes are incomparably the best. They can be expensive, but I find that even a small lime can yield more juice than a large but thick-skinned lemon. Other acid flavors come from using dried apricots and pomegranate seeds. These need to be soaked before use, and the soaking water is included in the dish: see, for example, the recipes for stuffed vegetables (see pages 92–5) or Lahme bi Ajeen (see page 30). Tamarind may be used the same way. Use your imagination to make the most of fresh ingredients available locally. Living in England, I have found rhubarb to be a marvelous, if non-traditional, alternative to lime juice for stuffed vegetables.

Dried limes My most exciting discovery, which I made a few years ago, was dried limes. I had not known of these in Egypt. They were given to me by a French friend married to an Iraqi, who called them *lamoun Basra*. Since then, I have found that they are used in other parts of the Middle East, and you can find them at ethnic grocery stores, usually imported from Pakistan. You can add them whole to a stew and they will soften as it cooks so that you can cut them up and eat them with it; or while still dry they can be crushed to a powder and added like a spice. They also make delicious hot drinks (see page 141).

Rose and orange flower water can be used interchangeably as delicate flavorings for fruit dishes, desserts and various sweet dishes. The best brands come from Cyprus, and a lovely French variety is usually sold in dark blue bottles.

Mastic or mastika is a resin used for flavoring milk puddings and a famous Turkish ice cream (see page 120). In Egypt it is also added with other spices and herbs to chicken broth. It should be used in very small amounts, and crushed with sugar or salt. A piece the size of a small pearl will flavor at least five cups of milk. It is best to use only a little at first, taste and add more if necessary. Too much will impart a bitter taste. The best mastic for cooking comes from the Greek island of Chios.

Bulgar wheat or pourgouri, though sometimes loosely termed 'cracked wheat', is not the same as the plain cracked wheat available from health food stores. Rather, it has been cooked and dried before crushing, and is eaten like rice, or used in salads, or serves as the basis of the classic Lebanese Kibbeh (see page 110).

Kishk or trahanas The first is the Egyptian name, the second the Greek Cypriot one, for cracked wheat cooked with yogurt or sour milk, then dried in the sun. Sold either in granular form or in small sticks at Greek or Middle Eastern grocery stores, it is used to thicken soups and sauces, and imparts a delicately acid flavor.

Tahina or tahini is sesame seed paste, usually sold in jars. It forms the basis of dips and sauces, and some kinds of *halva*, a popular snack, are made from tahina.

Samna or smen is a clarified, slightly sour butter used particularly in Egypt and North Africa. In the recipes here I have substituted clarified butter, made by heating butter very gently to evaporate the water in it.

Olive oil is also much used in the region. I generally use sunflower or corn oil for cooking, and reserve olive oil for the times I feel its special flavor is really necessary.

Vinegar In my experience, wine vinegar is not much used in the Middle East and I find that its distinctive flavor sometimes clashes with other ingredients. You will see that my usual salad dressing is made with lime or lemon juice rather than vinegar, with the exception of some eggplant and pepper salads. For these, and other dishes that call for vinegar, such as Higado con Vinagre (see page 73) and Zemino (see page 136) I use a good distilled malt vinegar – not the highly colored and caramelized type.

Filo (phyllo) and konafa pastries These two types of pastry dough are widely used throughout the Middle East, and are available in many ethnic grocery stores and even some supermarkets. They are both made from flour and water only, and fat is added at the time of use. Filo pastry comes in ultra-thin, tissue-like sheets, and is familiar to all who love Baklava (see page 130). It can be made at home by very skillful and patient cooks, but is usually manufactured commercially. Konafa looks like white Shredded Wheat and is always bought ready-made. Both are now often produced with large-scale factory processes, but they are still also made by hand, and I have recently seen this done with great panache both in Cairo and Alexandria.

The filo maker is called a *fatayri*. He rolls and stretches the dough by throwing it into the air and passing it from hand to hand with incredible speed. You may have seen pizza makers doing something similar, but filo is far thinner and each sheet is much wider. The completed sheets are cut to size, and filled and fried to order on the spot.

The konafa maker is even more skillful. He has in front of him a huge, round heated tray. On his right is a bowl full of thin batter. In his hand he has a perforated ladle, though some konafa makers disdain such an aid and use their fingers. They take some batter and very swiftly dribble it across the tray. The moment the batter hits the tray, it sets into something like extra-fine white vermicelli. At once, before it starts to color, he gathers it up with

The date harvest in the Tafilalet Oasis in Morocco. Dates are a mainstay of the diet in many parts of the Middle East. Fresh dates, served on their own or with nuts, make a simple but luscious end to any meal. Dried of fresh, they form the basis of a number of classic desserts and pastries.

his left hand and adds it to a pile on the table. Meanwhile, his right hand is already pouring the next batch of batter. It is breathtaking to watch.

Outside the Middle East, konafa is sold vacuum packed and often frozen. Instructions for handling it are given on page 131.

When fresh, filo is easy to handle and should be soft and pliable. But even then, its thinness and lack of fat allow it to dry out quickly so that it becomes brittle. When using filo pastry in large pieces, as for Baklava or for chicken or meat pies, this does not matter. Dried-up scraps of leftover filo can be used to make bases for tartlets or even larger quiches. However, you can prevent the filo from drying out.

Take the package of filo out of the refrigerator about 30 minutes before use. Open the package, but do not unroll or separate the sheets. Cover them with a soaked and well wrung-out dish towel, draping this over two cups, one placed at each end of the roll of filo so that the wet towel does not touch it. When you are ready to used the pastry, unroll just enough to cut off what you need. If you need whole sheets, take them out one at a time, then roll the rest back up again and immediately replace it under the towel.

Further instructions are given in those recipes where filo is used.

I hope that this book will give people who do not know Middle Eastern cooking a good general appreciation of it. I also hope that readers who cook these dishes will not follow the recipes slavishly, but will adopt them as a basis for experiment. Personally, I feel flattered when someone tells me that a recipe I gave them turned out perfectly; but I am more deeply pleased when they tell me that they have been using my dressing for their own salads or my pie dough for their quiches, or that they made small mince pies for Christmas using filo pastry in coils like borek. I would like people to use this book as a source of inspiration to widen their everyday repertoire. In particular, vegetarians should find exciting ways to vary their diet, not only from the Vegetables and Legumes chapter, but also by adapting dishes from the other sections.

As for those who are already familiar with Middle Eastern cooking, and even Middle Eastern cooks themselves, I hope that they will find ideas for variations on a well-loved dish, even if they are convinced that their own special version of other dishes cannot be improved upon.

Harvesting peanuts in Anamur, on the southern coast of Turkey. The Middle East as a whole produces nuts of all kinds, and they form an intrinsic part of the region's cooking, from sauces, stuffings and pilafs to cakes, cookies and pastries.

In the Middle East, where some form of refreshment is an essential part of any social visit or business transaction, time-honored rituals for the making and serving of coffee – distinctively rich, dark and strong – are observed to this day. Here, the green coffee beans are roasted in a long-handled iron pan over an open fire before being pulverized, briefly boiled and served in the traditional tiny cups without handles. Instructions for making coffee in the Middle Eastern way are given on page 141.

CHOOSING THE RIGHT SAUCEPAN

It is very important to use a saucepan of the right type and size for a particular dish.

Weight Especially for dishes that are cooked slowly, a heavy-based pan is essential. When buying a pan, make sure you aren't misled by one with a heavy handle only. Stainless steel is a very poor conductor of heat, and a pan of this metal must have a thick copper bottom; this doesn't apply to cast-iron or aluminum pans.

If you have to use a pan with a base that is not heavy enough, the defect can be largely overcome by setting it on a wire mesh heat diffuser, which works on both gas and electric stoves. Asbestos mats are a health hazard and should not be used.

Size Inexperienced cooks often use too small a pan and pile the ingredients up so that the food at the top remains uncooked while that at the bottom burns. I have worked out the following reliable rules. When cooking on top of the stove, the saucepan should be small enough for the ingredients to completely cover the bottom, and large enough for all the ingredients not to fill it more than half full. In this way, you will find that my recipe instructions to line the base of the pan with oil will automatically give you the amount of oil needed.

FRYING

The quantity of oil you use for any method of frying is entirely a matter of depth, and thus varies with the size of the pan. The following is an explanation of the terms I use in this book.

Shallow frying or sautéing The oil should just coat the base of the pan when it is poured in and swirled around.

Deep frying The food that is being fried should be completely submerged in oil, and covered to a depth of about $\frac{3}{4}$ in.

Semi-deep frying There should be a fair amount of oil, but it need not cover the food. Here you have to turn the food over to brown it evenly. For frying in this way it is a great help to use a wok: it needs much less oil than a flat-bottomed pan. In any recipe that calls for deep frying, you can semi-deep fry the food provided that you turn it, but not vice versa.

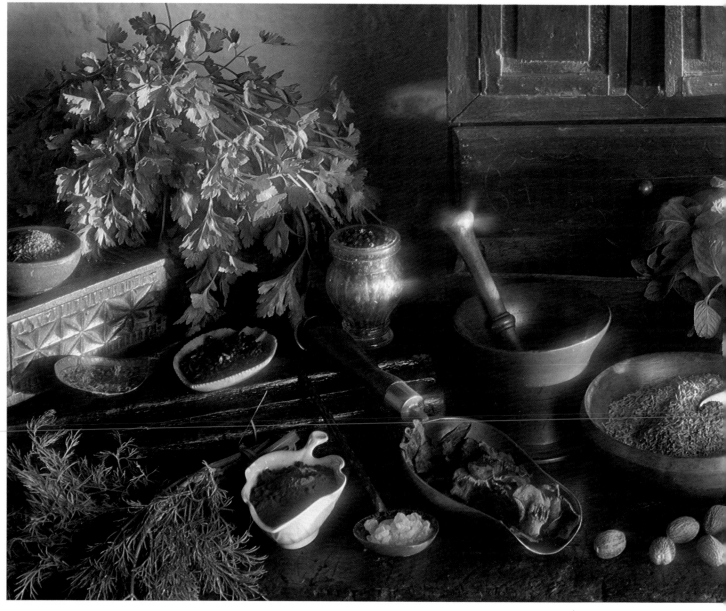

HERBS AND SPICES

Herbs, spices and condiments are an essential part of both savory and sweet Middle Eastern dishes. Good cooks seldom decide in advance exactly which ones and how much of each they will use, but rather taste at different stages of cooking. She or he knows how flavors develop as food cooks, or once it has cooled off if it is eaten cold.

Herbs are used fresh or dried, and spices are bought whole or ground; dried herbs or ground spices must be used while still fresh and not allowed to become stale. Often the dried product has quite a different taste from the fresh one and sometimes, as with dried mint and dried ginger root, this is preferable. Some spices, notably coriander, caraway and cumin seed, are roasted before use to develop their flavor. Traditionally, cooks in the Middle East have bought their spices from the special spice section in the market, where they can find them roasted to the exact degree they require, and freshly ground. The spice sellers, the best of whom attract faithful customers,

also make up their own blends. For Western cooks, who cannot always buy freshly roasted spices, it is better to buy spices whole, and to roast, grind and blend them at home. Heat them in a small frying pan without oil, shaking the pan continually until you smell the fragrance developing. A pestle and mortar is ideal for grinding small quantities of spice; you can also grind them in a small electric grinder.

In all the recipes in this book which include parsley, the flat-leafed variety is infinitely preferable. Like fresh cilantro, it is generally available from Middle Eastern food shops and markets. To store any that you do not need at once, wash it thoroughly, dry very well and cut off the stems, reserving them. Chop the leaves finely and place in a plastic box in the freezer. They will stay separate, so when you need the herb for flavoring you can just take a handful straight from the freezer box and throw it in. I also keep the stems in the freezer and use them, tied in bundles, to add flavor to soups and sauces.

1 Dill weed 2 Saffron
3 Oregono 4 Flat-leafed
parsley 5 Pomegranate seeds
6 Paprika 7 Black peppercorns
8 Mastic 9 Tamarind slices
10 Cumin seed 11 Nutmegs
12 Dried lemons and limes
13 Mint 14 Sea salt
15 Caraway seed 16 White
cardamom pods 17 Green
cardamom pods 18 Fennel
seeds 19 Cinnamon sticks
20 Ground ginger
21 Powdered chili 22 Sumac
23 Coriander seed
24 Turmeric 25 Allspice
berries 26 Cilantro

MEZZE

Mezze might be translated as 'appetizers', 'hors d'oeuvres' or 'snacks'. But these words can't begin to convey the range of delicacies, cooked and uncooked, which fall into the *mezze* category; and, more important, they do not give the full flavor of the way of life common to all Middle Eastern countries in which they play a part.

I firmly believe that it is impossible to learn about or judge the food of a country or region only through restaurants. Yet in this case I would say that the best and quickest way to introduce someone to the food of the Middle East is to treat them to a *mezze* meal in a Greek, Lebanese or Turkish restaurant. There are several reasons for this. An enormous variety of fare is offered, up to twenty different items, all in small portions. They range from familiar fresh vegetables [or *crudités*] served with exotic dips and cubes of cheese, to more unusual items: rissoles [meat, fish or bean patties], grilled or fried, with or without sauces; grilled prawns or chicken livers; small savory pies made of different pastries with various fillings, baked or fried. In fact, any dish of sufficient taste and interest can be presented as a *mezze* if it is small or can be served in small portions. Thus, in one sitting, you can get an idea of the range of the region's food.

This diversity reveals something else about Middle Eastern food. Meals are not served as a sequence of fixed courses, with each course calculated to feed a given number of people. Instead, the food is usually spread out on the table in a great variety of dishes and everyone helps themselves, choosing items with contrasting flavors and textures. The quantity of food depends on the variety of dishes offered.

Three typical dips for the *mezze* table (*left to right*) Bessara, Hummus Dip and Tahina Dip, with a bowl of crunchy Fried Fava Beans (*top*)

TAHINA DIP

PREPARATION TIME
10 minutes

1 clove garlic
2 Tbsp tahina [sesame seed]
    paste
juice of 1 lemon, or to taste

TO GARNISH
a few sprigs parsley, chopped

[picture on page 15]

Tahina, a thick sesame seed paste known under various spellings, is eaten both as a dip in its own right and added to other dips. One very popular combination is Hummus bi Tahina [see below], a dip made with garbanzo beans. I prefer tahina on its own, diluted and flavored in the most traditional Egyptian manner, as described here.

1 Crush the garlic with the salt in a mortar. Stir the tahina well so that the oil on top blends with the thick paste at the bottom of the jar. Add the tahina to the mortar if it is large enough, or put both the tahina and garlic into a bowl. Stir well.
2 Add the lemon juice gradually, stirring continuously. The color and texture will change; don't worry, just keep stirring until thoroughly mixed. Add some water a little at a time, stirring to incorporate each addition completely before adding more, until the paste is slightly thicker than whipping cream and even in color and consistency.
3 Taste, and add more lemon juice if necessary – it should taste quite lemony. When you are satisfied, stir in a little more water until the tahina is as thick as mayonnaise. Serve in shallow bowls, garnished with chopped parsley.

I sometimes add $\frac{1}{2}$ teaspoon of ground cumin, or a little vinegar, as well as the lemon juice. But I never add any oil. Tahina is in itself an oily paste, and in fact often replaces oil when added to other dips.

Tahina Dip should be stored in a bowl covered with saran wrap, to prevent its drying out. Should this happen, just mix in a little water or lemon juice.

HUMMUS DIP

PREPARATION TIME
8 hours soaking
1 hour 30 minutes, including 1
    hour 10 minutes cooking

$\frac{1}{4}$ lb dried garbanzo beans
1 medium onion
1 clove garlic or more, to taste
4 tsp olive oil
$\frac{1}{2}$ tsp turmeric
salt, to taste
juice of $\frac{1}{2}$–1 lemon, to taste

[picture on page 14]

This plain but agreeable dip made from garbanzo beans is popular all over the Middle East, and is becoming more and more popular in the States too. I like to brighten the taste by cooking the garbanzo beans with some flavoring: turmeric imparts a subtle aroma and also gives the beige paste a more attractive color.

1 Wash the beans and leave to soak for 8 hours in plenty of water.
2 Remove any floating debris and drain the garbanzo beans, reserving the water. If necessary, peel the garbanzo beans by rubbing them between your hands.
3 Chop the onion and garlic. Gently cook them over medium to low heat in enough of the oil to cover the bottom of a saucepan until the onion is transparent. Then stir in the turmeric and a little soaking water from the garbanzo beans. Add the garbanzo beans and enough of the soaking water to cover them by a good inch. Bring to a boil, reduce the heat and simmer until done, about 1 hour. [If you are using a pressure cooker, add just enough water to cover the garbanzo beans by 2 in. and cook for only 25 minutes.]
4 When the garbanzo beans are soft, drain and reserve the liquid. Mash them with a fork, add a little of the reserved liquid and then purée to the consistency of mayonnaise. [If you are using a blender or food processor, there is no need to mash the garbanzos first.]
5 Transfer to a bowl and add the salt, lemon juice and the remaining oil, tasting and mixing to get the right balance. If you find you would like more garlic, first crush some garlic with salt in a mortar, add a little of the hummus, mix well and then scrape out into the main bowl.

HUMMUS BI TAHINA This well-known and delicious variation is made simply by replacing the oil added at the end with a tablespoonful of tahina [sesame seed] paste.

PEELING DRIED GARBANZO BEANS
This is much easier than it sounds. After they have been soaked, just rub the garbanzo beans between your hands and return to the soaking water. The peel will float to the surface and can be easily discarded.

BESSARA [FAVA BEAN PURÉE]

Bessara is a purée made from dried fava beans and herbs. It is traditionally garnished with Ta'leya [see page 140], a dressing of garlic and fried crushed coriander seed. Use ready-peeled fava beans.

PREPARATION TIME
8 hours soaking
2 hours, including $1\frac{3}{4}$ hours cooking

$\frac{1}{4}$ lb peeled dried fava beans
2 green onions
1 clove garlic
1 Tbsp chopped cilantro
1 tsp crushed dried mint
1 tsp ground cumin seed
salt and pepper, to taste
a dot cayenne pepper or powdered red chili [optional]

TO SERVE
1 medium onion
olive oil for shallow frying

TA'LEYA:
1 Tbsp crushed coriander seed
1 clove garlic

[*picture on page 14*]

1 Wash the beans and leave to soak for 8 hours in plenty of water.
2 Remove any floating debris, drain the beans, and transfer them to a saucepan. Add enough water to cover by 1 in., and bring to a boil.
3 Meanwhile, chop the green onions [including the green tops] and the garlic. When the beans are boiling, skim off any froth. Then add the onions and garlic, and stir. Bring back to a boil, half cover the saucepan and reduce the heat. Simmer until the beans are soft [about $1\frac{1}{2}$ hours], stirring from time to time and adding more water if necessary. [If using a pressure cooker, cover the beans with 2 in. of water and cook for about 25 minutes.]
4 Purée the mixture, return it to the pan, cover and continue cooking. If it is too liquid, cook uncovered so that it dries out to a fairly thick purée consistency.
5 Add the cilantro, mint, cumin, salt and pepper and, if you like, a little cayenne pepper or powdered red chili. Stir well, taste and adjust the seasoning. Leave to cool.
6 For the garnish, slice the onion into rings and fry in hot olive oil until brown and crisp. Remove from the pan and reserve. To make Ta'leya, first chop the garlic very finely. Pour away most of the oil, leaving just enough to gently fry the garlic and the coriander until it gives off a sweet smell – be careful not to burn it. Serve the Bessara in a fairly shallow dish, topped with the Ta'leya and onion rings.

Bessara is also served with olive oil, lemon wedges and extra cayenne pepper [or powdered red chili] or red pepper [chili] sauce, so everyone can season it to suit themself.

FRIED DRIED FAVA BEANS

These crunchy, golden-brown beans are eaten like peanuts or roasted pumpkin seeds.

PREPARATION TIME
8 hours soaking
5 minutes, including cooking

$\frac{1}{4}$ lb peeled dried fava beans
salt
oil for deep frying

[*picture on page 14*]

1 Wash the beans and leave to soak for 8 hours in plenty of water.
2 Remove any floating debris, drain the beans, peel them if necessary, roll them in salt, then dry with paper towels.
3 Heat oil in a deep-fat fryer until quite hot. Use a large slotted spoon to lower the beans, a few at a time, very slowly into the hot oil. Fry each batch until golden brown. Drain on paper towels and eat cold.

Garbanzo beans can be deep fried and eaten in exactly the same way.

Radishes and green onions are often served with other raw vegetables as part of a *mezze* spread. RIGHT Huge radishes and green onions on sale at the Yemenite market in Tel Aviv, the largest city in Israel.

FALAFEL

PREPARATION TIME
8 hours soaking
2¾ hours, including 2 hours
    resting and 10 minutes
    cooking

½ lb dried fava beans
1 Tbsp very finely chopped
    parsley
1 Tbsp very finely chopped
    cilantro
4–5 green onions
1 clove garlic
½ tsp ground cumin seed
salt and pepper, to taste
a small pinch baking soda
    [optional]
oil for semi-deep frying

Falafel are small fava bean, garbanzo bean or lentil rissoles good with Tahina Dip [see page 16] as a 'mezze', or in pita bread with Egyptian Salad [see page 25]. They form part of the staple diet in Egypt, where they are usually eaten with Foul Medames [see page 100], a dish made with the same small brown bean I like to use for falafel. Since these beans need to be peeled after soaking – a tedious job – I recommend using larger dry fava beans which are sold ready-peeled and have a similar flavor.

1 Wash the beans and leave to soak for 8 hours in plenty of water.
2 Remove any floating debris, drain the beans and dry with paper towels. Grind in a mincer or meat grinder, using the fine disk, or in a food processor. They should have the consistency of a fairly dry, slightly grainy purée.
3 Mix the parsley and the cilantro in a bowl with the bean purée. Finely chop the green tops of the green onions and the garlic. Add these to the mixture, along with the cumin, salt, pepper and baking soda [if used]. Knead well, taste and adjust the seasoning. [Don't worry, it is quite nice raw.] The mixture will be a lovely pale green color, speckled with dark green. It will be easier to shape if you leave it to rest, uncovered, in the refrigerator for a couple hours.
4 Dampen your hands slightly. Take a marble-sized piece of the mixture, knead it in your palm to form a ball [see page 77], then set it on a plate or tray and flatten slightly with your finger. Make all the mixture into rissoles this way.
* Falafel may be prepared in advance to this stage and stored in the refrigerator or freezer. Freeze them loose on a tray, then pack into bags. Fry straight from the freezer.
5 Pour oil into a frying pan to a depth of 1 in., or use a wok if you have one. Heat the oil, then fry the rissoles, turning them, until they are golden brown on both sides. If they begin to turn dark brown, lower the heat. Drain the cooked Falafel on paper towels.

You can also make larger falafel for sandwiches or snack lunches by using walnut-sized pieces of the mixture. As each rissole expands in the hot oil, flatten it to make sure it cooks through.
    Falafel mixes are available in some stores. Although quite adequate, the addition of a little parsley and cilantro after soaking brings them to life.

LABAN CHEESE BALLS

PREPARATION TIME
15 minutes
1–2 days wait

1 tsp salt
1 cup 2 Tbsp thick natural
    yogurt
olive oil

[picture on page 27]

Laban cheese balls are often rolled in coarsely ground black pepper, paprika or crushed dried mint, making a colorful addition to the 'mezze' table.

1 Mix the salt into the yogurt, strain the mixture through cheesecloth, then tie the cheesecloth up into a bundle and hang it over a sink for a day or two, to allow moisture to drain out.
2 Refrigerate the Laban Cheese until it has dried out, then roll it into small balls and store them in a jar of olive oil.

EGGPLANT PURÉE

PREPARATION TIME
45 minutes, including 15
    minutes salting and 20–25
    minutes cooking

3 medium or 2 large eggplants
salt, to taste
1 clove garlic
½ small onion
lime or lemon juice, to taste
1–2 Tbsp olive oil
2 Tbsp chopped parsley

This delicious 'mezze' combines unusual flavors and spices. Choose medium or large eggplants, the long kind rather than round ones if possible. They have to be cooked until they are soft inside and rather charred outside. When grilling the eggplants to char them, a wire rack can be used instead of a griddle, though I find it less convenient.

1 Wash and dry the eggplants. Put a cast-iron griddle on a burner. If the eggplants are large, start grilling them whole over medium heat, turning frequently, until they begin to soften. Then increase the heat and keep grilling and turning until the skin is charred all over and broken in places. Medium eggplants can be grilled over high heat, as they will soften in the time it takes for the skin to char, about 20 minutes.
2 Hold each eggplant carefully by its stem and split it open lengthwise with a sharp

Eggplant Purée (*back left*) and Falafel, traditionally served with a bowl of Tahina Dip

knife. Some liquid will ooze out; wait until it stops dripping. Sprinkle the cut surfaces with a little salt and stand the eggplants upright, stem uppermost, in a colander for about 15 minutes. This procedure removes more moisture from the eggplants, improving the texture of the purée, and it was once necessary to make the eggplants less bitter, something seldom required with modern eggplant.

3 Crush the garlic with some salt in a mortar, and transfer to a bowl. Grate the onion and mix in. [A food processor can be used for all the chopping and mixing.] Spoon the eggplant pulp out of the rind, chop up the fibrous parts and add the pulp to the bowl.

4 Mix thoroughly, add some lime or lemon juice, taste and add more juice or salt if necessary. Then add the oil very gradually, as you would when making mayonnaise, stirring continuously. Stop adding oil as soon as the surface of the purée begins to shine. Taste again. Stir in some parsley and serve in bowls, sprinkled with the rest.

You can vary the seasoning by using vinegar instead of lemon juice, or a combination of the two. A touch of cayenne pepper [or powdered red chili] or red pepper [chili] sauce is sometimes added, or a tablespoonful of natural yogurt. Another seasoning you can add is T'atbil [see page 140].

BABAGHANOUSH Add 1 tsp tahina [sesame seed] paste instead of the oil.

Fried Eggplant, Onion and Tomato Salad (*left*) and Pepper Salad

PEPPER SALAD

PREPARATION TIME
30 minutes, including 5–10
    minutes cooking
1 hour wait

1 each sweet green, red and
    yellow bell peppers
1 clove garlic
salt, to taste
about 1 tsp vinegar
about 1 Tbsp olive oil

TO GARNISH
black olives [optional]

The peppers for this salad are charred to make them more digestible and – more importantly – to improve the flavor. Choose long peppers rather than round ones if possible; they are easier to grill evenly.

1 Wash and dry the peppers. Grill on a hot cast-iron griddle, turning from time to time, until the skins are charred and split on all sides. Transfer to a bowl, cover with a cloth and leave to cool. This makes peeling easier.

2 Peel the peppers, cut them open, discard the seeds and slice into strips. Wipe away bits of charred skin with paper towels, and arrange them in a shallow serving bowl. Chop the garlic very finely and sprinkle it on top. Sprinkle with salt, trickle the vinegar over the bowl, making sure to cover the salt. Leave for a few minutes, until the vinegar has dissolved the salt, then swirl the dish around gently to spread the seasoning all over the peppers.

3 Trickle the olive oil over the surface. Taste, and adjust the seasoning. If possible, leave for an hour or so before serving. Serve garnished with black olives if you like.

Alternatively, chop the peppers very finely, season as above, then arrange them in piles of different colors [see page 50]. Garnish with chopped hard-boiled egg whites and yolks. Vary the seasoning by using lime or lemon juice instead of vinegar, or by adding a small touch of red pepper [chili] sauce or cayenne pepper [or powdered red chili].

Some years ago, during a visit to Belgrade, a friend offered me a pepper salad very similar to this one, to 'introduce me to typical Serbian food', not realizing how familiar this kind of dish was to me. Her version, however, included eggplant, and the flavors blend extremely well. Now, I often make Eggplant Purée [see page 18] and this Pepper Salad separately, then combine the leftovers for the following day.

FRIED EGGPLANT, ONION AND TOMATO SALAD

PREPARATION TIME
**overnight salting
30 minutes, including 15–20
   minutes cooking**

**2 medium eggplants
salt
1 large onion
4–5 tomatoes, or a large can
oil for semi-deep frying
1 Tbsp vinegar
1 clove garlic**

TO GARNISH
a few sprigs parsley, chopped

This delicious eggplant dish is superb, either as an hors d'oeuvre, as a salad to accompany simply broiled meat or cold cuts, or as part of a vegetarian meal.

1 Prepare the eggplants the night before you want to cook them. Cut off and discard the tops and bottoms. Pare thin lengthwise strips off the outer peel about 1 in. apart to prevent the eggplant slices from buckling up when fried. Cut into slices about $\frac{3}{8}$ in. thick, put in a colander and sprinkle with salt. Cover with a plate, weight it down well and leave for at least 10 hours. If possible, turn the slices over after a few hours and press down again.

2 Dry the eggplant slices by pressing them between paper towels. Slice the onion into fairly thin rings. Slice the tomatoes if fresh, or drain canned tomatoes if you are using them.

3 Pour about $1\frac{3}{4}$ in. oil into a large frying pan. [A wok requires far less oil, which should be about $1\frac{1}{2}$ in. deep in the middle.] Heat the oil, and test the temperature with a piece of eggplant. When it sizzles to the surface, fry the eggplant slices in batches until brown on both sides. As you remove each batch, drain on paper towels. You may have to raise or lower the temperature of the oil as you cook.

4 When all the eggplant slices are done, remove the pan from the heat and strain the oil through a metal sieve lined with paper towel into a metal or other heat-proof bowl, so that you can reuse it. Return 1 to 2 tablespoonfuls of oil to the pan, and reheat until hot but not sizzling. Quickly fry the onion rings until golden and drain them on paper towels.

5 Make sure the pan is hot, then add all the tomatoes and mash them down quickly so that they are just scorched but not cooked. Remove and reserve them. Pour the vinegar into the pan. Bring to a boil, scraping the bottom of the pan with a spoon or spatula, then remove the pan from the heat.

6 Arrange the eggplant slices, tomatoes and onion rings in a shallow bowl. Chop the garlic very finely and sprinkle over the salad. Sprinkle the salad evenly with a little salt, and trickle the pan juices over to dissolve it. The salad will probably not need any more oil than this. Taste a little to judge for yourself, add oil if necessary, and adjust the seasoning at the same time. Allow the salad to cool completely, then serve garnished with chopped parsley.

Fried eggplant slices are also delicious with a dressing of natural yogurt mixed with a little crushed garlic.

Sweet bell and hot peppers of many kinds play an important part in all the cuisines of the Middle East. BELOW Red peppers drying in the sun in Nabeul, Tunisia

FRYING EGGPLANT

This is an improvement on the classic method of salting eggplant slices to make them absorb less oil in frying. Put the slices in a colander over a bowl, sprinkle them with salt and cover with a plate. Instead of leaving them only 10 minutes, or even 2 hours – which is the longest time usually recommended – leave them for at least 10 hours or overnight. Then dry them with paper towels. Although they will have withered, they will recover their shape when fried and you will be astonished at how little oil they take up.

FRIED EGGPLANT AND PEPPER SALAD

PREPARATION TIME
1 hour 35 minutes, including 1
   hour salting and 30 minutes
   cooking

1 medium eggplant
salt
3–4 sweet green bell peppers
3 Tbsp oil
1 tsp coriander seed
1 clove garlic
3 tomatoes
1 Tbsp vinegar

TO GARNISH
1 Tbsp chopped parsley

1 Cut the eggplant into 1 in. cubes. Put them in a colander, sprinkle with salt, cover with a weighted plate and leave for about an hour.
2 Cut peppers into pieces about 1 in. square, discarding the seeds. Fry them in the oil until the skins begin to crack, then lower the heat.
3 Take the eggplant cubes, one handful at a time, and dry by pressing between paper towels. Add each dried handful to the pan, stir and dry the next handful. Let the mixture cook over medium heat. If the vegetables stick to the pan, add a little water and scrape thoroughly.
4 Roast the coriander seed gently in a non-stick or Teflon pan, rolling it around frequently, until light colored. Crush and add to the vegetables. Chop the garlic very finely, add to the pan and fry for a few minutes.
5 Skin and chop the tomatoes and add to the pan. Cook over medium heat for about 15 minutes, until the eggplant cubes and tomatoes are fairly mushy, and the pepper pieces are cooked but still holding their shape.
6 Transfer the cooked vegetables to a bowl, add the vinegar, stir gently, taste and add more vinegar or salt as required. Tip into a shallow serving bowl and serve cold, sprinkled with chopped parsley.

For a piquant flavor, cook a small fresh chili pepper, de-seeded and chopped, along with the peppers.

YOGURT AND CUCUMBER SALAD

PREPARATION TIME
10 minutes

1 clove garlic
10 Tbsp [5 fl oz] natural yogurt
salt, to taste
1 cucumber
1 tsp crushed dried mint

1 Crush the garlic into a bowl. Add the yogurt, beat until smooth and add the salt.
2 Chop the cucumber into cubes and mix into the yogurt with the mint. Taste and adjust the seasoning. Serve cool.

YOGURT AND ONION SALAD This combination, using onion rather than cucumber, is not strictly Middle Eastern, being Indian-inspired, but it makes a delicious *mezze*. Slice 1 large or 2 medium onions very thinly. Put in a bowl, sprinkle with salt and the juice of $\frac{1}{2}$ lemon and leave to marinate for at least 1 hour. Add the yogurt and beat very well. Flavor the salad with crushed dried mint, and a pinch of cayenne pepper if you like. Serve cool.

GREEN BEAN SALAD

PREPARATION TIME
30–40 minutes, including
   20–30 minutes cooking

1–2 Tbsp olive oil
$\frac{1}{2}$ lb green beans
salt, to taste
juice of $\frac{1}{2}$–1 lime or lemon, to
   taste

For this salad, you should use very young, fresh beans which do not have strings that need removing.

1 Choose a heavy-based pan which can hold the beans in one layer and pour in enough oil to thinly coat the bottom. Wash the beans and cut off the ends. Add to the pan along with the salt and lime or lemon juice – you can add more later if necessary. Barely cover the beans with water. Shake the pan well and bring to a boil, then immediately lower the heat and cover the pan.
2 Shake the pan from time to time. After about 20 minutes, check to see if the beans are cooked. This depends on how you like your vegetables; to my taste they are ready as soon as they turn olive green. They will still be crunchy, but will have just lost their raw taste, after 20 to 30 minutes. If you prefer to cook the beans longer, you may need to add a little more water.
3 Arrange the beans in a serving dish. Reduce the liquid left in the pan by boiling and pour it over them. Taste, and add a little more salt or lime or lemon juice if needed. Serve cold.

If made in larger quantities, this green bean salad could serve as a delicious simple vegetable dish. The flavoring can be varied by adding thinly sliced garlic, chopped parsley or chopped cilantro.

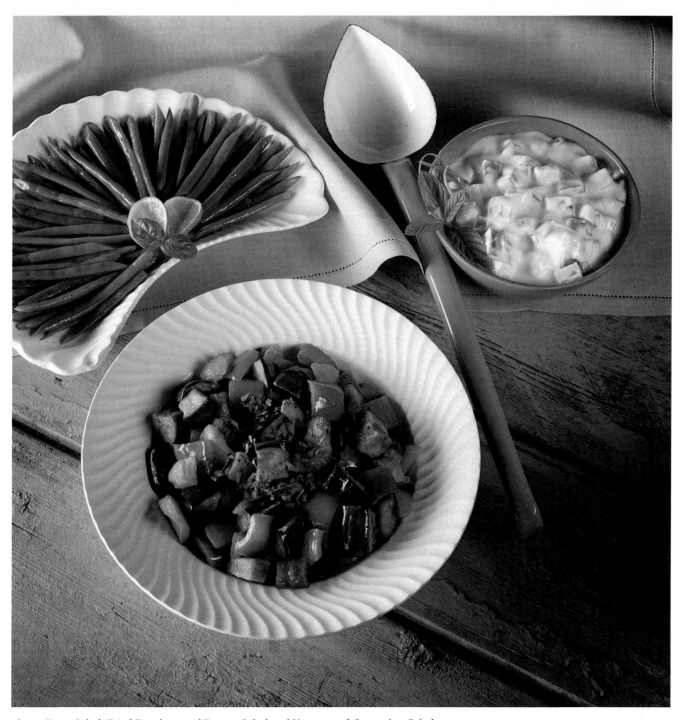

Green Bean Salad, Fried Eggplant and Pepper Salad and Yogurt and Cucumber Salad

SKINNING TOMATOES
This method is
particularly appropriate
for tomatoes used in
salads. Spike each
tomato on a wooden-
handled fork and hold it
over a naked flame. The
skin will crack and curl
up in no time.

SPINACH OR SWISS CHARD SALAD The stems of spinach or Swiss chard are also delicious cooked this way. Discard any discolored stems, trim the remaining stems and, in the case of Swiss chard, cut into strips. Cook as described for green beans in the recipe above for 10 to 15 minutes.

ZUCCHINI SALAD This recipe can be used to cook very small, young zucchini no larger than your thumb. It can be difficult to find zucchini this small unless you grow them yourself.

CELERY SALAD Cut celery into 2 in. sticks and cook as above, but add just enough turmeric to slightly color the vegetables and impart a delicate flavor.

All these salads may be eaten hot or cold.

Left to right Two bowls of Tabbouleh, made with varying proportions of bulgar wheat to greenstuff, Fattoush and Egyptian Salad

TABBOULEH

PREPARATION TIME
30 minutes, including 15
minutes soaking

2 Tbsp bulgar wheat
1¼ cups finely chopped parsley
2 Tbsp finely chopped cilantro
4 green onions
1 cucumber
about 1 Tbsp fresh mint, or 1
tsp crushed dried mint
salt and pepper, to taste
juice of 1–2 lemons, to taste
2 tsp olive oil

This delicious lemony salad of Lebanese origin has become deservedly popular in the West in recent years. Bulgar wheat is readily available in health food stores. The salad should be predominantly green with white specks.

1 Soak the bulgar wheat for about 15 minutes in a bowl of water.
2 Line a colander with cheesecloth and tip the bulgar wheat into it. Lift out the cloth and squeeze hard to remove as much moisture as possible. Put the bulgar wheat in a salad bowl and add the parsley, cilantro, green onions, cucumber and mint, all either chopped or cut up into very small pieces. Mix well.
3 Add salt, pepper and lemon juice to taste, and again mix well. Add half the oil, mix thoroughly, then add the rest if necessary and mix again. Use just enough oil to make the salad glisten. Taste, and adjust the seasoning if necessary.

When made with a much larger proportion of bulgar wheat, this salad looks much like a rice salad: white with green specks. If you want to make it this way, use 1¼ cups bulgar wheat and adjust the seasoning accordingly.

EGYPTIAN SALAD

PREPARATION TIME
30 minutes
1 hour wait

½ head romaine lettuce
2–3 cucumbers
2–3 green onions or 1 small sweet red onion or ½ large white Spanish onion
2 firm tomatoes
salt, to taste
juice of 1 lime or ½ lemon
about 2 Tbsp olive oil

TO GARNISH
a few sprigs parsley, chopped

Salads of this kind are made not only in Egypt, but all over the Middle East, from Greece through Turkey to Lebanon and beyond. The main feature is that the ingredients are cut into very small pieces. The dressing is made with lime or lemon juice rather than vinegar, tastes strongly of the juice and the salad is prepared in advance to let the flavor infuse. This suits Middle Eastern lettuces, which are of the romaine type, crisp but a bit tough. If you are using a round onion, it should be mild; best of all are the sweet red Italian type.

1 Dice the vegetables, and sprinkle with salt, then with the lime or lemon juice, and mix well to dissolve the salt. Add the oil a little at a time, mixing after each addition. I find there is enough oil when the salad glistens, but you might like more.
2 Taste, adjust the seasoning, and leave in a cool place for an hour. To serve, sprinkle chopped parsley over the salad.

The dressing can be varied by adding a pinch of ground cumin seed or a little crushed dried mint, and the salad garnished with chopped cilantro instead of parsley.

FATTOUSH [TUNISIAN SALAD]

PREPARATION TIME
1 hour, including 10 minutes cooking

2 thick slices dry brown bread
3 Tbsp vinegar
2 Tbsp water
1 large green bell pepper
2 medium tomatoes
2–3 green onions
¼ lb mild cheese
1 small can tuna fish
a few olives
capers [optional]
salt, to taste
1 clove garlic
1 tsp crushed coriander seed
½ tsp crushed caraway seed
a dot Harissa [see page 140]
2 Tbsp oil

This is a traditional Tunisian salad, a version of 'salade niçoise', whose ingredients vary according to taste and availability.

1 Cut the bread into small cubes and moisten with 1 tablespoonful of vinegar diluted with twice that amount of water. Broil the peppers until their skins are blistered and black. To make peeling the peppers easier, transfer to a bowl and cover with a cloth for a few minutes.
2 Peel and coarsely chop the peppers. Cut the tomatoes into cubes, discarding the pulp if watery. Chop the green onions, including the green tops. Drain the tuna. Cut the cheese into small cubes. Pit the olives.
3 Put the soaked bread in a salad bowl with the peppers, tomatoes, onions, tuna, cheese and olives, plus a few capers, if you like. Add salt to taste and toss the salad gently to mix the ingredients.
4 Crush the garlic. Fry the coriander seed, caraway seed, Harissa and garlic in the oil until the garlic is golden, then add the rest of the vinegar and pour the mixture over the salad.

You can also add a Preserved Lemon [see page 139], rinsed and chopped or cut into strips.

CABBAGE SALAD

PREPARATION TIME
3 hours salting
10 minutes

½ small white cabbage
salt
juice of ½ lemon or 2 tsp vinegar, or a mixture of the two
2 tsp olive oil, or as required
1 tsp crushed dried mint

[*picture on page 26*]

This cabbage salad is not of the crisp type that you sometimes find in Greek restaurants. It is very finely shredded and softened, so that it absorbs the dressing.

1 Shred the cabbage as finely as possible and put in a colander. Sprinkle some salt over it, put a weighted plate on top and leave for at least 3 hours. A fair amount of liquid will come out and the cabbage will soften.
2 Squeeze the cabbage hard with your hands to remove as much moisture as possible. Transfer to a bowl and add the lemon juice or vinegar, or a mixture of the two. Mix thoroughly. Add half the oil, mix well, then add the rest and mix again if necessary. Use just enough oil to make the salad glisten.
3 Taste, add more salt if necessary, and the mint.

You can use this cabbage salad as the basis for a mixed salad by adding some or all of the ingredients from Egyptian Salad [see above].

If you don't have time to wait 3 hours for the cabbage to soften, press the liquid out after about 30 minutes, squeezing and rubbing hard against the colander, and repeat after another few minutes.

THE MEZZE TABLE

The *mezze* idea is well worth adopting for the first course of a dinner party or a barbecue buffet. A large selection of appetizing delicacies awaits the guests as they arrive, allowing people to come at their convenience without leaving the early guests to starve.

The great advantage for the cook is that she or he can prepare most of the dishes for a *mezze* in advance, and, indeed, many of them require little or no preparation. You can therefore plan a range of dishes according to how much time you have, and how much you want to spend. It is also easy to cater for unexpected guests – simply bring out more dishes of olives and bread to supplement what is already on the table.

Preparing a *mezze* spread is also great fun because you don't have to make a large quantity of each dish. Select a number of dishes contrasting in texture, shape, color and, of course, flavor: crisp spinach borek, stuffed vine leaves, succulent chicken wings, dips, pickled vegetables and preserves, and plenty of good bread, home-made or otherwise.

Of course, there is no need to follow a *mezze* first course with other Middle Eastern courses: you could make any familiar main course, perhaps a roast or a casserole, and finish with fruit, cheese or your favorite dessert. And I do not want to give the impression that you have to offer lots of items for a *mezze*; any one, two or three of the recipes in this chapter would be quite enough before a traditional Western meal.

Above, from left to right, front row Filo Borek with Spinach Filling, Baked Borek with Cheese Filling, Chicken Wings in Garlic and Lime Sauce, Laban Cheese Balls. *Middle row* Falafel, bowls of feta cheese and olives, Grilled Chicken Livers, Filo Pastry Tarts, Poached Brains in Turmeric and Garlic Sauce. *Back row* Cabbage Salad, Hummus Dip and Spiced Carrots

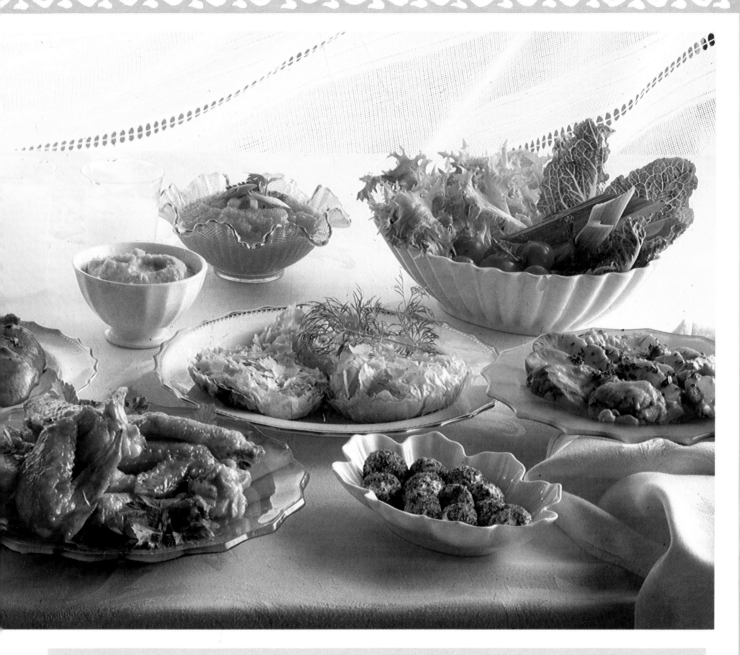

BOREK
Shaping Shortcrust Pastry Borek

1 Roll out the pastry into a thin circle, and put a teaspoonful of filling just off center on it. Be careful not to let the filling spread out.

2 Fold the pastry over the filling and press all around the edge (not too close to the filling) with your thumb to seal.

3 Trim the surplus pastry from the edge of the seam with a cup and knife or the rim of a glass.

4 Seal again by crimping all along the edge of the seam with a fork, or by pinching with your finger and thumb.

TARTS MADE FROM LEFTOVER FILO PASTRY

1 Grease an individual tart case. Arrange rectangles of leftover filo in the center of the case in overlapping layers.

2 Brush each rectangle lightly with melted butter as you go along. Add more overlapping layers until there are about 4 or 5 in all.

3 Spoon a heap of filling, such as the cheese filling on page 34, mixed with another beaten egg, into the center. Crumble the edges of the overlapping layers of filo over the filling, and any other scraps, to cover the filling. Bake in a moderate oven, 350°F, for 20–30 minutes.

CHICKEN WINGS IN GARLIC AND LIME SAUCE

PREPARATION TIME
1 hour 25 minutes, including 1 hour marinating and 20 minutes cooking

8 chicken wings
1 clove garlic
salt, to taste
juice of 1–2 limes or ½–1 lemon

[*picture on page 27*]

My family arrived in London in 1948 to find postwar rationing still in force. We used to buy enormous bags of chicken wings every week from a famous Indian restaurateur who owned a chicken farm; until we came along, he had thrown them all away. Contrary to what you might expect, we never tired of them. My mother devised countless ways to cook them, using chicken wings in almost any meat or poultry dish. And to this day I never fail to order the 'mezze' of chicken wings with lime and garlic served in Lebanese restaurants. You can substitute lemon juice if limes are not available.

1 Wash the wings, cut them in halves, and transfer to a bowl. Finely chop or thinly slice the garlic and sprinkle over the wings, followed by salt and plenty of lime or lemon juice. Leave to marinate for at least 1 hour, turning from time to time.
2 Put the wings and their marinade in a heavy-based saucepan wide enough for them to fit snugly together in a single layer. Barely cover them with water and bring to a boil. Lower the heat immediately and cover the pan. Simmer for about 15 minutes. Shake the pan from time to time to prevent sticking. If they do stick, add a little water and scrape the pan. When the dish is ready, the juices should have reduced to a thick sauce. Serve the wings hot on a small *mezze* plate with the pan juices poured over them.

GRILLED OR BROILED CHICKEN LIVERS

PREPARATION TIME
7 minutes, including 2 minutes cooking

8 chicken livers
salt and black pepper, to taste

[*picture on page 26*]

1 Rinse and dry the livers, and separate each into its two lobes.
2 Heat the broiler to high or, if using a cast-iron griddle on top of the stove, oil it and get it very hot, then oil it lightly with a brush or piece of wadded paper towel. Broil or grill the livers on both sides as quickly as possible to avoid drying them out. Take care not to over-cook them; each side will take about 1 minute. Sprinkle with salt [sea salt is particularly good] and black pepper, and serve.

The livers may also be sautéed in hot butter, seasoned and served with a squeeze of lemon juice.

POACHED BRAINS IN TURMERIC AND GARLIC SAUCE

PREPARATION TIME
**30 minutes soaking
30 minutes, including 20
 minutes cooking**

**2 sets calf's brains
1 Tbsp vinegar
1–2 Tbsp oil
juice of 1 lemon, or more to
 taste
1 clove garlic
1 tsp turmeric
salt and pepper, to taste**

TO GARNISH
a few sprigs parsley, chopped

[picture on page 27]

1 Wash the brains in cold running water. Soak them in cold water and vinegar for about 30 minutes. Rinse and remove the membrane. [With frozen brains, the membrane disappears anyway.]

2 Choose a pan into which the brains will fit in one layer. Put in just enough oil to coat the bottom, and the juice of a lemon. Slice and add the garlic. Lay the brains carefully in the pan and barely cover them with water. Add the turmeric, salt and pepper, and swirl the pan to spread the liquid over the brains. Bring to a boil, then reduce the heat to a gentle simmer and cover the pan. Check after a few minutes that the liquid is not drying up, and add more water if necessary. The brains are ready as soon as they are firm, after about 20 minutes. Be careful not to overcook them.

3 Put the brains on a plate to cool, and reduce the liquid in the pan by boiling if necessary; it should be fairly thick. Cut the brains into slices with a sharp knife. Arrange them on an hors d'oeuvre dish and pour the liquid over them. Add more lemon juice and chopped parsley if you like. Serve cold.

FRIED BRAINS Prepare the brains as above, then poach in salted water with a little vinegar. Allow them to cool, then cut into slices. Put a beaten egg yolk on a small plate, and some flour or very fine dried breadcrumbs on another. Coat each slice in the egg, then the flour. Fry gently in hot oil or clarified butter for a few minutes. Serve hot with wedges of lemon.

Below A market stall at Djerba, on a small island off the Tunisian coast, selling cinnamon bark, powdered green henna, lime blossom tea and other cooking and medicinal herbs

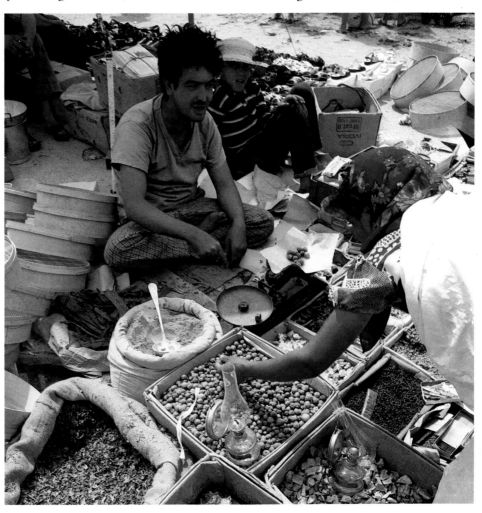

LAHME BI AJEEN [LEBANESE MEAT TARTLETS]

These are like miniature meat pizzas. Use the dough on page 134 or your favorite bread dough.

PREPARATION TIME
30 minutes, including 15
   minutes cooking

MAKES ABOUT 20 TARTLETS

BASE
bread dough made with 1⅔
   cups flour

FILLING
¼ lb minced lamb or beef, or a
   mixture of the two
1 medium onion
salt and pepper, to taste
1 tsp ground allspice
1 Tbsp finely chopped parsley
juice of ½ lemon, or to taste
1 oz pine nuts

TO BAKE
a handful of bran

1 When you have prepared the dough, make the filling. Put the meat into a mixing bowl and grate the onion straight into it. Add the salt, pepper, allspice, parsley and lemon juice. Taste, and adjust the seasoning.

2 Preheat the oven to 450°F. Quickly fry the pine nuts in a dry pan until slightly brown, and add to the mixture.

3 Knead the dough very well [see page 77]. Oil your hands lightly, take a walnut-sized piece of dough and knead it well. Roll or flatten it with your hand into a circle no thicker than a nickel, about 1/10 in. Draw your thumbs across the dough from the center to the edges to make a slightly raised rim to hold the filling.

4 Make all the bases and put a pile of filling in the middle of each. Sprinkle a dry baking sheet with bran and set the tartlets on it in rows. Bake for about 15 minutes, until the meat is done and the bread bases are cooked but still soft.

The filling may be flavored with a small amount of crushed dried limes [see page 10] or a sprinkling of sumac instead of lemon juice.

MEATLESS TARTLETS Mix one of the herb or spice mixtures on page 140 with a little olive oil and spread on the bases instead of the meat mixture above. A sprinkling of sesame seeds gives a nice crunchy texture.

BRIK À L'OEUF

Brik, the famous Tunisian snacks, are a special kind of deep-fried borek [see page 32]. In fact, the word 'brik' is simply the North African pronunciation of the original Turkish 'börek'. They may contain an infinite variety of fillings, the most spectacular of which is a whole egg [Brik à l'Oeuf, below]. Fillings may also be made of any suitable leftovers.

The wafer-thin pastry, called 'malsouga', comes in circles. It is sold in Tunisia and France. Chinese egg roll pastry is an ideal substitute; filo and strudel pastry are also satisfactory.

Brik are tricky to make at first, but once you have acquired the skill, they make a quick and very delicious snack. It is vital to have the filling ready first. The skill lies in the speed with which you fold the pastry into a package and slip it into the hot oil. If you are a beginner, it is probably a good idea to practice using the same ingredients [but only 2 eggs], mashed together, first. The mixture should be soft but not runny; if it is, add more cheese.

PREPARATION TIME
30 minutes, including 5–10
   minutes cooking

MAKES 4 BRIK

1 can tuna
8 small sheets Chinese egg roll,
   filo or strudel pastry
1 Tbsp oil + oil for deep frying
4 eggs
1 cup grated cheese
capers
salt and pepper, to taste

1 Drain and crumble the tuna. Cut the pastry into 5 in. squares and use two thicknesses of pastry for each brik. Put one of the squares on a plate; brush it lightly with oil and put the other square on top of it.

2 Put a large tablespoonful of tuna onto the square of pastry, to one side of the center. Make a hollow in the mound of tuna and break an egg into the hollow. Sprinkle cheese and capers on top, and add salt and pepper to taste. Fold the pastry over the filling to make a rectangular package, or a triangular one, whichever is easier. Moisten the seams with water to seal.

3 Heat the oil. Test the temperature by adding a small piece of filo pastry: when it sizzles, the oil is ready.

4 Slide the brik carefully into the oil and fry until golden brown, basting and turning once if it is not completely submerged in oil. It cooks almost immediately. Drain on paper towels.

Eating this brik also requires practice. The idea is to suck out the runny egg, at the same time getting a mouthful of tuna and crispy pastry.

OPPOSITE Brik à l'Oeuf, rectangular or triangular pastry package (*top left*), Lahme bi Ajeen (*bottom left*) and Baked Borek with Khandrajo Filling (*right*)

FISH AND POTATO BRIK No less delicious, but easier to make and eat! The filling may be made with leftovers from the Fish Stew on page 53, or some similar dish. Mash together cooked fish and a cooked potato. Add 1 tablespoonful chopped parsley, ½ tsp turmeric, and a dot of Harissa [see page 140] or other red pepper [chili] sauce. Beat an egg into the mixture. There should be enough filling for several briks.

BOREK

In Turkish 'borek' means, roughly, a pasty. The Arabic word is 'faytir'. There are many kinds, small and large, savory and sweet. Small savory borek are highly popular as *mezze*. The smaller and more delicate you can make them, the better they are. Fillings are endlessly varied: four are given below, and the other fillings elsewhere in this book should give you plenty of ideas for creating your own. Let your imagination be your guide. Borek may be made with pie crust dough or ready-made filo pastry dough. There are almost as many variations for the crust as there are for fillings, and each cook uses her own favorite. My own favorite recipe for pastry is not only very good, but also extremely easy to make, though it defies all conventional notions of pastry making: the quantities in the recipe are governed by volume and the absorbency of the flour you use, so they should be regarded as rough guidelines. The French principal of one cooking school was really shocked the first time she saw me making it, but she was so impressed by the result that now she insists that I include it in all my demonstrations. You can use this pastry for quiches, savory tarts and so on, as well as for borek. At that particular school they use it, made with sugar instead of salt, for Christmas mincemeat pies.

BAKED BOREK WITH KHANDRAJO FILLING

The Khandrajo filling, which my grandmother used to make, is rather like 'ratatouille'.

Filling

1 Cut the onion into small chunks and put it in a heavy-based pan with a thin layer of oil. Cook over a medium to low heat to soften it. Meanwhile, wash and dry the eggplants and, without peeling them, cut into 1 in. cubes. When the onion begins to color, mix in the eggplant, salt and pepper.

2 If you are using fresh tomatoes, peel them and remove any watery bits; if you are using canned tomatoes, drain and reserve the liquid. When the mixture gets a little darker, add the tomatoes and stir very thoroughly. Continue cooking on medium heat, stirring from time to time.

3 After about 20 minutes, increase the heat and stir constantly until the mixture becomes fairly dry and on the dark side. If it sticks to the pan, add a little water or reserved tomato liquid and scrape well. When the mixture is really quite dry, transfer to a bowl and leave to cool. It must be absolutely cold before you can use it. If any oil rises to the surface, spoon it off or soak it up with paper towels.

Pastry

4 Cut up the butter and melt it very gently over low heat, taking care not to cook it. Pour it into a small cup standing on a flat surface, then into a large mixing bowl. The butter will have left a mark inside the cup; this is the measuring mark.

5 Fill the cup with oil up to the same mark and pour this into the bowl. Measure an equal quantity of water in the same way. Add with the salt to the bowl and stir.

6 Using a large wooden spoon, add one large spoonful of the flour at a time, stirring constantly to mix it in. It looks rather unpleasant, like a sauce full of lumps, at first; but don't worry. Just go on adding and mixing, and the mixture will start to look more like dough. The proportions are about right when the pastry dough comes away from the sides of the bowl, leaving it clean. By then it will have taken up very roughly $1\frac{2}{3}$ cups of flour. Gather the pastry dough into the center of the bowl with your hands, and transfer it to a work surface. If the pastry dough is too soft, and needs more flour, put some in a pile on one side. Roll the ball of pastry dough in the flour. Then, with a quick, firm twist of your hand, incorporate the flour. French cooks call this *fraiser*.

7 The pastry dough is now ready to use; unlike others, it does not need a resting period. * However, it can be prepared in advance to this stage, wrapped in foil and stored in the refrigerator. It is easier to handle after refrigeration.

8 Just before you start filling the borek, preheat the oven to 375°F. To make small borek, take a piece of pastry dough about the size of an egg. Press it into a flat disk in your hand, ensuring that there are no cracks in it. Then flatten it more on a board and roll it into a thin circle. [See the step-by-step instructions opposite.]

PREPARATION TIME
1 hour 25 minutes, including 1 hour 10 minutes cooking

MAKES 20 BOREK

FILLING
1 large onion
1–2 Tbsp oil
2 large eggplants
salt and pepper, to taste
6–7 tomatoes, or a large can peeled tomatoes

PASTRY
2 oz [½ stick] butter
same volume oil and water [see right]
1 tsp salt
$1\frac{2}{3}$ cups flour

TO GLAZE
milk or egg yolk

[picture on page 31]

SOME BOREK SHAPES

Pastry for frying
CONES

1 Cut a circle of pastry 5 in. in diameter in half and moisten the straight edge.

2 Form the semicircle into a cone by folding the straight edge in half and sealing it.

3 Open out the cone and put in about half a teaspoonful of filling.

4 Close the top with wet fingers.

5 Crimp the seams with your finger and thumb.

With Filo Pastry
FINGER SHAPES

1 Put a sausage-shaped roll of filling diagonally across one corner of a double layer of filo, about 9 in. by 5 in.

2 Starting from the same corner, roll the pastry diagonally, folding in the sides as you go along to make a small, neat, finger-shaped package.

With Filo Pastry
COILS

1 Spread a narrow line of filling along one edge of a double layer of filo, about 12 in. by 5 in., leaving a small border of pastry uncovered at each end.

2 Fold in the two short edges and one long edge to enclose the filling.

3 & 4 Starting at the filling edge, roll the pastry into a long thin sausage shape.

5 & 6 Form a tight coil by holding one end of the pastry and twisting the rest of the roll around it.

All Pastries
TRIANGLES

1 Put a teaspoonful of filling in a small heap on a double layer of filo about 12 in. by 3 in.

2 Fold into a triangle as shown, making sure that the filling remains completely enclosed in the pastry.

9 Put one teaspoonful of the filling off-center on the pastry. Be careful to drop it in a neat pile. If it spreads out over the pastry you will not be able to seal the borek. Fold the pastry over to make a semicircle, and press all around with your thumb to seal it. Don't press too close to the filling. There must be space around it to allow for expansion during cooking. Trim the edge of the seam with the rim of a glass or a pastry cutter. Add the trimming to the main lump of pastry dough. Make sure of a good seal by crimping all along the seam with a fork, or by pinching with your finger and thumb.

10 Brush the borek with milk or beaten egg yolk and put them on a baking sheet. With this pastry, you do not need to grease or flour it. Bake for 30 to 40 minutes. Check that they are done by lifting one up. The underside should be just beginning to color. Transfer to a cooling rack and serve warm or cold.

CHEESE FILLING FOR BOREK

PREPARATION TIME
10 minutes

MAKES ENOUGH FOR 20 BOREK

½ lb grated cheese [see right]
breadcrumbs [if necessary]
1 large egg
1 tsp crushed dried mint
   [optional]

Cheese is one of the traditional fillings for all kinds of borek, baked or fried. The flavor must be well balanced: mild cheeses are too bland when cooked, strong ones too overpowering, so it is usual to mix them. A very strong mixture can be toned down by adding a small amount of fresh breadcrumbs. A few experiments will help you to achieve a good flavor with whatever cheese you have available. You might begin by trying the following combinations: 3 parts mild Cheddar to 1 part feta; or 3 parts strong matured Cheddar to 1 part feta plus a handful of fresh breadcrumbs; or one of the mild cheeses with just ½ oz of very strong blue cheese; or 6 parts mild cheese to 1 part each Parmesan and cream cheese. Combine the grated cheese with the egg. The consistency should be softish, but firmer than dropping consistency. Adjust it with more cheese or breadcrumbs. Add mint if you like.

FRIED BOREK WITH MEAT FILLING

PREPARATION TIME
1 hour 10 minutes, including
   30 minutes wait and 25
   minutes cooking

MAKES 30 BOREK

FILLING
1 medium onion
about 1 Tbsp oil
1 clove garlic
¼ lb minced lamb or beef, or a
   mixture of the two
1 tsp ground allspice
¼ tsp grated nutmeg
salt and pepper, to taste
1 egg
1–2 Tbsp chopped parsley

PASTRY
1⅔ cups flour
1 tsp salt
2 Tbsp oil
5 Tbsp lukewarm water

oil for deep frying

[picture on page 31]

Make the filling first so that it has time to cool before you use it. My favorite pastry dough [see page 32] is too rich for frying. The one given here is more suitable.

Filling
1 Grate or chop the onion very finely, put in a saucepan with a little oil, and cook over medium heat for 10 to 15 minutes, or until soft and transparent.
2 Chop the garlic very finely and add to the onion. Increase the heat and cook, stirring, until the onion turns golden brown. Add the meat, squashing it against the side of the pan. If it sticks to the bottom, scrape well. Keep stirring until the meat begins to brown. Add the pepper, allspice, nutmeg and salt. Mix well and keep stirring until the meat is nicely brown. If it sticks, scrape the pan thoroughly and add a little water.
3 Transfer the mixture to a bowl. Beat the egg and mix it in to soften the mixture. Stir in parsley to taste. Let the mixture cool thoroughly before using it.

Pastry for frying
4 Sift the flour and salt into a bowl. Make a hole in the center. Pour the oil and water into the hole and mix with two knives or a pastry blender until all the flour is combined. If you use a food processor, add only the oil at first, and pour in water a little at a time, as you may not need it all. Gather the pastry dough with your hands and knead very well until it is even and soft. This takes a good 10 minutes. Form the dough into a smooth ball, cover the bowl with a damp cloth and leave to rest for about 30 minutes in the refrigerator.
5 Put a little oil on your hands and rub it into a rolling pin. Take a lump of dough the size of a walnut. Knead very thoroughly until it is perfectly smooth, and form it into a round ball without creases. Roll the pastry out into a circle, as thinly as you can; it must be really transparent. Put a saucer about 5 in. diameter on the circle and trim around it. Save the trimmings to use later. Cut the circle in half with a sharp knife. You may prefer to roll out all the pastry circles before shaping and filling. If so, brush one side of each circle with a little oil, then stack them.
6 Wet your finger and run it along the straight edge of a piece of pastry. Fold the pastry in two and close to form a cone shape. Open out the cone, hold upright and put in about half a teaspoonful of filling. Close the top with wet fingers. Crimp the seams at intervals with your thumb and forefinger to make a frilly edge.
* This pastry can be prepared in advance, and is actually improved by freezing, which lightens the texture. You can freeze the uncooked borek first loose on a tray, then packed in bags, and fry them straight from the freezer.
7 Deep fry for less than a minute, until puffed up and golden, then drain on paper towels. Serve hot.

Traditional additions to the filling are some chopped cooked spinach with a squeeze of lemon juice; or a hard-boiled egg cut up into very small pieces [not chopped]; or a handful of pine nuts quickly browned in a dry frying pan. You can also replace the egg with a set of cooked calf's brains [see page 29], which gives a distinctive flavor.

TESTING OIL
TEMPERATURE

Cut off a small piece of whatever you are frying or take a pinch of breadcrumbs if you are using them, and drop into the oil. When it sizzles to the surface, the oil is hot enough. For safety, I use a long-handled spoon to slowly ease the food into the hot oil.

Baked Borek with Cheese Filling and Filo Pastry Borek with Spinach Filling

FILO PASTRY BOREK WITH SPINACH

PREPARATION TIME
1 hour 15 minutes, including
  30 minutes cooking

MAKES 16–18 BOREK

2 lb fresh spinach or 1 lb frozen
  leaf spinach
salt, to taste
3 cups grated Cheddar cheese
4 Tbsp [2 oz] cream cheese
2 large eggs
juice of 1 lemon, or to taste
pepper and grated nutmeg, to
  taste
1 lb package filo pastry
oil or melted butter

The traditional coil shape can be achieved only if using very fresh and pliable filo pastry [see the advice on handling filo pastry on page 130]. These borek are slightly larger than others.

1 If you are using fresh spinach, wash it well, tear it up and put in a saucepan. Sprinkle with the salt, cover the pan and cook on low heat, turning frequently, for a few minutes. Turn the pan on its side and squeeze the spinach to remove as much moisture as possible, then turn up the heat to dry it more. Tip it into a sieve and press out the last remaining water. If using frozen spinach, thaw it in a pan with salt, then dry it out as above. It is important that the salt is added in the first stages of cooking; if added later, there is a risk that it will draw moisture out of the spinach.

2 Chop the spinach roughly and put it in a bowl with the cheese, eggs and lemon juice. Stir well; it should be quite firm. Taste, and add more salt, pepper and a little nutmeg.

3 Cut the filo sheets into rectangles about 12 in. by 5 in. Roll up the cut sheets together and keep them covered with one or two damp cloths. Put a bowl at each end of the rolled-up sheets, and hang the cloths over them so that they do not touch the pastry. Remove one sheet at a time, as needed.

4 Preheat the oven to 375°F. Brush one side of a filo sheet lightly all over with oil or melted butter. Place another filo sheet on top of it. Take about a tablespoon of filling and spread it in a line as thick as your little finger all along one long edge of the rectangle [follow the step-by-step instructions on page 33]. Leave about $\frac{3}{8}$ in. at each end of the pastry free of filling. Roll the pastry lengthwise into a cigar shape, then form into a tight, flat coil. Put on an oiled baking sheet and brush the top and sides with oil. The borek should be packed tightly together on the sheet to keep them from uncoiling when baked.

5 Bake in the oven for 25 to 30 minutes, or until golden brown on top.

35

SOUPS

In the Middle East, like anywhere else, soups are enjoyed in every home. But, I am embarrassed to confess, until I started cooking when I was in my twenties, I avoided soups. Now they are among the things I most enjoy making and eating, as they allow such great creative scope. All kinds of legumes, fresh vegetables, meats, poultry or fish and their scraps or bones, herbs and spices available in this country, can be turned into exciting soups with a Middle Eastern flavor.

There is often very little difference between a soup and a stew; the quantity of water is what distinguishes one from the other. I have grouped the soup recipes into a few general categories. First come those based on meat, chicken or fish broths and stocks. For these I provide a simple basic stock recipe – something well worth making whenever you have the chance, and storing in the freezer. Second are meat and vegetable soups. Third are those based on purées of legumes. The fourth category comprises what I call special soups: Melokheya Soup from Egypt and Trahanas Soup from Cyprus. The former is an old favorite of mine and the latter, a recent discovery I have adopted with enthusiasm.

Two rich vegetable soups and two stock-based soups (*clockwise from the top*) Shorba, Rich Meatless Soup, Yogurt Soup with Chicken Rissoles and Parsley and Egg and Lemon Soup with Meat Balls

STOCK AND BROTH

I usually make stock with whatever is available: bones and meat or poultry, or fish bones, heads and trimmings, and with a couple of carrots, a leek, an onion, some parsley stalks [which have more flavor than the leaves], and salt and pepper. I never include any extra flavoring when making basic stock in advance, since I intend to use it for different soups or other dishes, each of which will have its own flavoring.

I find it better not to add the vegetables to the pot at the beginning, but after the water boils and all the scum has been skimmed off. Floating vegetables make this difficult. After adding the vegetables, whole or cut into chunks, I bring the water back to a boil slowly, add salt and pepper, and simmer very gently with the lid set on the pan at a tilt to let out some of the steam.

If I am making a broth to be used immediately, I cook it until it no longer tastes watery. When making meat or poultry stock in advance, however, it is better to continue cooking until the liquid is reduced to about half its original volume, making a really strong stock, which is a fine basis for soups and other dishes. This is then diluted when needed to make broth.

When the stock is ready, I strain it through a sieve into a bowl, let it cool, then leave it in the refrigerator overnight. The fat rises to the surface and congeals into a solid mass which is easy to remove. After this, I warm the stock and strain it again through a sieve lined with paper towel into a saucepan. This has to be done gently so that the sediment stays at the bottom of the bowl. Then I boil the stock for a couple of minutes and leave it to cool. The result is a pure, strong stock, well worth all the trouble.

When making a poultry broth with an entire bird rather than just the carcass or trimmings, I save the meat as soon as it is cooked, cutting it off the carcass and returning the carcass to the pot. The meat can either be used for another dish, or added to the stock at a later stage. This is because the meat of factory-farmed chicken cooks long before any flavor is imparted to the broth. Of course, if you use a boiling fowl or a corn-fed bird, this does not apply.

For making a fish broth, the bones and heads of white fish are ideal. The fish should not be simmered for more than 20 to 30 minutes. To reduce it to keep for later use, I strain the stock and continue simmering without the solids.

Although I do not like bought stock cubes as the only basis of a soup, they are useful for adding to a dish that needs to be enriched, or used to stretch a soup if unexpected guests arrive.

Right A wide range of spices and grains on sale in the souk at Fez. Many spices are sold whole, then mixed, roasted and ground for use in a particular dish. Those shown here include root ginger, sweet red bell peppers, cloves and allspice berries. The grains include couscous and various sizes of bulgar, or cracked, wheat.

EGG AND LEMON SOUP WITH MEAT BALLS

PREPARATION TIME
1 hour 15 minutes, including
    45 minutes cooking

about 4 $\frac{1}{2}$ cups meat or chicken
    broth
3–4 sticks celery
4 small potatoes, or 1–2 larger
    ones
$\frac{1}{4}$ lb lean veal, lamb, beef or
    chicken
1 small onion
2 cloves garlic
3 Tbsp chopped parsley
salt and pepper, to taste
a pinch ground allspice
juice of 1–2 lemons
2 eggs

TO GARNISH
a few sprigs parsley, chopped

TO SERVE
lemon wedges

[picture on page 36]

The combination of egg and lemon with a rich broth to give a distinctive, tangy flavor is a favorite all over the Middle East, both for soups and for sauces. In Arabic it is known as 'beid bi lamoun', in Greek 'avgolemono'; both simply mean 'egg and lemon'. The broth may be made from a chicken, veal or fish stock; the soup may include rice, vermicelli [or other small pasta], pieces of meat, chicken or fish, minced meat or chicken balls or fish rissoles, and vegetables, usually celery and potatoes. Here is one recipe from the immense variety: do not hesitate to try changes to suit your taste.

1 If you are using stock which has been prepared in advance, dilute it with enough water to make up the amount required and bring it to a gentle boil. If using freshly made broth, simply bring it to simmering point. Trim and wash the celery, saving some leaves if you want to add them to the meat balls instead of parsley. Cut the celery into 2 $\frac{1}{2}$ in. lengths, removing any tough strings, and add to the broth. Wash the potatoes, peel them if you like, cut into chunks if they are large, and add to the broth.
2 Prepare the meat balls. Mince the meat and put into a mixing bowl. Grate the onion and garlic into the bowl. Add the parsley or chopped celery leaves, salt pepper and allspice. Knead the mixture thoroughly, then taste and adjust the seasoning. Damp your hands slightly and form the mixture into walnut-sized balls, kneading each well until quite smooth. Keep your hands just damp and they will not stick [see page 77].
3 When the vegetables are cooked, gently slide the meat balls into the soup and continue simmering gently for about another 15 minutes.
4 Meanwhile, beat the juice of 1 to 2 lemons, according to taste, with the eggs in a bowl. Add a ladleful of the hot broth and continue beating, then add several more ladlefuls, beating all the time.
5 Carefully remove the meat balls and vegetables from the soup with a slotted spoon. Put them in a soup tureen and keep warm. Remove the pan from the heat and pour the egg and lemon mixture gradually into the soup, beating all the time. Return the pan to a low heat to thicken the soup gently, taking care not to let it boil or it may curdle. Pour into the tureen and garnish with a little chopped parsley. Serve with wedges of lemon, for those who like the lemon flavor even more pronounced.

You can vary the seasoning of the meat balls with any herb or spice that appeals to you, or use a fish broth as the basis of the soup and make some Fish Balls [see page 52].

YOGURT SOUP WITH CHICKEN RISSOLES AND PARSLEY

PREPARATION TIME
1 hour 15 minutes, including
    45 minutes cooking

5 $\frac{1}{3}$ cups chicken or veal broth
$\frac{1}{4}$ lb cooked chicken
1 medium onion
1 $\frac{1}{3}$ cup cooked long grain rice
1 egg
1 tsp crushed dried mint
salt and pepper, to taste
5 Tbsp very finely chopped
    parsley
1 egg yolk
1 $\frac{1}{4}$ cups natural yogurt

[picture on page 36]

Another way of giving a tangy flavor to a soup is to use yogurt rather than lemon juice. Take care that the soup does not boil, or the yogurt will separate.

1 Pour the broth into a large, heavy-based pan with a lid. Cover, and bring to a gentle boil.
2 Meanwhile, make the chicken rissoles. Mince the cooked chicken, grate the onion and mix both with the rice. Knead very well to blend evenly. Beat an egg and add, a little at a time, to bind the mixture. It should not be sloppy; if it is, add some fresh breadcrumbs. Mix in the mint, salt and pepper.
3 Scatter the parsley all over a tray. Form the chicken mixture into walnut-sized rissoles and gently roll them in the parsley until they are completely covered.
* The dish can be prepared in advance to this stage.
4 About 15 minutes before serving, carefully lower the rissoles into the broth, which should be simmering. Keep it simmering gently for the rest of the cooking time. Some of the parsley will come off, but you will be surprised how much will stick to the rissoles if it has been chopped very finely.
5 Carefully transfer the rissoles to a soup tureen and keep warm. Beat the yogurt and egg yolk together in a bowl and add some hot broth, a tablespoonful at a time, stirring constantly. [This will prevent the yogurt from separating, provided that it is not allowed to boil.] Add the yogurt mixture to the broth, heat gently to serving temperature and pour over the rissoles.

RICH MEATLESS SOUP

PREPARATION TIME
55 minutes, including 45
    minutes cooking

1 fresh or dried chili pepper
1 medium onion
5 cloves garlic
1 tsp crushed caraway seed
4 tomatoes, or a small can
1 Tbsp oil
3 Tbsp chopped cilantro
salt and pepper, to taste
about $\frac{2}{3}$ cup coarse farina or
    long grain rice

TO GARNISH
a few sprigs fresh mint,
    chopped

[picture on page 37]

This is sometimes called 'poor man's soup' because it is meatless. I've renamed it for its rich flavor.

1 If using a dried chili, soak it for a few minutes until soft. Chop the onion finely, and crush the garlic. Remove the seeds from the chili, chop it finely, and mix well with the garlic, onion and caraway seed. A food processor will do the whole job in one step, but remember to remove the chili seeds first.
2 If using canned tomatoes, drain them and reserve the liquid; if using fresh ones, chop roughly.
3 Fry the onion and spice mixture gently in the oil in a heavy-based saucepan. When the onion is transparent, add the tomatoes, a little of the cilantro, salt and pepper to taste. Simmer for about 30 minutes, or until the farina or rice is tender, being careful not to overcook it.
4 Add enough water to make a soup consistency, bring to a boil, then reduce the heat again and simmer until the watery taste completely disappears. Add the farina or rice and simmer for another 10 or 15 minutes until it is cooked. Taste, and adjust the seasoning. Serve garnished with the rest of the chopped cilantro and mint.

The rice or farina can be replaced by a handful of presoaked, precooked dried garbanzo beans or navy beans added at step 3.

You could use canned beans for this, but they will yield inferior flavor.

SHORBA

PREPARATION TIME
8 hours soaking
1 hour 5 minutes, including 50
    minutes cooking

2 oz garbanzo beans
2 Tbsp oil
2 medium onions
1 lb stewing lamb
5–6 medium tomatoes or 1
    large can
$\frac{1}{4}$ lb green beans
2 medium potatoes
$\frac{1}{4}$ lb fava beans, fresh or frozen
4–5 sprigs each fresh mint and
    cilantro
pepper, to taste
1 tsp paprika
2 Tbsp tomato purée
$1\frac{1}{4}$ cup water
salt, to taste
1 medium zucchini
1 medium sweet green bell
    pepper
$3\frac{1}{2}$ oz vermicelli

[picture on page 36]

Though 'shorba' is the Arabic word for soup, the Algerian friend who cooked this dish for me insists that Shorba is its name, since other soups, such as Lentil Soup and Navy Bean Soup, are named after their main ingredients.

1 Wash the garbanzo beans and leave to soak at least 8 hours in plenty of water.
2 Pour enough oil into a heavy-based saucepan to line the bottom and set it over a medium heat. Roughly chop the onions and add them to the pan. Cut the meat into cubes and add. Stir thoroughly after every addition. Leave to cook over medium heat, stirring from time to time.
3 As you prepare the vegetables, add them to the pan. If using fresh tomatoes, skin and chop them; drain and chop canned ones, reserving the liquid. Trim the ends off green beans, removing any strings, and halve them. Wash and peel the potatoes [or I prefer to keep the skin on] and, if they are large, cut into chunks. If using fresh fava beans, pod them; frozen ones may be added straight from the freezer. If necessary, peel the garbanzo beans by rubbing them between your hands. Remove the leaves from the mint and cilantro and reserve them. Tie the stalks into a bundle and add to the pan.
4 Add the pepper and paprika to the pan after the vegetables. Add the tomato purée, diluted with $1\frac{1}{4}$ cup water or liquid reserved from the canned tomatoes. Bring to a boil, then lower the heat to simmering point. Cook, half covered, for about 1 hour or until the garbanzo beans are tender. Add salt to taste.
5 Slightly scrape the zucchini, de-seed the green pepper and cut both into large chunks. Add to the soup with enough water to cover the vegetables by 2 in., about $6\frac{2}{3}$ to $8\frac{3}{4}$ cups. Bring to a boil. Taste, and adjust the seasoning. Lower the heat and simmer, half covered, for another 20 minutes or so. Taste again and, if the soup still tastes watery, increase the heat and reduce further.
* The soup may be prepared in advance to this stage.
6 Crush the vermicelli into the soup and cook for another 5 minutes or until it is tender. Remove the bundle of herb stalks, chop the mint and cilantro leaves, add them and serve.

You can substitute beef for the lamb: foreshank of beef imparts a delicious flavor to the soup, but of course requires a longer time to cook. Stewing chicken will produce yet another stock. Fresh peas and carrots can also be added.

Clockwise from the top Lentil Soup, Trahanas Soup, Navy Bean Soup and Melokheya, a classic Egyptian dish

LENTIL SOUP

PREPARATION TIME
1 hour 15 minutes, including 1
  hour cooking

6 oz dry red lentils
about 1 Tbsp oil or clarified
  butter
1 medium onion
salt and pepper, to taste

TA'LEYA
2–3 cloves garlic
1 tsp ground cumin seed
1 tsp oil or clarified butter

This is another splendid soup for vegetarians. Others can use a chicken or meat stock or, as I often do, add a smoked ham bone at the beginning.

1 Spread the lentils out on a large plate and pick out any stones. Wash in several changes of water.

2 Add just enough oil or clarified butter to a large saucepan to coat the base, and set over a medium heat. Chop the onion very finely, add it to the pan and cook until soft and transparent. Then raise the heat and stir until the onion browns. Add the lentils and enough water to cover them by 1 in., bring to a boil and then lower the heat to simmer. Half cover the pan and simmer for about 30 minutes, or until the lentils are very tender.

3 Remove the lentils, leaving any remaining liquid in the pan. Purée them and return to the pan, adding more water if necessary to make a good creamy soup consistency.

5 Prepare the Ta'leya. Chop the garlic very finely. Heat the oil or clarified butter in a small pan and add the garlic. Stir; as soon as it colors, add the cumin, taking care not to burn it. Stir quickly and tip into the soup.

6 Add salt and pepper to taste, and simmer the soup for another 15 to 20 minutes.

MELOKHEYA

PREPARATION TIME
3 hours, including 2½ hours
    cooking

about ¼ lb dried *melokheya*

STOCK
1–2 marrow bones
1½ lb beef foreshank
1 medium onion
2 carrots
1 leek
salt and pepper, to taste
6 cracked cardamom pods
½ tsp crushed mastic
8¾ cups water

TA'LEYA
4–5 cloves garlic
1 Tbsp crushed coriander seed
2 tsp clarified butter

TO SERVE
lemon juice, to taste [optional]

[*picture on page 41*]

This universally popular soup is a classic Egyptian dish. It is made from the leaves of a species of mallow plant, known as 'melokheya'. The dried leaves can be found in Middle Eastern food shops – the spelling of the name on the package varies widely. Fresh bunches of 'melokheya' are also sometimes available in summer; the leaves look a bit like mint. The soup is usually made with a base of chicken stock to which you add some marrow bones. On feast days in Egypt, this is replaced by a goose, which makes it extra special. I like to use beef foreshank, which gives a very rich stock.

The way in which Melokheya is served and eaten varies greatly. Each family, and indeed each individual, has their own set ritual. I like to eat Melokheya first as a soup – on its own or maybe with a small piece of meat – into which I dunk pieces of Arabic Bread [see page 134]. For the next course I eat it as a sauce poured over rice, with Egyptian Salad [see page 25]. Others like to have it as a soup, with the meat that was cooked in it and some rice added to it, all seasoned with a dash of lemon juice. Still others cut up pieces of bread, moisten them with Melokheya, mix in some rice and pour more Melokheya on top. When the stock is made with a whole goose or a whole chicken, the bird is removed, browned in the oven after the soup is cooked and served separately.

If you are using fresh 'melokheya', the preparation is slightly different. For the quantities here you would need about 1½ lb fresh leaves. You can also use half fresh and half dried, which saves expense and some of the labor of preparation, and still gives a superior flavor. Wash the 'melokheya', shake off excess water, strip the leaves from the stems [which should be discarded] and spread the leaves out on a cloth to dry thoroughly, which takes several hours. Then chop them finely: the traditional tool is a half-moon cutter, but a food processor does it much more easily.

1 Make the stock with the ingredients on the left, following the method on page 38. Simmer for about 2 hours or until the meat is very tender. [In a pressure cooker it takes 25 to 30 minutes.] Leave to cool, then remove all the fat.

2 Crush the dried *melokheya* leaves to a powder, preferably in a blender or food processor. There should be 1¼–1½ cups powder. Take a ladleful or two of the cold stock and pour it onto the powdered *melokheya*. Soaking the *melokheya* helps to restore its fresh flavor.

3 Bring the stock to a boil in a very large saucepan. [The *melokheya* swells when cooked.] Add the soaked *melokheya* mixture to the stock and stir thoroughly to mix it in. Bring to a slow boil, half cover and cook for about 45 minutes. Stir from time to time and check that nothing is sticking to the bottom of the pan. A good beating is also necessary, particularly when using dried *melokheya*, as the soup tends to separate. The ideal final result is a well-blended green soup.

4 Prepare the Ta'leya. Crush the garlic and fry quite briskly with the coriander in clarified butter until you can smell the fragrance of the coriander. Add to the soup, with a squeeze of lemon juice if you like, just before serving.

The amount of Ta'leya varies according to individual preference, and some people also add ground cumin seed and cayenne pepper.

CROÛTONS
I find that the traditional method of making *croûtons*, by frying cubes of stale bread in butter, makes them too rich, for they absorb an enormous amount of butter. I have devised a quick way of making lighter *croûtons* with a flavor of butter but using a fraction of the amount. Cut thick slices of bread and spread both sides with butter. Cut these into cubes and bake in a moderate oven, about 350°F, until they are crisp.

FREEZING STOCK AND SAUCE
Home-made stock and tomato sauce can be frozen in an ice cube tray, and the frozen cubes transferred to a plastic bag and kept in the freezer. These basic ingredients are then always available and ready for immediate use, no matter how little you need.

NAVY BEAN SOUP

PREPARATION TIME
8 hours soaking
2¼ hours, including 2 hours cooking

1 lb navy beans
1 Tbsp clarified butter
1 large onion
salt and pepper, to taste

TA'LEYA
3 cloves garlic
1 tsp clarified butter
1 tsp crushed coriander seed
1 Tbsp paprika
½ tsp cayenne pepper

TO SERVE
croûtons
lemon wedges
butter

TO GARNISH
a few sprigs parsley or cilantro, chopped

[*picture on page 41*]

1 Rinse the beans in two or three changes of water, cover with water and leave to soak at least 8 hours.
2 Melt the clarified butter in a saucepan. Chop the onion finely, add to the pan and soften over medium heat. When the onion is transparent, raise the heat and fry until golden, stirring continually. Add the beans with their soaking water. Bring to a boil, then lower the heat, half cover the pan and simmer for about 1½ hours. In a pressure cooker, this will take only about 25 minutes.
3 When the beans are soft enough to be squashed with a fork, drain them, reserving the liquid, and liquidize them with enough of the cooking liquid to achieve the consistency of a cream soup. Return to the pan and set over a low heat. You may need to add a little more liquid to thin the soup down to your liking. Bring to a boil, then reduce the heat and simmer for about 30 minutes.
4 Prepare the Ta'leya. Chop the garlic very finely. Melt the clarified butter in a small pan. When it is sizzling, add the garlic, coriander, paprika and cayenne pepper or powdered red chili, stir and fry quickly for about half a minute, then tip into the soup. Ladle a little soup into the pan and stir to mix in the last fragments, then pour back into the saucepan. Add salt and pepper, taste and adjust the seasoning.
5 Serve with *croûtons*, and some wedges of lemon and some butter on the side, since some people may like to add a little lemon juice, or a dab of butter in the French manner. Sprinkle the soup with a little chopped parsley or cilantro if you like.

Black-eyed peas can be used instead of navy beans to make an equally fine soup.

TRAHANAS SOUP

PREPARATION TIME
2 hours soaking
45 minutes, including 30 minutes cooking

½ cup trahanas
5 cups broth [see right]
salt and pepper, to taste
3–4 tomatoes
¼ lb halumi or mozzarella cheese

TO SERVE
lemon wedges

[*picture on page 41*]

The recipe for this splendid soup was taught to me by a London Cypriot friend, Sylva Kofu. She insisted that it should be made with a plain broth of beef and marrow bones only, without any additions at all. Other people will swear that you need a good chicken broth with all the usual additions. I've tried both and like them equally; see what you think.

Trahanas comes in pieces or crushed. If halumi cheese is not available, mozzarella is an adequate substitute.

1 If the trahanas is in large pieces, crush it. Cover with water and soak for two hours.
2 Bring the broth to a boil and add the soaked trahanas, stirring constantly until completely blended. The purpose is to thicken as well as to flavor the soup. Taste and adjust the seasoning. Skin and chop the tomatoes, add them and cook for about 30 minutes on a low heat [using a heat diffuser if possible], stirring occasionally.
3 Cut the cheese into small cubes, add to the soup and cook for 5 minutes. The cheese should be melting but still holding its shape. Serve with wedges of lemon, as some people like to give the flavor an extra tang.

An Egyptian soup or stew would never be served without the soft, round, flat bread found throughout the Arab world. Traditionally the bread is never cut; pieces are torn off by hand and used to scoop up food from the plate. *Right* Two Egyptian women making bread at home. The pastry is shaped into large circles, then baked in a brick and clay oven.

FISH

No one, I think, will ever forget, even if they have enjoyed it only once, the aroma and flavor of a freshly caught Mediterranean fish grilled over charcoal. You may eat it in any of countless harbor-side restaurants in Alexandria or Athens, Algiers or Istanbul. The succulent fish, redolent of the sea, needs only a hint of flavoring from a little garlic, lemon juice and olive oil to be perfect.

In the Middle East, fish is also baked, with or without vegetables, and fried, either whole if small or medium-sized, or cut into slices or fillets if larger. There are a variety of sauces to accompany grilled, baked or fried fish [see pages 136–138]. Fish make delicious stews and soups, and can also be braised in the style known as *sofrito*. They can be minced, made into loaves and rissoles and cooked in fish sauces. All these recipes can be applied to most fish available locally throughout the United States.

For a while it looked as if fresh fish was going to disappear completely from the stores and fishmongers became an endangered species. But now fresh fish is making a comeback, and fish markets are springing up across the country. Even in the landlocked Mid-West you can find not only freshwater fish, but delicious fresh saltwater fish and seafood as well.

As American towns become increasingly cosmopolitan, we are beginning to see the return of the fishmonger offering a wide variety of fish.

Grilled Freshwater Trout (*top*) and Baked Gray Mullet, served with Tahina Dip. Other classic sauces (pages 136–8) are also good with fish.

45

The design of Turkish cäiques, traditional Mediterranean fishing boats, has not changed since ancient times. *Above* Dikili, a small fishing village on the Aegean coast. Turkish fish dishes rely on the superb quality of the fish, which is very often simply grilled over charcoal.

GRILLED, BROILED AND BAKED FISH

There are a few very simple guiding principles for grilled, broiled and baked fish. First, while most types of fish can be grilled or broiled, they should be cooked this way only if they are really fresh. Small and medium-sized fish, such as smelt, fresh sardines, red and gray mullet, mackerel, snapper and small sea bass, should be grilled or broiled whole. Larger fish, such as cod, halibut and hake, can be sliced into steaks, then marinated and broiled, as can fresh or frozen fillets.

Second, any fish that can be grilled or broiled can equally well be baked – and vice versa, assuming absolute freshness. In the recipes that follow, any named fish can be changed for another whole fish, slice or fillet of the same size or type. I have given a few hints on the slight difference in procedure necessary when using steaks or fillets of larger fish instead of whole smaller fish. The various fish do differ in oiliness, and where this matters I have also mentioned it in the recipe. The important point is that all the recipes are for firm-fleshed fish.

To flavor fish in a Middle Eastern way, marinate it in lime or lemon juice and olive oil, with some garlic, maybe a piece of fresh ginger, fresh herbs such as parsley or fennel leaves, and salt or pepper. There is a simple guiding principle: the more delicate the fish, the more delicate the marinade should be.

Of course, a marinade is ideal for giving a Middle Eastern flavor to fish cooked over charcoal on a barbecue. Fish can also be grilled on a lightly oiled cast-iron griddle over high heat.

GRILLED OR BROILED FRESHWATER TROUT

PREPARATION TIME
45 minutes, including 15
   minutes marinating and 15
   minutes cooking

4 river trout, each about 1 lb
   before preparation
2 cloves garlic
¼ cup chopped parsley
salt and pepper, to taste
juice of 1–2 lemons
1 Tbsp olive oil

TO GARNISH
lemon slices

[picture on page 44]

This is a perfect example of a local fish cooked in a Middle Eastern way.

1 Prepare the fish, or have it prepared, as described on page 48.
2 Cut a piece of foil for each fish to rest on. This will be a great help in turning them over during grilling or broiling. Make a couple of small cuts on each side of the fish and insert thin slivers of garlic. Chop the rest of the garlic, mix with half the parsley and stuff the fish with it. Sprinkle the fish with the salt, pepper and lime or lemon juice and rub this all over the fish with your hands. Leave to marinate for at least 15 minutes. Trout, being oily, do not require any oil at this stage.
3 Turn the broiler up high or make sure the grill is ready. When it is very hot, put each fish, on its foil, on the broiler rack or grill and cook on each side until the skin starts cracking, about 6 or 7 minutes a side in the case of a fair-sized trout. If the fish seems to be drying up, squeeze on a little lemon juice, or any leftover marinade.
4 Pour the olive oil into a cup, add the remaining parsley and beat to combine. Spread half this mixture on the serving dish. Tip the cooked fish onto the dish, top with the rest of the mixture and garnish with lemon slices.

If you cook white fish in this way, add one tablespoonful of oil to the marinade.

   Cilantro or fennel leaves can be used instead of parsley. Also, if you have some Preserved Lemons [see page 139], you can cut them into small pieces and add them to the stuffing, and use the liquid from the preserve instead of lemon juice – but remember that it is rather salty, so omit salt from the marinade. Slivers of fresh ginger can be inserted with the garlic, and chopped ginger added to the stuffing.

BAKED GRAY MULLET

PREPARATION TIME
1 hour 10 minutes, including
   30 minutes marinating and
   30 minutes cooking

1 gray mullet, about 3 lb
   before preparation
1 medium onion
3–4 cloves garlic
1 large sweet green bell pepper
3–4 Tbsp chopped parsley
juice of 1 lemon
salt and pepper, to taste
2–3 Tbsp olive oil

TO GARNISH
lemon wedges

[picture on page 45)

When baking fish, the larger the fish, the more you get for your money. Ask your fishmonger not to cut off the head and tail and to gut it through the smallest possible incision.

1 Wash the fish and remove any remaining scales.
2 Choose a baking dish that will take the fish whole. Slice the onion very thinly and spread it over the dish.
3 Chop most of the garlic very finely and cut the pepper into the thinnest possible strips. Mix well in a bowl with the parsley, lemon juice, salt and pepper. Stir in the oil. Pour most of this mixture over the onions, but reserve just enough to put inside the fish – to flavor it, it isn't meant to be a full-scale stuffing
4 Cut one or two slits on each side of the fish and insert slivers of garlic. Spoon the reserved mixture inside the fish. Put it on the dish and turn it over and over so that it gets coated with the marinade. Leave in a cool place for at least 30 minutes.
* The dish may be prepared in advance to this point, covered with foil or saran wrap and stored in the refrigerator.
5 Preheat the oven fairly hot, 375°F. Bake the fish, basting it a couple of times and turning it once after 20 minutes. It should be done in about 30 minutes, but check a little earlier.
6 Serve garnished with lemon wedges and parsley, with the marinade as a sauce.

Whole fish are very good marinated in a simple mixture of olive oil, lemon juice, salt and pepper, served with an Egg and Lemon Sauce [see page 136], Tahina Dip [see page 16] or mayonnaise. It can be covered with the sauce and garnished with parsley, pine nuts, paprika, olives or anything that you feel is suitable.

FISH BAKED WITH VEGETABLES A whole fish can be marinated as described above, and baked on a bed of sliced potatoes, onions, tomatoes and peppers. The marinade can be flavored with thyme, oregano, bay or fennel leaves. But don't overdo the mixture of herbs: it is better to have two or three in harmony than a cacophony.

BAKED FISH FILLETS OR STEAKS Fish fillets can also be baked in any of the above ways. They are also good baked in a cooked sauce, such as the Tomato Sauce on page 137. Reduce the sauce until quite thick, cover the fillets with it, wrap in foil and bake.

STUFFED SEA BASS

PREPARATION TIME
1½ hours, including 1 hour
   cooking

1 sea bass, at least 2¼ lb
   before preparation
¾ cup fine, soft breadcrumbs,
   made from stale bread
6–10 olives, depending on size
½ cup coarsely ground walnuts
¼ cup chopped parsley
1 Tbsp tomato purée
salt and pepper, to taste
1 tsp paprika
1 tsp turmeric
1 tsp ground allspice
1 large onion
juice of 2 lemons
6 tomatoes, or a large can
2–3 Tbsp olive oil
2–3 Tbsp fish stock [optional]
a dot cayenne pepper or
   powdered red chili

TO GARNISH [optional]
small sprigs parsley
lemon slices
olives

I first saw a fish boned through the back, with superb skill, at a demonstration of West Indian food by the professional cook Rosamond Grant. Your fishmonger may be able to bone a fish in this way; but if not, with a little practice and following the step-by-step instructions below, you should be able to do it yourself.

1 Wash and scale the fish thoroughly.
2 Prepare the stuffing. Quickly crisp the breadcrumbs in a dry frying pan. Put them in a bowl. Pit the olives, cut into small pieces and add to the bowl with the walnuts and some of the parsley. Add the tomato purée, salt, pepper, paprika, turmeric and allspice. Grate about 2 tablespoonfuls off the onion into the bowl. Add the juice of one lemon, mix thoroughly and adjust the seasoning to your taste.
3 Bone and gut the fish, rinse and dry it, put in as much stuffing as it will comfortably hold and sew it up. [See the diagrams for guidance.] Reserve any spare stuffing.
4 Preheat the oven to 350°F. Choose an oven-proof dish that will take the fish whole. Slice the onion into rings and spread them out in the dish. Chop the tomatoes if fresh, or drain and crush if canned, reserving the liquid from the can. Add the tomatoes to the dish and sprinkle with the rest of the parsley and any remaining stuffing.
5 Mix the olive oil in a jug with the fish stock if you have any, or some of the reserved liquid from the canned tomatoes, or water. Add the juice of the other lemon: there should be a generous ½ cupful of liquid in all. Also add salt, pepper and a small dot of cayenne pepper [or powdered red chili]. Beat well and pour half of it onto the dish. Lay the fish on the bed of vegetables and pour the rest of the liquid over it.
6 Bake the fish for about 1 hour in all, basting after 30 minutes. When it is cooked, taste the sauce and adjust the seasoning if necessary. Serve with the sauce spooned over. If you like, garnish it with sprigs of parsley along the spine of the fish, thin slices of lemon and whole olives. It will look superb and taste even better.

You can vary the herb and spice combinations in the stuffing by adding to or replacing those listed with, for example, a little ground cumin seed and a dot of Harissa [see page 140], red pepper [chili] sauce or cayenne pepper [or powdered red chili], and adding small pieces of Preserved Lemon [see page 139].

BONING A FISH THROUGH THE BACK

1 Using a sharp knife, cut along each side of the backbone.

2 Ease out the backbone, snip it with scissors at the tail and head ends, and remove it completely. Remove the guts.

3 Remove the gills and wash the fish in cold running water.

4 After stuffing, sew up the slit with a needle and thread.

BUYING AND SCALING FISH

If you are going to cook your fish whole or stuffed, make sure that the fishmonger leaves on the head, and if he is gutting it for you ask him to do this through the smallest possible incision, which will ensure that the fish retains its shape.

Always make sure that there are no scales left on a fish. Using the blunt back of a knife, scrape off the remaining scales, working towards the head.

Small Fried Fish and Stuffed Sea Bass with a spicy tomato and herb stuffing

SMALL FRIED FISH

Fresh sardines [larger than the canned ones] or small red mullet are ideal for this dish. Allow two sardines or one mullet per person.

PREPARATION TIME
50–55 minutes, including 30 minutes marinating and 5–10 minutes cooking

4 fresh small red mullet, or 8 fresh sardines
2 cloves garlic
½ rounded tsp ground cumin seed
3 Tbsp finely chopped parsley
salt and pepper, to taste
flour for coating
oil for semi-deep frying

TO GARNISH
lemon wedges

1 Wash, scale and gut the fish if necessary.
2 Chop the garlic very finely and mix with the cumin, parsley, salt and pepper. Stuff the fish with at least half the mixture. Rub the rest on the outside, and leave for about 30 minutes in a cool place, or covered in the refrigerator, to allow the fish to take up the flavor.
3 Heat enough oil for semi-deep frying in a heavy pan or wok. Test the oil by adding a pinch of breadcrumbs. As soon as they sizzle to the surface, the oil is hot enough. Coat the fish with flour and shake off the excess. Fry the fish for 5 to 10 minutes or until cooked. Serve either hot or cold with wedges of lemon.

Slices or steaks of larger fish such as gray mullet or sea bass can be cooked in the same way. Coat the slices with the mixture and leave to stand as above. Then moisten them with beaten egg, dip in flour and fry. They can be served with Egg and Lemon Sauce [see page 136], Tahina Dip [see page 16] or mayonnaise.

SLICED FISH IN TOMATO SAUCE

PREPARATION TIME
1½ hours, including 50 minutes
cooking

3 lb white fish, e.g. cod, hake or
halibut [see right]
1 egg, beaten
about 4 Tbsp dry breadcrumbs
1 large onion
oil for semi-deep frying
1 Tbsp water
1 clove garlic
3 Tbsp chopped parsley
1 large can tomatoes
salt and pepper, to taste
1 Tbsp tomato purée
1 Tbsp vinegar
1 tsp sugar, or to taste
[optional]

This is a delicious way of preparing large, firm fish. The piquant tomato sauce suits both a plain white fish such as cod or hake, or halibut, turbot, gray mullet or sea bass. Buy steaks, or cut the fish into slices about ¾ in. thick.

1 Slice the fish if necessary, dry it, dip in beaten egg and coat with breadcrumbs. Chop the onion very finely. Pour oil into a heavy sauté pan large enough to hold the fish in one layer and having fairly high sides and a lid, to a depth of about 1 in. Heat it quite hot: test by dropping in a pinch of breadcrumbs, which would sizzle up to the surface. Fry the fish slices quickly until brown on both sides. Remove them and drain on paper towels.
2 Carefully pour away most of the oil, leaving just enough in the pan to coat it well. Reduce the heat to medium, add the onions and cook until transparent. If some of the breadcrumbs left in the pan stick, scrape them off with a spoon and mix with the onions. Add a tablespoonful of water or juice from the can of tomatoes, bring to a boil, then reduce the heat to simmer. Meanwhile, chop the garlic, then add it and the parsley to the pan.
3 Drain and add the tomatoes and mash them with a fork, then add the salt, pepper, tomato purée and vinegar. Stir and taste: you may like to add a little sugar. Bring to a boil, then reduce the heat and simmer for 15 to 20 minutes.
4 Add the fish slices, turning them over to coat them with the sauce. If the sauce is too thick, dilute it with some water or juice from the can, or a little more vinegar if needed. Cover the pan and simmer for about 20 minutes. This dish is best served with rice.

You can also use the Tomato Sauce on page 137, if you have some already made, or canned tomato sauce. Warm it up and add fresh parsley and, if you like, some cilantro. You might also add small pieces of Preserved Lemon [see page 139] or a dot of cayenne pepper or powdered red chili. Fry the fish in a separate pan, add it to the sauce and simmer for about 20 minutes.

ESCABECHE

PREPARATION TIME
30 minutes, including 25
minutes cooking
2 days marinating

3–4 lb fish, e.g. mackerel [or
see right]
flour for coating
1–2 Tbsp oil, + more for semi-
deep frying
2 medium onions
1 large sweet green bell pepper
2–3 cloves garlic
a pinch cayenne pepper
1 rounded Tbsp whole allspice
3 Tbsp chopped parsley
a pinch dried thyme
2 bay leaves
salt and pepper, to taste
1¼ cups vinegar

Various versions of this dish of marinated or quickly pickled fish are found all around the Mediterranean under various names; another one is 'scabetch'. It crossed the Atlantic to Jamaica, where it is called 'escovitch', and to South America, where a version is made with completely raw fish [but 'cooked' by the acid marinade] is known as 'seviche' or 'ceviche'. In Mexico, the marinade for 'escabeche' often includes orange juice and chili peppers. The recipe I have given here is for my favorite version, which is splendid made with mackerel; you can use almost any small or medium-sized, firm-textured whole fish, from large sardines to smaller John Dory. Larger fish can be sliced and cooked in the same way, too. The dish improves with a period of refrigeration, and should be made at least two days in advance.

1 Wash, scale and gut the fish as necessary. Dry and roll in flour.
2 Put a little oil in a frying pan and set it over medium heat. Finely slice the onions, add them to the pan and let them cook gently while you cut the pepper into strips and chop the garlic. Add these, and the cayenne pepper, whole allspice, parsley, dried thyme rubbed in your hands to release the flavor, bay leaves, salt, pepper and vinegar, to the pan. Bring to simmering point and cook for 10 to 15 minutes.
3 Meanwhile, fry the fish in about a 1 in. depth of oil in a separate pan until golden brown, and drain on paper towels. Transfer it to a fairly deep dish. Pour the sauce over it and leave to cool. Cover and leave in the refrigerator for at least 2 days. Serve cold.

You can also cook the dish in one pan, if you prefer. Fry the fish first, then remove it from the pan and pour most of the oil away. Add the onions to the pan and continue making the sauce as above.

Here are a few tips for recognizing a really fresh fish. Its eyes should be bright, the skin should be shiny and the area under the gills should be red. The fish should be firm to the touch and smell of the sea.

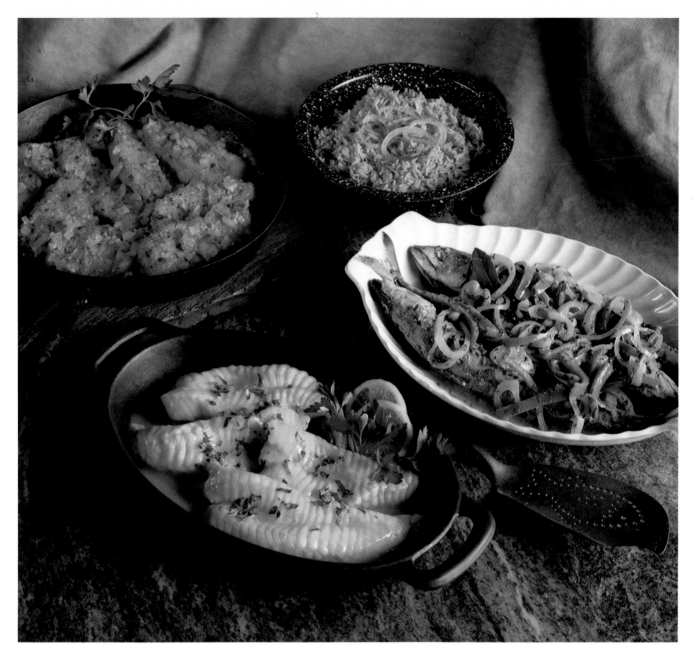

Left to right Sliced Fish in Tomato Sauce, Fish Sofrito, made here with angelfish, and Escabeche, served with a special Rice for Fish (*recipe on page 104*)

FISH SOFRITO

PREPARATION TIME
20–30 minutes, including 15 minutes cooking

about 2 Tbsp oil
1 clove garlic
juice of 1 lemon
½ tsp turmeric
5 Tbsp water or fish stock
4 slices angelfish, each about 7 oz
5 Tbsp fish stock or water

TO GARNISH
a few sprigs parsley, chopped

This is a delicious and very quick way to cook fillets, slices or steaks of large fish. I like it best made with angelfish, but I've also cooked a much coarser fish, conger eel, in this way with good results. It may be eaten hot or cold. If you use good fish stock rather than water for the sauce, it will set to a delicious jelly when it cools.

1 Choose a frying pan which will take all the fish in one layer, and pour in just enough oil to coat the base. Slice the garlic very finely, add it to the pan with the lemon juice, turmeric and a little water, and bring very gently to a boil.
2 Meanwhile, wash and dry the fish. Raise the heat, and add the fish to the pan when the liquid is just beginning to tremble. Add the fish stock if you have some, or otherwise water, to just cover the fish. Bring it to simmering point and cook very gently until done, which will be no more than 10 minutes.
3 Transfer the fish to a deep dish. The sauce should be quite thick; if not, reduce by boiling before pouring it over the fish. Sprinkle with the parsley.

FISH LOAF SOFRITO

This delicious fish loaf is an example of a traditional dish which used to be time-consuming and messy to prepare but which, when made with a modern gadget such as a food processor, presents no such problems. The 'sofrito' sauce, made as in the previous recipe, is used for poaching the fish loaf. The dish is excellent as a buffet spread.

1 Mince the fish finely; it will be easier if you poach it a little first. Finely grate the onion and garlic. Mix the parsley and most of the breadcrumbs well with the fish. [If using a food processor, first chop the onion and garlic, then add the parsley and breadcrumbs and finally the fish and process until all is well combined.] Add the salt, pepper, cumin and turmeric, mix again and check that the consistency is just firm enough to handle.

2 Transfer the mixture to a mixing bowl. Taste and adjust the seasoning if necessary. Knead it with your hands [see page 77]. If it is too soft to be formed into a roll, stiffen it with more breadcrumbs. Damp your hands slightly, take half the mixture and form it into a roll about 2 in. thick and as evenly cylindrical as possible – but don't worry if it is a bit thicker in the middle. Make a second roll with the rest of the mixture.

3 Fry the two loaves in fairly hot oil, turning them once, for a few minutes or until lightly browned all over. Remove the loaves from the pan and drain them on paper towels.

4 Use a frying pan [or a saucepan into which both fish loaves will fit comfortably] to prepare the *sofrito* sauce in the same way as in the previous recipe. [You can use the pan and oil from frying the loaves if you like, but remember to pour away most of the oil.] Add enough fish stock, if available, or water to make the sauce fairly thin. There should be about $1\frac{1}{4}$ cups of sauce. Add the two loaves to the pan and poach gently. Shake and tilt the pan from time to time to spread the liquid around, and turn the loaves over. Cook them for about 30 minutes.

5 Remove the loaves from the pan and leave to cool. Cut them into slices about $\frac{3}{4}$ in. thick and arrange them on a dish. Reheat the sauce, reduce it by boiling until thick and pour it over the slices.

*The dish may be prepared in advance to this stage. Store in the refrigerator until shortly before serving.

The sauce for this recipe goes equally well with the Fish Balls below, while the tomato sauce in that recipe can replace the *sofrito* sauce for the loaf.

PREPARATION TIME
1 hour, including 40 minutes cooking

1 lb fish fillets [haddock, hake or cod]
1 large onion
1 clove garlic
3 Tbsp chopped parsley
about 1 cup soft breadcrumbs
3 Tbsp chopped parsley
salt and pepper, to taste
1 tsp ground cumin
$\frac{1}{2}$ tsp turmeric
oil for shallow frying

SOFRITO SAUCE
about 2 Tbsp oil, if not using oil from frying loaves
1 clove garlic
juice of 1 lemon
$\frac{1}{2}$ tsp turmeric
$1\frac{1}{4}$ cups fish stock or water

FISH BALLS IN TOMATO SAUCE

These fish balls are made from a mixture very similar to that used for the fish loaf in the previous recipe.

1 Mince the fish finely. Add the breadcrumbs, cilantro, cinnamon, parsley, salt and pepper. Mix well. Add extra breadcrumbs if the mixture is too soft, and form it into round rissoles the size of a marble, or little finger shapes if you prefer, so long as they are not too large [see page 77].

2 Choose a frying pan that will take all the fish balls in one layer, pour in just enough oil to coat the base of the pan and set over high heat. Grate the onion into the pan. Finely chop the tomatoes, reserving the liquid if using canned tomatoes, and add them to the heated pan. Bring the liquid to a boil, then lower the heat to medium and leave to cook for a few minutes.

3 Meanwhile, de-seed the chili and chop it very finely. Chop the garlic finely. Add these, along with the salt, pepper and cumin, to $1\frac{1}{4}$ cup water or reserved tomato liquid, and pour into the pan. Add the paprika and turmeric. Bring back to a boil, then lower the heat to simmer.

4 Gently roll the fish balls into the sauce and poach gently for about 15 minutes. Serve on a bed of rice.

The fish balls can also be coated in dried breadcrumbs and fried separately until golden before adding them to the sauce.

PREPARATION TIME
45 minutes, including 20 minutes cooking

1 lb fish fillets [haddock, hake or cod]
about 1 cup soft breadcrumbs, or more if needed
a few sprigs cilantro, chopped
1 tsp ground cinnamon
3 Tbsp chopped parsley
salt and pepper, to taste

SAUCE
about 2 Tbsp oil
1 medium onion
6 tomatoes, or a large can
1 fresh chili pepper
1 clove garlic
salt and pepper, to taste
1 tsp ground cumin seed
1 Tbsp paprika
$\frac{1}{2}$ tsp turmeric

Fish Stew piled over a mound of Couscous, with the rest in a separate bowl (*back left*), Fish Loaf Sofrito (*front*) and Fish Balls in Tomato Sauce (*right*)

FISH STEW FOR COUSCOUS

I have eaten this stew as part of a whole fish meal – brik, fish soup and couscous – cooked by a young Tunisian friend in London. She chose the fish from a selection at the local fishmonger. Although couscous, the national dish of the North African countries, is usually associated with meat stews, the Tunisians also cook it with fish. The other North Africans tease them by calling them the 'fish couscous eaters'.

PREPARATION TIME
1 hour, including cooking

2 Tbsp oil
1 large onion
2 cloves garlic
1 large can tomatoes
1 tsp ground cumin seed
salt, to taste
1 tsp cayenne pepper
1 tsp turmeric
1 Tbsp tomato purée
1 large sweet green bell pepper
2½ cups water
4 small potatoes
2 fresh sardines [or smelt]
2 small mackerel
½ lb angelfish
1 lb couscous

TO SERVE
a little Harissa [see page 140]

1 Put the oil in the bottom part of a couscous steamer or a large, heavy-based pan and set over medium heat. Finely chop the onion and garlic and add to the pan. Drain the canned tomatoes, chop, and add them to the pan along with the cumin when the onion begins to brown. Add the salt, cayenne pepper, turmeric and tomato purée to the mixture. Bring to simmering point and leave to cook with the pan half covered.
2 Cut the green pepper into large pieces, discarding the seeds. Leave the potatoes whole, peeled or with their skins on, as you prefer. Add both to the mixture along with the water, bring to a boil, then simmer for about 15 minutes. Meanwhile, prepare the fish. Gut the sardines but leave them whole. Cut the mackerel into halves, discarding the heads, and cut the angelfish into large chunks.
3 When the vegetables are cooked, remove them and keep them warm. Add enough water to the pan to cover the fish. Bring to a boil, put in the fish, cover and simmer until the fish is done, about 30 minutes. Return the vegetables to the pan. Following the instructions for Couscous on page 108, give it the second steaming over the fish stew.
4 Taste, and adjust the seasoning if necessary. Serve the fish and vegetables on a mound of couscous with the rest of the stew in a separate bowl.

This stew goes equally well with rice. You can vary it by adding other vegetables at the appropriate time so that they are all ready together: carrots near the start of cooking, zucchini near the end, and so on. Serve the stew and couscous as any real Tunisian would, with a small bowl of Harissa.

POULTRY

Chicken, poussin, duck, goose, turkey, pigeon and quail, cooked in a thousand and one different ways, are popular throughout the Middle East. Young, tender birds are simply grilled or broiled. Larger fowl are made into stews with vegetables, fragrant with herbs and spices and often enriched with dried fruits. They are stuffed before being cooked as a casserole, roasted or steamed, and are also made into spectacular festive dishes.

Apart from quickly grilled or broiled dishes, most traditional recipes call for long, slow cooking so that the liquid and accompanying ingredients will have developed their full flavor by the time the fowl is tender. However, the factory-farmed poultry sold in most American supermarkets tend to cook in a fraction of this time. I often stipulate that you should remove the bird if it is done before the sauce has attained its full richness, and reduce the sauce until it no longer 'tastes of water'. Many times, when using chicken pieces rather than a whole bird, for example, it is advisable to make the sauce to a midway stage, and then add the chicken, having first fried it if appropriate.

If possible, buy 'free-range', corn- or grain-fed chickens. Fortunately, we are beginning to see the come-back of these 'real' birds. They take longer to cook than factory-farmed birds, so if you do use one, increase the cooking times given in the following recipes accordingly. When you are cooking a chicken whole and want to test for doneness, stick a sharp knife or skewer into the center of the thigh; there should be no trace of pinkness.

Chicken Sofrito (*top left*), Chicken Tajine with Olives and Lemon (*bottom left*) and Grilled Poussins, with a chopped Pepper Salad (*recipe on page 20*)

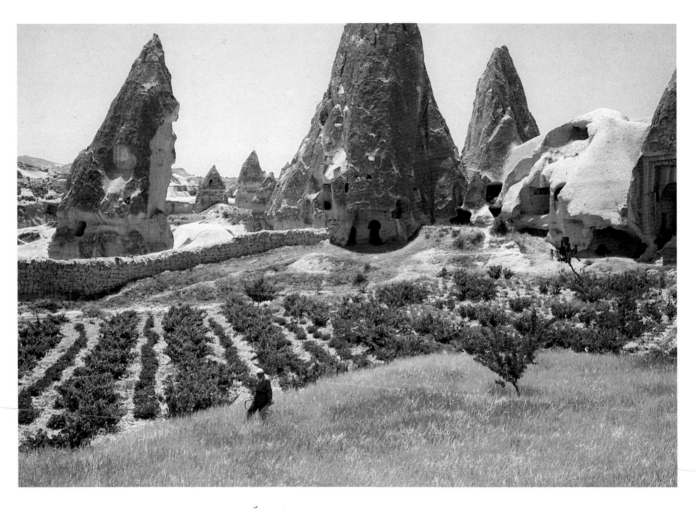

Raisins are used in savory dishes – pilafs, stuffed vegetables, chilled soups, or cooked with meat or poultry – throughout the Middle East. *Above* The vineyards and distinctive cone dwellings of Cappadocia, centuries ago a volcanic region and now one of the three main vine-producing areas of Turkey.

GRILLED POUSSINS

PREPARATION TIME
1 hour 5 minutes, including 30
   minutes marinating and 30
   minutes cooking

2 poussins
salt and pepper, to taste
1–2 cloves garlic
juice of 1 lemon
2 Tbsp olive oil

[*picture on page 55*]

Delicate-flavored poussins, like fish, are eminently suited to grilling outdoors over charcoal [see pages 78–79] or to more prosaic indoor methods.

1 Split the poussins open down the back and flatten by beating with a rolling pin. If they are large, remove the legs. Slice the garlic thinly. Put the poussins [including the legs] in a shallow bowl, sprinkle with the salt, pepper and garlic, pour over most of the lemon juice and turn to make sure they are evenly coated. Pour on the oil and leave to marinate in the refrigerator for at least 30 minutes, or several hours if more convenient.
2 Heat a cast-iron griddle really hot and oil it. Put the poussins on and press down well so they make good contact with the surface. After about 5 minutes turn them over, press down again and grill for a few minutes over high heat. Reduce the heat to medium and cook for about another 10 minutes; turn and cook the other side for 10 minutes or until the inside of the leg is done. Transfer the poussins to a serving dish. Deglaze the griddle with a little water and a squeeze of lemon juice. Pour the liquid over the poussins and sprinkle with a little more salt. Serve with rice or French fries, and a green salad.

Farm pigeons and quails are also delicious split, marinated and grilled in this way. Naturally you will need more of the smaller birds. Breast of chicken or turkey can also be marinated and grilled for a couple of minutes on each side; served with a generous green salad, this makes an interesting, quickly prepared lunch – and a low-calorie one for anyone on a diet.

CHICKEN SOFRITO WITH POTATOES

PREPARATION TIME
2 hours, including 1½ hours
  cooking

2 Tbsp oil
1 tsp turmeric
3–4 cloves garlic
juice of 2–3 lemons
1 cup 2 Tbsp good stock, or
  more as required
1 medium chicken, about 3 lb
salt and pepper, to taste
1½ lb potatoes
oil for deep frying

TO GARNISH
a few sprigs parsley, chopped

[*picture on page 54*]

This very simple way of cooking chicken is a great favorite of mine. Both this recipe and the one below can be easily adapted for veal. The best cut to use is the knuckle, but instead of having it cut into slices, osso buco style, it is better to bone it and cut it into chunks with the marrow bone added separately for extra flavor. It should be tender enough to cut with a fork and will take a good two hours to cook.

1 Choose a heavy-based saucepan or flame-proof casserole into which the whole chicken will fit comfortably. Pour in a thin layer of oil, add the turmeric, whole garlic cloves, lemon juice and stock, and set over medium heat. Put in the chicken, sprinkle with salt and pepper, and turn it over to coat it with the contents of the pan. Leave the breast down and cook, half covered, on medium heat, for about 1 hour. Turn from time to time, and add more stock if necessary to keep at least 1 in. of liquid in the bottom of the casserole.

2 Preheat the oven to 400°F. Transfer the chicken to a roasting pan and put it in the oven to brown, about 30 minutes.

3 To cook the potatoes, first peel them and, if small, leave them whole; if large, cut into chunks or strips. Deep fry until golden but not cooked through. Drain on paper towels, put them in the casserole and shake well to coat with liquid. Continue cooking until the potatoes are done. This should not take very long; check for doneness after about 5 minutes.

4 When the chicken is nicely browned, serve with the potatoes arranged around it in the sauce. A sprinkling of chopped parsley brings out the color.

Although it gives an attractive finish, it is not necessary to brown the chicken in the oven. Instead, the whole dish can be cooked on top of the stove: add the fried potatoes to the cooked chicken, shake the casserole and simmer briefly until the potatoes are cooked.

Chicken pieces can also be cooked in this way, without the potatoes. Serve with rice instead.

COLD CHICKEN SOFRITO A chicken cooked in a casserole as above, but without the potatoes, can be cut up when done, and the pieces skinned and arranged in a shallow bowl. Reduce the liquid in the casserole to a thick consistency and pour it over the chicken. When it cools it will form a delicious aspic.

CHICKEN TAJINE WITH OLIVES AND LEMON

PREPARATION TIME
1 hour 50 minutes, including
  1¾ hours cooking

2 Tbsp oil
1 medium chicken, about 3 lb
  with giblets [optional]
2 medium onions
1 clove garlic
1 lemon
a few strands saffron [or a
  pinch turmeric]
2 tsp ground ginger
salt and pepper, to taste
3 Tbsp chopped parsley
⅓–1⅔ cups green olives, to taste

[*picture on page 54*]

This and the following 'tajine' recipe were given to me by Fatima Ma'toughi. However, I have adapted them both by drastically reducing the amount of oil.

1 Pour enough oil into a heavy-based saucepan or flame-proof casserole to coat the bottom. Put in the whole chicken. Grate the onions, crush the garlic and slice the lemon. Add these, along with the saffron, ginger, salt and pepper. Turn the chicken over to coat it with the mixture, set over medium heat, and cook, covered, for about 30 minutes, turning several times. If the mixture becomes too dry, simply add a little water.

2 Add the parsley and as many olives as you like. If you have the giblets, chop them into small pieces and add. Cook for another 45 minutes or so, turning from time to time, until the chicken is cooked through.

* The chicken can be prepared in advance to this stage, and reheated while browning in the oven. Reserve the chicken and the sauce separately.

3 Preheat the oven to medium, 375°F. Transfer the chicken to a roasting pan or oven-proof serving dish and put it in the oven to brown, about another 30 minutes.

4 Reduce the mixture remaining in the pan to a thick sauce. To serve, pour the sauce over and around the chicken and arrange the lemon slices on top.

If you have a Preserved Lemon [see page 139] use half of it, chopped, instead of lemon slices, but add to the chicken with the parsley [step 2].

Chicken Tajine with Raisins and Almonds and Chicken with a Rich Bulgar Wheat Stuffing

CHICKEN TAJINE WITH RAISINS AND ALMONDS

PREPARATION TIME
2 hours, including 1½ hours
  cooking

1 medium chicken, about 3 lb
2 Tbsp oil
salt and pepper, to taste
a few strands saffron [or a
  pinch turmeric]
2 tsp ground ginger
1 tsp ground cinnamon
2 medium onions
1 cup water
⅓ cup whole peeled almonds

RAISIN SAUCE
3–4 medium onions
4 Tbsp [½ stick] butter
¼–⅓ cup raisins
1 tsp ground cinnamon
2 tsp sugar
1 Tbsp water

[picture on page 58]

1 Cut the chicken up and put the pieces in a large, heavy-based saucepan with the oil, salt, pepper, saffron, ginger and cinnamon. Finely chop the onions and add to the pan. Set over a medium heat, half cover and cook for 30 minutes, turning the chicken from time to time.

2 Add the water, bring to a boil, lower the heat and simmer, half covered, for a further 30 minutes until just cooked.

3 To make the raisin sauce, first chop the onions very finely and put in a smaller saucepan with the butter, raisins, cinnamon, sugar and water. Cook, uncovered, over medium heat, stirring from time to time, for about 45 minutes or until the onions have melted away and the whole mixture becomes thick, glossy and golden brown. If the sauce is thick enough but the onions are still visible, add a little more water and continue cooking until they disappear.

4 Add the almonds to the chicken and continue simmering until it is tender. Arrange the pieces on a dish [or in a *tajine* pot if you have one] and pour the cooking sauce over, arranging the almonds on top. Serve the raisin sauce in a separate bowl.

CHICKEN TAJINE WITH PRUNES AND SESAME SEEDS Cook the chicken as above, but use prunes instead of raisins for the sauce, and roasted sesame seeds instead of almonds. Cook the prunes with a little liquid from the chicken and the other ingredients for the raisin sauce. Gently dry roast a handful of sesame seeds. To serve, pour the sauce over the chicken, arrange any whole prunes around and on top, and sprinkle with sesame seeds.

STUFFED POULTRY

Stuffed poultry is a great favorite in the Middle East. The main ingredients are usually rice, bulgar wheat or couscous with a variety of additions: nuts and dried fruits, herbs, spices and sautéed liver and hearts, subtly flavored or spicy to complement the bird.

CHICKEN WITH RICH BULGAR WHEAT STUFFING

PREPARATION TIME
1 hour soaking
2½ hours, including 1½ hours cooking

1 cup bulgar wheat
3 medium onions
¾ cup pine nuts
1 tsp ground cinnamon
6 Tbsp chopped parsley
½ cup raisins
salt and pepper, to taste
1–2 Tbsp oil
1–2 oranges
1 medium chicken, about 3 lb
2 Tbsp [¼ stick] butter
1–2 Tbsp clarified butter

TO GARNISH [optional]
orange slices

1 Soak the bulgar wheat in plenty of cold water for at least 1 hour.
2 Squeeze the bulgar wheat dry in a cloth and put in a mixing bowl. Dry fry the pine nuts gently until lightly colored and browned. Chop one of the onions very finely. Add the pine nuts, chopped onion, cinnamon, parsley, raisins, salt and pepper to the bulgar wheat. Mix well and check the seasoning. If the additions look sparse, add more: you can make the stuffing as rich as you like.
3 Chop the remaining onions very finely. Choose a saucepan or flame-proof casserole into which the chicken will fit comfortably and pour in just enough oil to coat the base of the pan. Cook the onion until transparent. Add the orange juice and simmer gently.
4 Stuff the chicken with as much of the bulgar wheat mixture as it will hold, adding small pieces of butter. Put some stuffing under the breast skin. Reserve the remaining mixture. Sew up the bird if necessary.
5 Put the chicken in the pan and add enough water to half cover the bird. Bring to a boil, lower the heat and simmer, covered, for about 1½ hours, or until the chicken is brown and the sauce thick and golden brown. Turn it over carefully from time to time and add a little water if the sauce is drying up.
6 Fry the remaining bulgar wheat mixture in very hot clarified butter, tossing it, for less than a minute. [A small wok is ideal, since you need less butter.]
7 Remove the chicken, carve it and keep warm. Tip the fried bulgar wheat mixture into the pan, mix well with the liquid and set over low heat. Taste the sauce, adjust the seasoning and add more orange juice if you like. If the orange juice is sour, add a little sugar to the sauce.
8 To serve, pile all the bulgar wheat mixture in the serving dish and arrange the pieces of chicken on top. Garnish with orange slices if you like.

STEAMED STUFFED CHICKEN

PREPARATION TIME
3 hours 20 minutes, including 2½ hours cooking

2 sticks celery
3 green onions
½ Preserved Lemon [see page 139], or 1 tsp dried lime, or juice of 1 lemon
3–4 small tomatoes
1 Tbsp tomato purée
1¼ cups finely chopped parsley
salt and pepper, to taste
1 tsp cayenne pepper
2 Tbsp [¼ stick] butter
3½ lb chicken
flour and water paste to seal steamer [see right]

TO SERVE
salt, pepper and ground cumin seed mixed to taste

[picture on page 61]

If you own a double steamer, you will be able to enjoy making this delicious Moroccan dish. Its subtlety of flavor calls for a good quality chicken, such as one of the 'free-range', grain-fed birds which are now becoming more readily available.

1 To prepare the stuffing, first finely chop the celery, green onions [including the green tops], lemon or lime [if used] and tomatoes. Mix these together and add the tomato purée, parsley, salt, pepper, lemon juice [if used], cayenne pepper and butter cut into small pieces. If you have the chicken liver and heart, chop into small pieces and add to the stuffing.
2 Fill the bottom of the steamer with plenty of water [but it must not touch the upper part when it boils]. Bring to a boil while you stuff the chicken with the mixture and sew it up if necessary. Insert some stuffing under the breast skin. When the water boils put the top on the steamer, lower the heat and carefully seal the join between top and bottom with flour and water paste. Put the chicken, breast down, in the top of the steamer, cover with a clean damp cloth and put on the lid. Steam for 2 to 2½ hours, or until the chicken is cooked.
3 To serve, cut up the chicken, arrange the pieces around the edge of a dish and spoon the stuffing into the center. Sprinkle with a mixture of salt, pepper and cumin seed.

If you are skilled at boning a whole chicken you can, of course, stuff and cook it in this way, reducing the cooking time accordingly.

GREEK CHICKEN PIE

PREPARATION TIME

3 hours, including 2 hours 20 minutes cooking

2 hours cooling and reheating

SERVES 8

1 lb leeks
$\frac{3}{4}$ cup [1$\frac{1}{2}$ sticks] butter
1 medium chicken, about 3 lb, jointed
salt and pepper, to taste
$\frac{1}{2}$ cup [1 stick] butter
4 Tbsp flour
2 cups milk
1 cup grated Cheddar or other medium-strong cheese
4 eggs
a pinch ground nutmeg
$\frac{1}{4}$ cup [$\frac{1}{2}$ stick] butter
$\frac{1}{2}$ lb filo pastry

This is my friend Mireille Attas' version of the classic Greek pies made with filo pastry. They come with a great variety of fillings: mixed cheeses and egg, or spinach, egg and cheese (very similar to those used in the 'mezze' section) and meat or poultry, with or without vegetables, usually held together with a highly seasoned white sauce.

1 Choose a pan large enough to hold the leeks and the chicken. Wash and finely slice the white parts of the leeks and cook them gently with $\frac{3}{4}$ cup butter until tender, about 20 minutes. Cut up the chicken and add, along with enough boiling water to cover by about 1 in. Add salt and pepper and simmer gently for another 1 hour or so, until the chicken is very tender.

2 Take the pieces out of the pan with a slotted spoon, leaving the liquid. Skin and bone them, and cut the meat into small pieces. Return to the pan and boil quickly to reduce the cooking liquid to a very thick consistency. Allow to cool while you make Béchamel Sauce with $\frac{1}{4}$ cup butter, the flour and milk [see page 138]. Add this and the grated cheese to the pan. Lightly beat the mixture and stir in the eggs and nutmeg; then mix thoroughly.

3 Preheat the oven to moderate, 350°F. melt $\frac{1}{4}$ cup butter and use some of it to grease a medium rectangular oven-proof dish. Cover the bottom with half the filo pastry sheets, lightly brushing each one with melted butter before setting the next one on top [see pages 28, 65]. Spread on the filling and cover with the other sheets, again brushing each one with melted butter and finishing by brushing the top with the last of the butter. Score the surface into squares with a razor blade. Sprinkle the pie with a little water to keep the leaves from lifting – I find a houseplant mister ideal for this – and bake for 1 hour or until golden.

* The dish should be prepared in advance to this stage.

4 Let the pie cool completely, then slice it without taking it out of the dish. Reheat and serve warm.

CHICKEN KISHK

PREPARATION TIME

1$\frac{1}{2}$ hours, including 1 hour cooking

1 medium chicken, about 3 lb
3–4 medium onions
2 sticks celery
1 carrot
salt and pepper, to taste
5–6 cracked cardamom pods
$\frac{1}{2}$ tsp crushed mastic [optional]
3 Tbsp flour
3 Tbsp natural yogurt
1–2 Tbsp clarified butter

[picture on page 62]

This is such a great favorite in Egypt that the name has become a term of endearment: you say that someone is 'a real kishk chicken'. Pieces of chicken are served with rice and a very thick, sharp yogurt sauce enriched with onions browned in clarified butter. The sauce is a modern urban adaptation of the traditional 'kishk' made in the country. It is always served with rice and isn't recommended for those who have to count calories. Although it is an extremely well-known dish, I only learned of it a few years ago from a friend in London. I probably missed it when I was a child because of my aversion to soft boiled food. Traditional kishk on its own is also appetizing: wheat is boiled in sour milk, then dried in the sun and crushed. Sometimes, while still damp, it is formed into small balls or sticks. This is also known as 'trahanas', and is used to enrich and thicken soups.

1 Cover the chicken in water and simmer for about 1 hour with one of the onions, the celery, carrot, salt, pepper, cardamom pods and mastic [if available]. When the chicken is done, remove from the pan, reserving the stock. Skin the chicken, cut the meat from the bones, chop it into large pieces and set aside. Return the carcass to the pan and continue simmering until the broth is flavorful.

2 To make the sauce, first stir together the flour and yogurt over low heat and add 4 or 5 ladlefuls of the hot stock one-by-one. When the taste of raw flour is gone and the sauce cooked, reduce to a very thick consistency. Chop the remaining onions, fry in clarified butter until brown and add, with the butter, to the sauce.

3 To serve, arrange the chicken pieces on a mound of rice and smother with the sauce. This dish can be eaten either hot or cold; if hot, it may be advisable to reheat the chicken pieces briefly in the sauce.

Steamed Stuffed Chicken and Greek Chicken Pie

FRIED CHICKEN WITH SESAME SEEDS

PREPARATION TIME
30 minutes, including 20
minutes cooking

4 chicken pieces
1 egg
4 Tbsp flour
$\frac{1}{2}$ tsp baking soda
salt and pepper, to taste
1 cup sesame seeds
oil for shallow frying

This dish is similar to Chicken Maryland, using sesame seeds instead of corn to give it a Middle Eastern touch. The recipe was given to me by Jacqueline Biancardi, a superb cook who also comes from Egypt and whose extensive travels are reflected in her cooking.

1 Skin the chicken. Beat the egg and mix in the flour and baking powder to make a thick, gluey batter. Dry the chicken pieces, sprinkle with salt and pepper, dip in the batter and roll in sesame seeds.

2 Heat the oil in a large, heavy-based frying pan. Add the chicken pieces and fry for about 10 minutes on each side, then drain on paper towels. Serve on a bed of watercress.

Left to right Chicken Kishk, Sfereya and Fried Chicken with Sesame Seeds, served on a bed of watercress

SFEREYA

This recipe for Sfereya, an Algerian dish, was given to me by my friend Dalilia. It is garnished with roasted almonds and served with cheese and bread rissoles.

PREPARATION TIME
8 hours soaking
1 hour 20 minutes, including 1 hour cooking

$3\frac{1}{2}$ oz garbanzo beans
6 chicken thighs
1 Tbsp 2 tsp clarified butter [or half oil, half butter]
1 tsp cinnamon
salt and pepper, to taste

RISSOLES
1 cup soft breadcrumbs
$\frac{3}{4}$ cup grated Monterey Jack
$\frac{1}{2}$ tsp baking soda
salt and pepper, to taste
1 tsp cinnamon
1 egg, beaten + 1 yolk

oil for shallow frying

TO SERVE
$\frac{1}{4}$ cup blanched almonds

1 Wash the garbanzo beans and leave to soak at least 8 hours in plenty of water. Drain and, if necessary, peel the garbanzo beans by rubbing them between your hands.
2 Sauté the chicken pieces in clarified butter in a heavy-based frying pan until golden brown on both sides. Add the cinnamon, salt, pepper, garbanzo beans and just enough water to cover. Bring to a boil, reduce the heat and simmer for about 45 minutes while you prepare the rissoles and almonds. If the chicken is tender before the garbanzo beans have cooked, remove and keep warm.
3 To make the rissoles, first mix the breadcrumbs with the grated cheese, baking powder, salt, pepper and cinnamon. Gradually beat the egg into the mixture. It must not be wet: you may not need all the egg. Mold the mixture into walnut-sized lumps. Shallow fry in oil until golden brown all over and keep warm. At the same time, gently dry roast the almonds until lightly colored.
4 If you have not already done so, remove the chicken pieces from the pan and place them on a serving dish. Keep warm.
5 To thicken the sauce, beat the egg yolk lightly in a cup, then beat in a little of the hot sauce, pour into the pan and heat gently, stirring. Taste, and adjust the seasoning. Pour the sauce over the chicken and scatter the roasted almonds on top. Arrange the rissoles around it.

PERSIAN CHICKEN WITH RICE

PREPARATION TIME
1 hour 45 minutes, including cooking

CHICKEN
8 chicken thighs
1 small stick celery
1 small carrot
1 small onion
2 cloves garlic
2–3 strands saffron [or a pinch turmeric]
salt and pepper, to taste

CARROTS IN CARAMEL
1 lb medium carrots
2 Tbsp [$\frac{1}{4}$ stick] butter
salt and pepper, to taste
1 large orange
2 Tbsp sugar
1 Tbsp water

1$\frac{1}{4}$ cups basmati [or long grain] rice
oil for mold

TO SERVE
$\frac{1}{3}$ cup whole peeled almonds

[picture on page 64]

This dish of chicken with carrots, candied orange peel and rice is one of my students' favorites. All the separate elements can be prepared in advance. I like to make it with chicken thighs, which yield neat, even pieces of meat. It can, of course, be made with a whole chicken cut up into pieces.

1 Skin the chicken thighs. Chop the celery, carrot and onion into large chunks, put in a saucepan with the garlic, saffron, salt and pepper, barely cover with water and poach for 20 to 30 minutes, or until the chicken is tender. Leave the chicken to cool in the stock to keep it from drying out.

2 Scrub the carrots and cut into matchsticks. Put into a heavy-based pan with the butter, salt, pepper and about a tablespoonful of stock from the chicken. Bring to a boil, then reduce the heat and simmer, covered, for about 10 minutes, or until cooked, shaking the pan from time to time.

3 Wash and scrub the orange, and peel it with a very sharp knife. Pare off most of the pith from the peel and cut it into very thin strips. Blanch them in boiling water for a few minutes, then drain.

4 Make a caramel syrup by boiling the sugar with water in a small pan until it turns a pale golden color. Add the blanched orange strips and continue cooking until the caramel becomes slightly more colored. Pour over the carrots and mix in.

5 Cook the rice Persian-style [see page 106]. Preheat the oven to moderate, 350°F. Remove the chicken pieces from the stock. Oil a large ring mold and arrange the pieces of chicken in it with some of the carrots in little clumps between them. Fill the mold with rice, packing it in firmly so that there are no gaps. [If you have managed to form crust in the rice pan, reserve it – uncovered.]

6 Heat the molded chicken and rice in the oven for a few minutes. Add a little stock to the carrots and caramel and reheat. Reduce the rest of the stock to make a thick sauce. Gently dry roast the almonds.

7 Turn the mold out onto a serving dish and fill the center with the caramelized carrots and orange peel. Pour some of the stock over to color it and sprinkle with chopped roasted almonds. If you have the rice crust, cut into triangles and set them around the edge of the dish. Serve the sauce separately.

If you prefer, simply pile the chicken pieces onto the rice and pour the sauce over it.

Middle Eastern cooking makes surprisingly exotic use of familiar ingredients, as with the caramelized carrots in this Iranian chicken dish (*above*). *Right* Huge piles of carrots, white turnips and pumpkins, with the green tops sold separately, at a Berber market in Morocco.

Two festive poultry dishes: Persian Chicken with Rice and Pastilla

PASTILLA

PREPARATION TIME
3 hours 10 minutes, including
   cooking

2 Tbsp oil
1½ lb onions
1 clove garlic
salt and pepper, to taste
6–8 strands saffron [or 1 tsp
   turmeric]
1½ tsp ground ginger
4 tsp ground cinnamon
1 medium chicken, about 3 lb
1¼ cups very finely chopped
   parsley
1⅔ cups peeled almonds
2–3 Tbsp sugar
1 Tbsp ground cinnamon
juice of ½ lemon
7–8 large eggs
2 Tbsp [¼ stick] butter
1 lb package filo pastry
1 egg, beaten

TO SERVE
3–4 tsp confectioner's sugar
3–4 tsp ground cinnamon

This famous Moroccan festive dish is usually made with pigeons. It takes a long time to prepare, and is quite complicated, though not actually difficult. The spectacular result is well worth the time and effort. This version was shown to me by Fatima Ma'toughi. If making Pastilla for the first time, I advise you to prepare the two fillings in advance. For general advice on handling filo pastry, see page 130.

1   Choose a saucepan or flame-proof casserole that will comfortably take the chicken pieces and onions: they should no more than half fill it, so that they will be easy to turn. Pour in oil to a depth of 1 in. and set over medium heat. Grate the onions and add, stirring from time to time. Thinly slice the garlic and add with the salt, pepper, saffron, ginger and a teaspoonful of ground cinnamon. Cut up the chicken and add. Raise the heat a little and cook for about 1 hour, turning the pieces from time to time.

2   Add the parsley. Cook for another 30 minutes, or until the meat comes easily off the bones.

3   Dry roast the almonds, grind them roughly and mix with the sugar and the rest of the cinnamon. Set aside.

4   When the chicken is cooked, remove the pieces with a slotted spoon and set aside to cool. Strain the contents of the pan through a double layer of cheesecloth into a bowl. Reserve the liquid and return the parsley and onions to the pan. Add the lemon juice, and break 6 or 7 eggs into the pan. Stir gently until they begin to set. The whole mixture should have the texture of a purée. Set aside while you skin and bone the chicken and cut into bite-sized pieces.

5   Melt the butter and use some to grease your largest roasting pan. Put a piece of filo pastry lengthwise in the center, moisten lightly all over with fingers dipped in reserved chicken stock, and set a second sheet of filo the same size on top. Follow the step-by-step instructions opposite. [Moisten each sheet of filo in this way to prevent their sticking together.] Arrange more sheets of filo radiating outwards like the petals of a flower, with

the inner end of each resting on the first two sheets and the outer end hanging over the edge of the roasting pan. Overlap the sheets until they are about 4 layers thick in all.

6 Pile the chicken pieces onto the filo in a tidy rectangle the same size as the first two sheets. Spread the parsley mixture on top. Cover with one sheet of filo. One by one, lift up the outer ends of the top layer of the overlapping filo sheets, fold each one over the rectangle and stick each one lightly in place by moistening with your fingers dipped into the beaten egg. Take care to keep the rectangle compact.

7 Add most of the rest of the melted butter to the almond mixture and check the balance of flavors: the almond, cinnamon and sugar should be distinct, without overwhelming each other. Correct the proportions if necessary. Spread this mixture on top of the now nearly completed pie and smooth it gently with your fingers. Place 2 more layers of filo pastry on top, lengthwise, exactly like the first 2 layers. Fold over and stick down the remaining outer sheets of filo as in step 6. Check that the filling is evenly protected by the pastry all around. To complete the package, place more sheets of filo crosswise over it and tuck underneath. Preheat the oven to 350°F.

8 Brush the pastilla with the remaining melted butter and bake for about 30 minutes or until golden brown. Let it cool a little, then decorate with alternating trails of confectioner's sugar and cinnamon.

PASTILLA

1 Lay a rectangular sheet of filo in a large roasting pan. (The rectangle should be a little smaller than the base of the pan.) Brush the pastry with chicken stock, and lay another sheet of filo the same size on top to form the base.

2 Arrange more sheets of filo in the pan so that they overlap like the petals of a flower, making sure the base is covered. Brush each sheet with stock as you go along. Add more overlapping sheets until they are about 4 layers thick all round.

3 Pile the chicken mixture onto the pastry, then spread on the parsley mixture. Cover with a rectangle of filo the same size as the base, and brush it with stock.

4 One by one, fold the top layer of the overlapping sheets of the filo into the center of the rectangle and stick each one lightly in place by moistening it with beaten egg. Spread the almond mixture on top, then a double layer of rectangles of filo the same size as the base. Fold over and stick down the remaining overlapping sheets of filo as before.

5 Lay two or three rectangles of filo crosswise over the package.

6 Tuck the edges of the crosswise sheets underneath the package, which should be neat, completely enclosing the filling.

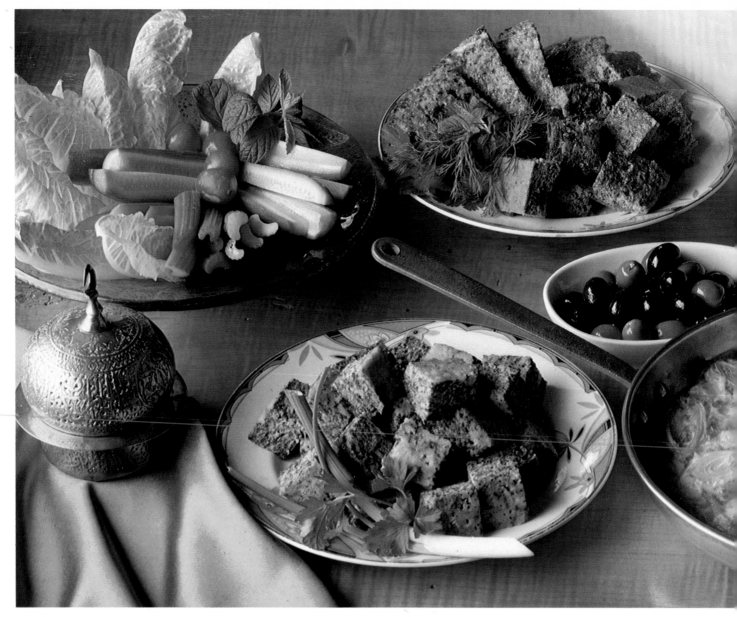

EGG DISHES

Eggah is a general term for a wide variety of egg dishes similar to Spanish omelettes found all over the Middle East. The name varies from country to country: *eggah* is the Egyptian word, while in Tunisia it is *tajine* and in Iran *kuku*. For all the dishes here I have used the names arbitrarily.

The beauty of *eggah* is its versatility. Any of them can be served cold, cut into small cubes, as *mezze*; or hot or cold as hors d'oeuvres; or as a light lunch dish with a salad. They are ideal for picnics. The quantities given here are for a light lunch for 4; as *mezze* they would do for 6 or 8.

The consistency of *eggah* varies, depending on how many eggs are used. With a large number of eggs, it has a light texture, almost like a soufflé; using fewer eggs makes it more solid. You will find *eggah* recipes in the vegetable chapter [pp. 96–97]. Another favorite is made with sautéed, well-spiced minced meat to which you add raw green onion, diced uncooked tomatoes and chopped parsley. These give the dish a blend of textures as well as flavors.

Cooking times for *eggah* are also variable, and you can choose the cooking method appropriate for the time you have. In a frying pan, an *eggah* takes only about 10 minutes; in a moderate oven, 350°F, it takes up to 45 minutes. The cooking time also depends on the thickness of the *eggah*. Ideally, aim for a depth of 1 in. when the mixture is poured into the pan. If baking, put the *eggah* mixture in its baking dish on a preheated baking sheet, as you would a quiche, to prevent the center or bottom from remaining undercooked or soggy. Test for doneness by touching the surface with your finger to see if it is firm.

Eggah sometimes have a tendency to become springy or rubbery in texture on cooling. I believe this is due to air bubbles, created by beating the eggs, forming a kind of foam cushion. For this reason, I recommend that you stir the eggs in gently with a palette knife or spoon.

HERB KUKU

This dish, made with fresh herbs, must be eaten cold. If you taste a piece hot, and another cold, you will see how the blend of gentle flavors has developed.

Mix 3 tablespoons chopped parsley with 2 tablespoons each chopped cilantro and mint. Add 2 tablespoons each coarsely chopped walnuts and whole raisins. Stir in 5 or 6 large eggs one by one. Add salt and pepper to taste and 1 teaspoon each ground allspice and crushed dill weed. Stir gently, taste and adjust the seasoning. Transfer the mixture to a greased oven-proof dish and bake in an oven preheated to 350°F for 30 to 40 minutes, or cook gently in a frying pan in a little oil and butter for about 10 minutes (see page 97).

TUNISIAN TAJINE

Heat 1 tablespoon oil in a heavy-based pan over low heat. Add 7 ounces lean minced lamb, 5 ounces chopped lamb's liver and salt and pepper to taste. Cook gently, stirring until the meat is brown. Stir in 1 cup chopped parsley, 1 tablespoon dried breadcrumbs and $\frac{1}{2}$ cup grated Monterey Jack and mix well. Stir in 6 large eggs one by one. Taste and adjust the seasoning. Transfer the mixture to a greased oven-proof dish and place in an oven preheated to 350°F. Bake for about 25 minutes. [Unlike most *eggah*, this dish must be baked.]

Front Spinach Eggah, Leek and Potato Eggah (*recipes on pages 96–7*) and Tunisian Tajine. *Back* Herb Kuku and Cabbage Salad (*recipe on page 25*)

MEAT

The meats most closely associated with Middle Eastern cooking are mutton and lamb, but veal and beef are also widely available. Pork is popular in Greece and Cyprus, but as it is forbidden under both Moslem and Jewish dietary law, it is little used elsewhere. With few exceptions, the recipes of the region call for 'meat', without specifying either the kind or the cut, and for most recipes in this chapter, it is in fact possible to substitute other meats for those specified.

The many ways of cooking meat include broiling or grilling for tender cuts, baking and stewing with vegetables and legumes, and braising with sauces flavored with spices and herbs and enriched with dried fruits and nuts. Minced meat of all kinds, which is much used throughout the Middle East, is often made into meat balls, which may be grilled, fried or broiled, or braised in delicious sauces.

Middle Eastern cooks excel in the art of cooking stews, blending different ingredients according to what is available and what they can afford, but most of all relying on the inspiration of the moment. A *tajine* is simply a stew cooked in a North African dish with a spectacular pointed lid rather like a hat, which is itself called *tajine* and which is very suitable for slow cooking on hot ashes.

Middle Eastern meat dishes usually include vegetables, dried fruit or grains in varying proportions: sometimes the meat is the main ingredient and in other recipes it is the flavoring. *Top left* Baked Leg of Lamb with Okra, *below left* Shoulder of Lamb Stuffed with Apricots and *right* Lamb with Pasta

BAKED LAMB

Lamb baked either on its own or with vegetables or pasta is a great favorite in the Middle East. When there is no oven at home, or when the oven is not large enough, the meat is often sent to the local baker, with very precise instructions as to how it should be cooked.

LEG OF LAMB WITH OKRA

PREPARATION TIME
2½ hours, including 2 hours 20 minutes cooking

½ leg of lamb
a little oil
salt and pepper, to taste
2 cloves garlic
1 large onion
4–5 tomatoes
1 Tbsp tomato purée
1¼ cups hot water
1 lb fresh okra
½ cup 2 Tbsp vinegar
oil for shallow frying
3–4 cloves garlic
1 Tbsp ground coriander seed
juice of 1 lemon

[*picture on page 68*]

Okra, a favorite in the Southern States, is known in Middle Eastern cooking as 'bamia' and in Indian cooking as 'bhindi'. The smaller and younger it is, the better. Choose fresh, young pods whenever possible. See page 87 for tips on preparation.

1 Preheat the oven to hot, 475°F. Trim excess fat from the meat with a sharp knife. Rub it with a little oil, salt and pepper. Cut 2 cloves of garlic into slivers and insert into small cuts in the meat. Put the meat in the oven while you prepare the sauce.

2 Grate the onion, and skin and chop the tomatoes. Dilute the tomato purée in the hot water, add the salt and pepper and mix with the tomatoes and onion. Spoon the tomato and onion mixture over the meat and turn it over once or twice to coat it. Return to the oven, lower the heat to moderate, 350°F, and cook for about 2 hours or until the meat is done to your taste – though for this kind of dish it is best to have the meat well cooked rather than underdone in the French way.

3 Wash the okra well, peel the tops in a cone shape and soak in the vinegar mixed with enough water to cover for about 30 minutes.

4 Rinse and dry the soaked okra. Crush 3 or 4 cloves of garlic and set aside. Pour oil into a deep-fat fryer to a depth of about 1 in. and heat until quite hot. Fry a few okra at a time until golden. [Be careful, since the oil tends to sputter. Using a deep-fat fryer with its basket keeps this problem to a minimum.] Use a slotted spoon to transfer the okra to a sieve for a couple of minutes to shed oil. Sprinkle with salt and finish draining on paper towels. Take the oil off the heat.

5 When the meat is cooked, take it out of the oven and keep warm. Put the okra into the roasting pan. To make Ta'leya, pour away most of the oil from the deep-fat fryer, leaving about a tablespoonful. Lightly fry the crushed garlic and coriander in the remaining oil, add a little of the juice from the roast meat, stir and tip the mixture over the okra. Add the lemon juice and mix gently with a large metal spoon. Taste and adjust the seasoning.

6 Clear a space in the middle of the roasting pan, put the meat back in and return to the oven for at least another 20 minutes, or until the okra is cooked. [It doesn't matter if some of the okra are a bit squashed.] This dish is delicious with rice, or just bread and a green salad.

RIGHT Sides of lamb hanging in the window of a traditionally tiled butcher's shop in Cairo. Lamb – and mutton – is the only meat eaten by the enormous majority of people in the Middle East: pork is forbidden by Moslem religious law and beef is only for the wealthy. The fattiest cuts of lamb are the most highly prized

BAKED SHOULDER OF LAMB STUFFED WITH APRICOTS

PREPARATION TIME
3–4 hours soaking
2 hours 20–40 minutes,
   including 2–2$\frac{1}{2}$ hours
   cooking

$\frac{1}{4}$ lb dried apricots
1 small onion
salt and pepper, to taste
1 shoulder of lamb [with or
   without the bone]
1 tsp coriander seed
a little olive oil, salt and pepper

[*picture on page 68*]

Lamb goes extremely well with dried fruits such as prunes, quinces and apricots. Ask your butcher to cut a hollow pocket in the shoulder to contain the stuffing; or do it yourself by whichever method you know best. You should also remove as much fat as possible from the shoulder, or ask the butcher to do so.

1 Cover the apricots with water and soak for 2 to 3 hours.
2 Drain the apricots, reserving the soaking water. Chop them and the onion very finely, add the salt and pepper and mix well. This can be done in a food processor; chop, rather than purée, it.
3 Preheat the oven to hot, 450°F. Prepare and trim the shoulder if necessary. Gently dry roast and crush the coriander seed. Oil your hands and use them to rub salt, pepper, coriander and oil into the outside of the lamb. Spoon the apricot mixture into the pocket, pushing it as far in as you can, and secure with skewers if necessary. Put the meat in an oven-proof dish: it should just fit the dish. If any stuffing is left over, put it around the meat. Add 1$\frac{1}{4}$ cups of the soaking water, and put the meat in the oven. Roast for about 30 minutes, turning it over after about 15 minutes. Then lower the heat to warm, 375°F, and cook for another 1$\frac{1}{2}$ to 2 hours, depending on size. After the first hour, check that the liquid is not drying up and add a little hot water if necessary. In any case, scrape around the dish so that the juice gets mixed with the stuffing and sticky pieces, and spoon over the shoulder. Serve with rice. Couscous [see page 108] or Pourgouri Pilafi [see page 107].

I often mix the apricots with prunes and sometimes add a handful of coarsely chopped walnuts.

You can, of course, also use this stuffing for traditional roast lamb made with a boned shoulder of lamb. A small leg of lamb or even loin chops can be given the same exotic flavor if they are surrounded by the fruit and pot-roasted.

LAMB WITH PASTA

PREPARATION TIME
1 hour 40 minutes, including
   1$\frac{1}{2}$ hours cooking

2$\frac{1}{4}$ lb lean lamb, either leg
   sirloin or any cut from the
   leg or shoulder
salt and pepper, to taste
juice of $\frac{1}{2}$–1 lemon
2 Tbsp olive oil
1 small onion
1 tsp crushed dried *rigani* [or
   oregano]
$\frac{3}{4}$ cup 2 Tbsp dry white wine
2 tsp tomato purée
1$\frac{1}{4}$ cup boiling water
14 oz orzo [small pasta grains;
   see page 109]

TO SERVE
5 oz grated Parmesan

[*picture on page 69*]

The recipe for this dish, known in Greek as 'arni youvetsi', is from Jacqueline Biancardi. 'Rigani', a type of oregano which grows in Greece, is normally used to flavor the meat. Ordinary oregano is a perfectly adequate substitute.

1 Preheat the oven to hot, 425°F. Trim the meat and cut into 2 in. chunks. Put it in a medium-sized oven-proof dish, season with salt and pepper, and add the lemon juice and oil. Toss well to coat the meat and put it in the oven for 10 to 15 minutes to brown, turning it over once.
2 Chop the onion, add to the meat along with the *rigani* [oregano] and pour the wine over the meat. Reduce the heat to warm, 325°F, and cook for another 40 minutes.
3 Remove the meat with a slotted spoon and set aside. Dilute the tomato purée with the boiling water and pour into the dish, then add the pasta and mix well. The pasta should be just covered with liquid; add more boiling water if necessary. Taste and adjust the seasoning. Return the dish to the oven for about another 30 minutes. Then return the meat to the dish and put it back in the oven for 15 minutes to reheat. Serve sprinkled with grated Parmesan.

If you want to use larger short pasta, such as shells or bows, parboil it before adding to the sauce.

In our family we used to make this dish differently. The meat and onions were browned and cooked [without tomatoes] in heavy-based saucepan on top of the stove, and the pasta browned separately by quick shallow frying in hot oil before being transferred to the saucepan to finish cooking with the meat and its juices.

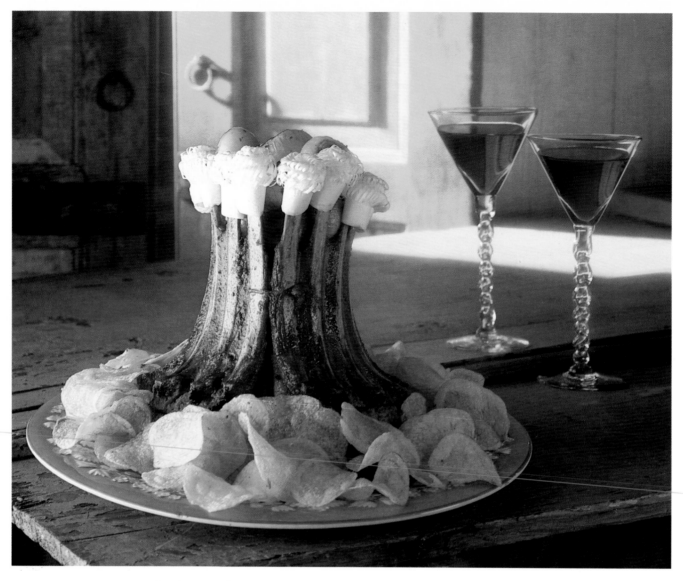

Spiced Crown of Lamb, served with potato chips

SPICED CROWN OF LAMB

PREPARATION TIME
1 hour 40 minutes, including
   1$\frac{1}{2}$ hours cooking

1 crown roast of lamb having
   12–14 chops
1 tsp ground ginger
2–3 strands saffron or 1 tsp
   turmeric
1 tsp ground cumin seed
salt and pepper, to taste
2 Tbsp oil
about 10 small onions
1 Tbsp water

This typically British dish is transformed and given a Middle Eastern flavor by altering the seasoning. It is an anglicized adaptation of a dish cooked for me by my Moroccan friend Fatima Ma'toughi. She makes it with loin of lamb and serves it with French fried potatoes added to the sauce [see below].

1 Preheat the oven to 350°F. Mix the ginger, saffron or turmeric, cumin, salt and pepper with half of the oil. Reserve a teaspoonful of this spice mixture and rub the rest into the meat. Put the meat in a baking dish and cook in the oven for about 1$\frac{1}{2}$ hours, or until the meat is tender.
2 Cook the onions separately in the rest of the oil, the water and the reserved spice mixture for a few minutes. Put them in the center of the crown and roast for another 10 minutes.
3 Serve with potato chips.

LOIN OF LAMB WITH FRENCH FRIES Rub a loin of lamb with the spice mixture described here and put in a flame-proof casserole with 2$\frac{1}{2}$ cups water. Bring to a boil over medium heat. Add the onions, reduce the heat and simmer, covered, for about 30 minutes, or until the onions are cooked. Transfer the meat and onions to an oven-proof casserole and brown in a hot oven, 475°F, for 15 to 20 minutes.

TUNISIAN KAMOUNIYA

PREPARATION TIME
1 hour, including 40 minutes
    cooking

2 Tbsp olive oil
1 large onion
½ lb each lamb's heart, kidneys
    and liver
2 tsp ground cumin seed
salt, to taste
6 tomatoes
2 tsp tomato purée
½ tsp Harissa [see page 140] or
    other red pepper [chili] sauce
2 tsp turmeric

[picture on page 75]

Kamouniya means 'with kamoun' – 'with cumin' – in Arabic. This delicious offal recipe was given to me by a Tunisian friend. There is also an Egyptian dish called 'kamouneya', made with stewing lamb or beef and cooked in a similar way.

1 Put the oil into a heavy-based pan. Finely chop the onion and cook gently until soft and transparent.
2 Cut the heart and kidneys in half, and carefully remove the skin and membranes. Cut the meat into cubes and add to the pan, along with half the cumin. Brown gently for a few minutes. Add enough water to just cover the meat, add salt, bring to the boil, then simmer, covered, for about 30 minutes.
3 Cut the liver into cubes, skin and de-seed the tomatoes and add to the pan along with the tomato purée, Harissa and turmeric. Bring back to a boil and simmer for a further 10 minutes.
4 Mix the rest of the cumin with a little water. Just before serving, tip this into the mixture, stir well and adjust the salt to taste.

HIGADO CON VINAGRE

PREPARATION TIME
40–50 minutes, including 15
    minutes cooking

1½ lb lamb's liver
fine dried breadcrumbs for
    coating
oil for shallow frying
2 cloves garlic
1 Tbsp fine dried breadcrumbs
1 Tbsp tomato purée
2 Tbsp vinegar
½ cup 2 Tbsp water
salt and pepper, to taste

[picture on page 75]

Usually the names of Sephardic Jewish dishes, like the Sephardis themselves, have come from medieval Spain. 'Higado con vinagre' simply means 'liver with vinegar' in Spanish; this version of the dish has a tomato-flavored sauce. This is how my grandmother always cooked liver. Generally, lamb's liver would be used, although I like it best with calf's liver, for which I have given instructions below.

1 Trim, wash and slice the liver. Coat the slices with fine dried breadcrumbs. Finely chop the garlic, and have the vinegar and tomato purée ready at hand.
2 Choose a frying pan into which all the liver slices will fit easily, and pour in oil to a depth of about $\frac{3}{8}$ in. Heat the oil until it sizzles and put in the slices. Cook for a few seconds on each side to brown. Remove and drain on paper towels.
3 Carefully pour away most of the oil. Return the pan to the heat and quickly fry the garlic and remaining tablespoonful of breadcrumbs. Add the tomato purée. As soon as the mixture starts sticking, pour in the vinegar and the water, and stir. Return the liver to the pan. Add salt and pepper to taste. Turn the slices over so that they are evenly coated with the sauce. Half cover the pan and simmer for about 5 or 10 minutes. If the sauce starts to dry out too quickly, add a little water.
4 When the liver is cooked, transfer it to a serving dish and keep warm. Taste the sauce and adjust the seasoning if necessary. If it is too liquid, reduce it by boiling; it should be rather thick. Pour the sauce over the liver and serve hot.

If you use calf's liver, which needs only a few minutes' cooking, don't fry it before the sauce is cooked. Prepare the sauce first by frying the garlic and a tablespoonful of breadcrumbs, then adding the tomato purée, vinegar and water. Simmer the sauce for about 10 to 15 minutes. Quickly brown the liver slices in a little very hot oil in a separate frying pan – not more than a minute each side – then transfer to the sauce and simmer for a couple of minutes in breadcrumbs, and poach in the sauce for about 5 minutes.

BREADCRUMBS

Leftover bread will dry in a few days uncovered in the refrigerator. I do not generally discard the crust, but while the bread is still soft I cut it into small pieces which can then easily be ground with a mortar and pestle, or food processor, then pushed through a sieve.
Soft breadcrumbs Traditionally, soft breadcrumbs are made from stale bread without crusts which is soaked in stock, milk or water, pressed to remove excess moisture, then crumbled. However, if you do this with modern mass-produced bread, the result is rather like wallpaper paste. So let it go slightly stale, but then do not soak it. Pass it through a meat grinder with a fine disk, or a rotary cheese grater or, best of all, use a food processor.

LAMB, FENNEL AND FAVA BEAN TAJINE

This is another dish cooked for me by my Moroccan friend, Fatima Ma'toughi.

PREPARATION TIME
1 hour 20 minutes, including
   50 minutes–1 hour 10
   minutes cooking

2 Tbsp oil
1 medium onion
$\frac{1}{2}$ lemon
1–1$\frac{1}{2}$ lb stewing lamb
salt and pepper, to taste
1 tsp ground ginger
3–4 tomatoes
2 medium heads fennel
1$\frac{1}{2}$ lb fresh, or $\frac{1}{2}$ lb frozen fava
   beans
3 Tbsp chopped cilantro
1$\frac{1}{4}$ cup water

1 Choose a flame-proof casserole large enough so that all the ingredients only half fill it. Pour in enough oil to coat the base, set over medium heat, and grate in the onion. Wash and scrub the lemon, cut into slices and add.

2 Cut the lamb into 2 in. cubes and add to the casserole along with the salt, pepper and ginger. Cook on medium heat, half covered, turning the meat occasionally, for 15 minutes. Skin and chop the tomatoes and add to the casserole. Cook for another 15 minutes, or until the meat is tender.

3 Meanwhile, wash the fennel heads, discarding any brown or withered parts. Cut each one into large chunks. Pod the fava beans if fresh; if frozen, leave unthawed. When the meat is tender, add the fennel, beans and cilantro. Add the water or, if using frozen fava beans, add only half the water. Bring back to a boil, lower the heat and simmer until the vegetables are cooked, about 10 minutes. Taste, adjust the seasoning and serve with rice, Couscous [see page 108] or Pourgouri Pilafi [see page 107]. Don't remove the slices of lemon; they should be tender and delicious.

Artichokes also go well with fava beans. For convenience, add canned artichoke hearts once the fava beans are cooked.

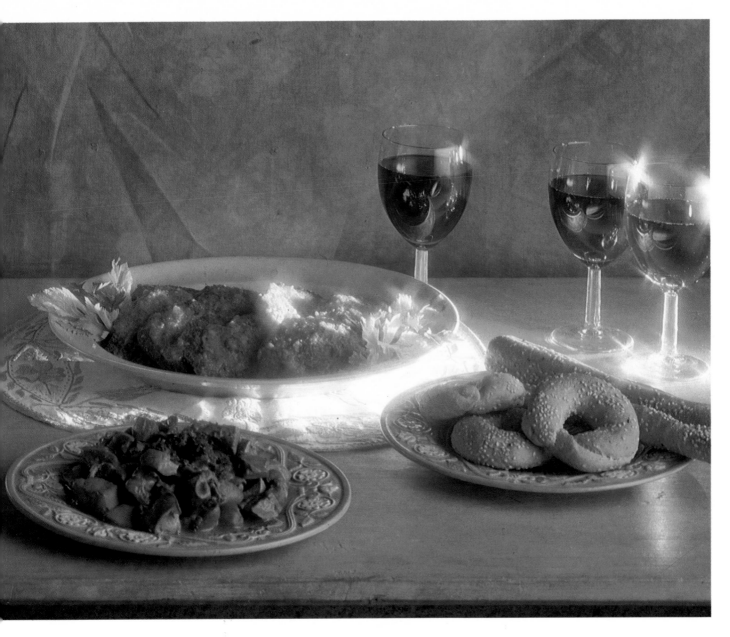

LAMB WITH PRUNES AND APRICOTS

PREPARATION TIME
3–4 hours soaking
1 hour 35 minutes, including 1
    hour 10 minutes cooking

¼ lb pitted prunes
¼ lb dried apricots
2 Tbsp oil
1 medium onion
1½ lb lamb steaks, sirloin or any
    cut from the leg or shoulder
1 tsp ground allspice
salt and pepper, to taste
1 Tbsp sesame seeds
1 recipe Plain Pilaf Rice [see
    page 104]

1 Rinse the prunes and dried apricots, cover with water and soak for at least 2 or 3 hours. Drain, reserving the liquid.
2 Pour enough oil into a heavy-based saucepan to coat the bottom thinly. Grate the onion into it and set over medium heat. Cut the meat into 2 in. chunks and add to the pan. Add the allspice, salt and pepper, and mix well. Half cover the pan and cook for about 30 minutes, turning from time to time. If the meat sticks, scrape the pan and add a little of the soaking liquid from the fruit.
3 When the meat is cooked, add the whole fruit and enough reserved soaking liquid to just cover, bring to a boil and reduce the heat to simmer. Cook for another 30 minutes or until the liquid has thickened. Meanwhile, gently roast the sesame seeds in a dry frying pan and prepare the Pilaf Rice.
4 To serve, use an oiled mould to form a ring of rice, and turn it out onto the serving dish. Spoon the meat and fruit in around the ring, sprinkle with roasted sesame seeds.

This dish is also delicious cooked with only one of the two fruits, or with pork instead of lamb. A more exotic ingredient to cook with lamb in this way is fresh quinces.

Left to right Lamb, Fennel and Fava Bean Tajine, Lamb with Prunes and Apricots, Tunisian Kamouniya and Higado con Vinagre

75

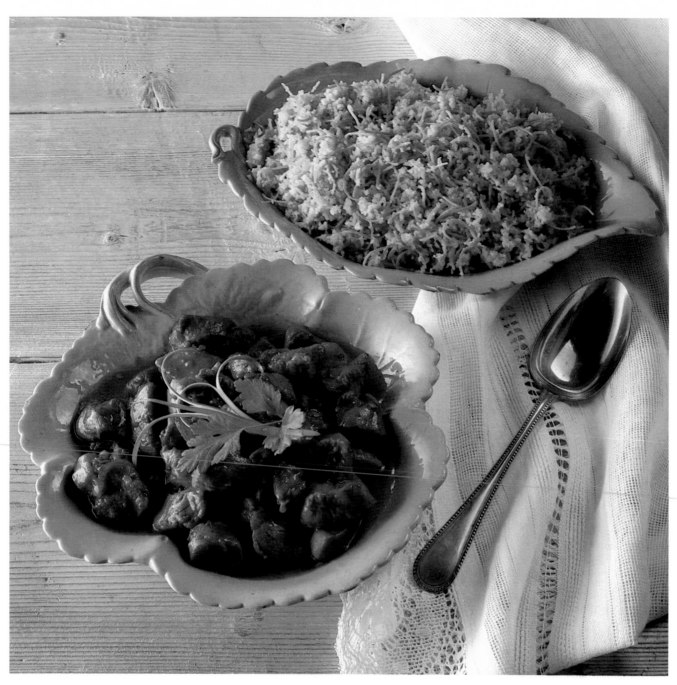

Pork Afelia may be served with rice or Pourgouri Pilafi (*recipe on page 107*)

PORK AFELIA

PREPARATION TIME
2 hours marinating
1¼ hours, including cooking

1 lb pork sirloin, tenderloin or
  any cut from the shoulder or
  leg
about ¾ cup red wine
2 Tbsp olive oil
2 tsp coarsely crushed
  coriander seed
salt and pepper, to taste

1 Trim the pork and cut into chunks. Put in a bowl, cover with red wine and leave to marinate for at least 2 hours.
2 Remove the meat from the marinade with a slotted spoon, reserving the marinade. Dry it with paper towels and brown in the olive oil in a heavy-based saucepan, in batches if necessary. Pour out most of the oil, leaving just enough to gently fry the coriander seeds until their fragrance develops. Pour in the marinade, scrape the pan and return the meat. Add salt and pepper to taste.
3 Bring the liquid to a boil, turn down the heat and simmer, covered, for about 1 hour or until the meat is tender. When the meat is cooked, the liquid should be reduced and thick. If it is too thin, remove the meat temporarily and reduce the sauce by raising the heat.

This dish goes well with Pourgouri Pilafi [see page 107], or rice.

KOFTA

'Kofta' is Arabic for minced rissoles, which are either grilled, broiled, fried or cooked in sauces, or added to soups or vegetables. The first time I introduce them to students I use a minimum of flavoring to show that if well prepared, Kofta are delicious. But they must be thoroughly kneaded [see below] so that all the flavors blend in and the mixture is soft and even. Try this simple seasoning first, then ring the changes with different spices.

I cannot overemphasize the importance of kneading the meat mixture until it is smoothly blended; this is the key to success for any Kofta recipe. Your hands will get sticky, but the illustrations below will show you how to avoid it.

GRILLED LAMB KOFTA

PREPARATION TIME
20 minutes including cooking [but depends on individual taste]

1 lb minced lamb [from shoulder or leg]
1 small onion
salt and pepper, to taste
2 Tbsp chopped parsley
$\frac{1}{4}$ tsp ground cumin seed

Ideally, it is best to use a cast-iron griddle.

1 Grate the onion into the meat and add the other ingredients. Knead well [see below], taste and adjust the seasoning.
2 Heat the griddle, broiler or grill. Form the kofta mixture into whatever shape you like. You can make small fingers about 1 in. long or flat rounds about 3–4 in. in diameter, not forgetting to knead well before shaping.
3 Place the shaped kofta on the griddle or grill, or under the broiler. The kofta should seize immediately and by the time you have put the last one in place, the first will be ready to turn over.
4 When brown all over and still juicy inside, remove and serve on a bed of shredded lettuce, or in pita bread with Tahina Dip [see page 16] and Egyptian Salad [see page 25].

If you shape the kofta like a hamburger you will find that even the most unadventurous children will like them.

You can vary the flavoring by adding any, or a combination, of the following: a grated clove of garlic, a touch of Harissa [see page 140] or powdered red chili or chopped cilantro. Or you can replace the cumin with ground caraway seed.

FORMING BALLS OR FINGER SHAPES

This method can be used with a variety of mixtures: minced meat and fish, nut or fruit pastes.

1 Knead the mixture thoroughly.

2 Wet one hand in a bowl of cold water, then shake off any excess. Rub your palms together so that they are just moist.

3 Take an egg-sized piece of the mixture and knead it until smooth. Wet your hands as in step 2 as soon as the mixture begins to stick to them.

4 Roll the mixture between your palms to make a ball or finger shape.

Note This tip on shaping minced meat also applies to minced or pounded chicken and fish mixtures [see pages 39 and 52] and to pastries and doughs for cookies and *petits fours* [see pages 125 and 128].

BARBECUES

Charcoal-grilled kebabs are the best known of all Middle Eastern dishes. Also popular for grilling are Kofta [minced meat rissoles; see the recipe on the previous page], small lamb chops, liver, poussins [baby chickens], quails and fish. They are served with dips, pickled vegetables and condiments, plenty of bread and salads. Their distinctively Middle Eastern character usually comes from steeping in simple marinades flavored with grated onion, garlic, parsley, salt and pepper. Other spices and herbs are often added: some people use *rigani* [Greek oregano], others cumin, coriander, allspice or Harissa [see page 140].

As children, our favorite treat was to be taken to a restaurant in Cairo which specialized in barbecuing. We ordered, not by portion, but by weight: a *ratl* [about 1 lb] of kofta; another of kebab; and two of *risha* – this means 'feather', and refers to the finest chops cut from the best end and trimmed of all fat. While we waited, we were tantalized by the aroma of the meats being cooked on a

charcoal grill in our full view, and our impatience was kept in check only by the constant arrival of *mezze*: pickled vegetables and tahina to eat with vast quantities of Arabic Bread. From time to time we would call the waiters and threaten to cancel our order if they did not hurry, as we had already satisfied our hunger. But they knew that the moment the fragrant grilled meats arrived, lying on huge beds of parsley, we would change our minds and dive in with renewed appetite. The restaurant never put onions or pieces of sweet bell pepper on the kebab skewers, and I still dislike such additions myself.

KEBABS AND CHOPS

Mix a finely grated medium onion with the same quantities of salt, pepper, cumin and parsley used in the Kofta recipe on the previous page. Spread this mixture over 1 pound cubed lamb and 4 small lamb loin chops trimmed of all fat. Refrigerate for at least 1 hour, turning from time to

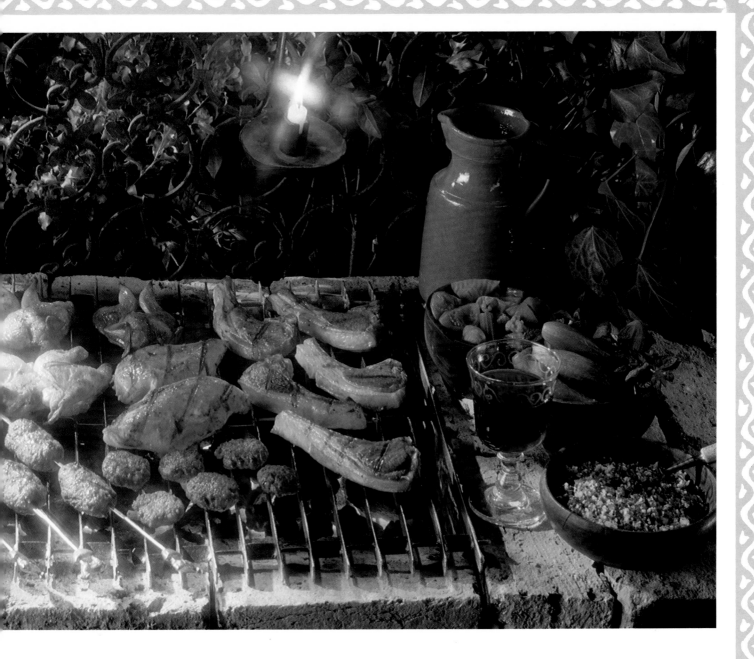

time to spread the mixture evenly over the meat. Grill on a barbecue until the meat is done to your taste and serve on a bed of chopped cilantro leaves.

Recipes for grilled fish and poussins, which are both also good barbecued, are on pages 46–7 and 58.

Kebabs, served on a bed of cilantro, eaten with a sprinkling of the red spice sumac, a dip such as Tahina, a mixture of pickled vegetables, bread and perhaps Tabbouleh (*recipe on page 24*), make a wonderful summer barbecue. On the barbecue above are quails, poussins, chicken breasts, large and small Kofta and chops. Pita bread may be heated through for a few minutes on the grill when the meat is cooked and you are ready to eat.

DRIED HERBS

When using dried herbs, always rub them between the palms of your hands before adding them to the dish. This releases the flavor and pulverizes the herb so that it blends in better. If the herb contains bits of twig, rub it through a wire mesh tea strainer.

HERBS, SPICES AND SALT

If, when tasting a dish to adjust the quantities of herbs and spices, you think it needs a bit more of everything, first try adding a little more salt. Taste again, and you will find that all the other flavors are enhanced.

MEAT BALLS [KOFTA] IN TOMATO SAUCE

PREPARATION TIME
1 hour, including 50 minutes
   cooking

2 Tbsp oil
1 medium onion
salt and pepper, to taste
1 tsp crushed dried lime, or
   juice of $\frac{1}{2}$ lemon
1 large can tomatoes
1 Tbsp tomato purée
$\frac{1}{4}$ cup soft breadcrumbs
$\frac{3}{4}$ lb minced beef or lamb, or a
   mixture of the two
a few sprigs fresh mint,
   chopped or 1 tsp crushed
   dried mint
2 Tbsp chopped parsley
1 tsp ground cumin seed

There is an infinite variety of meat ball dishes in the Middle East. In this recipe the meat balls are poached in a tomato sauce; you could also use Egg and Lemon Sauce [see page 136].

1 Take a heavy-based saucepan and pour in enough oil to cover the bottom. Set over medium heat. Grate the onion and add all but about a tablespoonful to the pan. Add the salt, pepper and dried limes or lemon juice. When the onion begins to brown, lower the heat. Drain the tomatoes and add to the pan along with the tomato purée. Continue cooking, half covered.

2 Meanwhile, prepare the meat balls. Mix the breadcrumbs with the minced meat, the rest of the grated onion, salt, pepper, mint, parsley and cumin. Knead well with dampened hands [see page 77], and form into walnut-sized balls: there should be enough for about 2 dozen meat balls.

3 Fry the meat balls in a little oil until brown and drain on paper towels. Tip them into the pan, shake well, taste and adjust the seasoning. Simmer, covered, for about 30 minutes. Serve with rice.

The tomato sauce can be flavored in a variety of other ways: for example, with roasted crushed coriander seed, a little red pepper [chili] sauce, turmeric and ginger. A handful of chopped parsley can be added to the sauce just before the tomatoes. The minced meat is often blended with cooked vegetables, such as leeks, eggplant or zucchini, very finely chopped, instead of breadcrumbs.

Garbanzo beans are one of the most characteristic ingredients of North African cuisine but legumes are a staple everywhere. BELOW Beans, lentils, seeds and nuts on sale in Nazareth market

Meat Balls in Tomato Sauce and Beef, Lamb, Garbanzo Bean and Egg Pie, served with a salad of tomatoes, cucumber and parsley.

BEEF, LAMB, GARBANZO BEAN AND EGG PIE

PREPARATION TIME
8 hours soaking
$1\frac{1}{2}$–2 hours, including 1–$1\frac{1}{4}$
  hours cooking if using a
  pressure cooker [add another
  40 minutes if not]

SERVES 8

3 oz garbanzo beans
1 small onion
1 Tbsp oil
$1\frac{1}{2}$ lb beef foreshank
pepper, to taste
1 tsp ground cinnamon
$\frac{1}{2}$ lb minced lamb
1 small onion
1 cup grated Cheddar, or other
  medium strong cheese
$\frac{1}{4}$ cup dried breadcrumbs
1 tsp single-acting baking
  powder
1 tsp ground allspice
3 Tbsp chopped parsley
salt, to taste
4 large eggs

This traditional North African dish involves such long and tedious preparation that I never bothered to cook it until I acquired a food processor. Thanks to this, it is now very easy to prepare. A pressure cooker also saves an enormous amount of time.

1 Wash the garbanzo beans and leave to soak for a good 8 hours in plenty of water.
2 Finely chop a small onion and put in a pressure cooker or saucepan with the oil. Set over medium heat, and cook uncovered. Trim the beef, cut into even chunks and add to the pan. Brown on all sides for about 10 minutes. Meanwhile, drain the garbanzo beans, reserving the soaking liquid and, if necessary, peel them by rubbing between your hands.
3 Add the garbanzo beans to the pan and enough reserved soaking water to cover to a depth of 1 in. Add the pepper [but no salt yet] and cinnamon. Cover the pan, bring the pressure up and cook for about 20 minutes [or about 2 hours in a saucepan]. The meat should be tender enough to cut with a fork; if not, simmer for a while half covered. There should be a fairly thick sauce. Adjust the amount of liquid by continuing to cook the meat uncovered or by adding water to the sauce. Add salt to taste.
4 Preheat the oven to moderate, 350°F. Process the minced lamb, a small onion, most of the cheese and the breadcrumbs to the consistency of a soft, even purée. Transfer to a mixing bowl, add the baking powder, allspice and parsley, then beat in the eggs one by one.
* The dish can be prepared in advance to this stage.
5 Put the beef and garbanzo beans in a medium-sized oven-proof dish: they should cover the bottom in one layer. Spread the processed mixture over the top. Sprinkle the rest of the grated cheese over it and bake in the oven for 30 to 40 minutes, until the mixture is set and the top is brown. Serve hot or cold with bread and a salad.

LAMB STEW FOR COUSCOUS

PREPARATION TIME
8 hours soaking
2 hours 10 minutes, including
 1 hour 50 minutes cooking

2 Tbsp dried garbanzo beans
2 Tbsp oil
1 medium onion
1½ lb stewing lamb
4 medium tomatoes
2 cloves garlic
1 tsp ground ginger
1 tsp crushed fennel seed
1 rounded tsp Harissa [see page
 140] or other red pepper
 [chili] sauce
1 rounded tsp turmeric
1¼ cup water
1 medium carrot
1 large zucchini
4 small potatoes
1 recipe pre-cooked Couscous
 [see right]

This lamb stew is one of an infinite variety that go with couscous. It is advisable to start by preparing Couscous on page 108, giving it the second steaming over this stew.

1 Wash the garbanzo beans and leave to soak at least 8 hours in plenty of water. Drain and, if necessary, peel the garbanzo beans by rubbing them between your hands.
2 Pour the oil into the bottom part of a couscous steamer or into a large, heavy-based saucepan. Chop the onion very finely. Trim the meat and cut it into 2 in. cubes. Cook the meat and onion gently in the oil for about 30 minutes, turning occasionally.
3 Skin, de-seed and chop the tomatoes. Crush the garlic and pound to a paste with the ginger, fennel seeds and turmeric. Mix with the tomatoes and Harissa. [A food processor is ideal for this.]
4 Turn up the heat to brown the meat, then add the tomato and spice mixture, garbanzo beans and water. Bring to a boil, reduce the heat, half cover and simmer for about 1 hour.
5 Peel or scrape the carrot and zucchini and cut into large chunks. Leave the potatoes whole, peeled or unpeeled as you prefer. Add the vegetables to the mixture and leave to simmer for about 20 minutes.
6 Put the pre-cooked Couscous [prepared to the end of step 3 of the recipe on page 108] in the top of the steamer and fit the two halves snugly together. Steam the couscous uncovered for 20 minutes, fluffing it up occasionally with a fork.
7 Warm a large serving dish in a warm oven. When the vegetables are tender, add salt to taste. Spoon the couscous into the serving dish, making a pile with a hollow in the center. Trickle some of the sauce over the couscous. Spoon some of the meat and sauce into the hollow in the center, and scatter a few pieces of the vegetables onto the mound. Serve the rest of the stew in a separate bowl.

For a different flavor, add a bouquet of parsley and cilantro to the stew with the tomato and spice mixture, and remove just before serving.

LAHME LAHLOU [SWEET MEAT]

PREPARATION TIME
3–4 hours soaking
1 hour 10 minutes, including 1
 hour cooking

¼ lb pitted prunes
½ cup 2 Tbsp granulated sugar
2 Tbsp orange flower water
½ tsp ground cinnamon
1 lb lean lamb, either leg sirloin
 steaks or any cut from the
 leg or shoulder

TO GARNISH
¼ cup blanched almonds

In Algeria, this is served at the end of a meal on very special occasions. It is eaten on its own, as the crowning moment of the meal; you might compare it to medieval mincemeat or blancmange, both of which were festive sweet dishes made with meat.

1 Rinse the prunes and soak in water for at least 3 or 4 hours.
2 Put half the sugar, half the orange flower water and the cinnamom into a heavy-based saucepan and heat gently for a few minutes.
3 Meanwhile, cut the meat into 2 in. cubes. Add to the saucepan and cook slowly for about 45 minutes or until tender, checking from time to time and adding a little water if necessary. When the meat is cooked, the sauce should have thickened to a syrupy consistency.
4 Broil the almonds gently until lightly colored and set aside. Add the prunes, along with the rest of the sugar, and simmer for about 10 minutes. Just before serving, stir in the remaining orange flower water. Taste, and adjust the seasoning. Serve garnished with roasted almonds.

OPPOSITE Lamb Stew for
Couscous (*left*) and Lahme
Lahlou, an Algerian sweet
meat

> ### SAUCES
> Middle Eastern sauces, whether on their own, in stews or similar dishes, are seldom thickened by adding flour. Instead, they are reduced to the correct thickness by boiling, which also intensifies the flavor.
>
> Onions used in sauces should always be chopped extremely finely or even grated so that when the sauce is cooked, the onions should be invisible. Always begin cooking them over a low or medium heat until transparent and soft. Then the heat can be turned up if you want to brown them.

VEGETABLES & LEGUMES

As a child, the only cooked fresh vegetables I ever ate were *bamia* [okra] in sauce, *melokheya* [see page 42] – and French fries! Other vegetables, especially when simply cooked, I dismissed as sick-bed fare. Now, after years of cooking, I have developed quite a taste for vegetables, and the more simply cooked the better.

By 'simple cooking', I do not just mean mere boiling, as you can see from the recipes that follow. To my taste, vegetables are best cooked in a little oil and flavoring, with hardly any water. A good, fundamental rule is that the younger and fresher the vegetable, the simpler the flavoring should be. Simplest of all is olive oil, salt [sea salt is best] and lime or lemon juice. You might also add a little garlic, turmeric and chopped celery leaves or parsley or cilantro; or some spices such as roasted and roughly crushed coriander seed, caraway seed, a very little Harissa [see page 140], ginger [fresh or ground] or just a little cayenne pepper or powdered red chili. Tomato purée can be added for a different color as well as yet another flavor.

In the Middle East, fresh vegetables are usually cooked in stews flavored with meat, poultry or fish, and some recipes – those with a higher proportion of meat or other ingredients – will be found in other chapters. Vegetables cooked and eaten without meat are not just for vegetarians. Fresh vegetables combine marvelously with legumes [beans and peas], and stuffed vegetables are delicious cold or hot. It is easy to put a number of dishes together for a well-balanced and exciting vegetarian meal; they are all just as good without meat.

Clockwise from top left Shredded Cabbage, Braised New Potatoes, Green Bean Stew and Okra with Veal, with a bowl of Preserved Lemons (*recipe on page 139*) and pickles

BRAISED NEW POTATOES

PREPARATION TIME
**1 5 minutes, including at least
    1 0 minutes cooking**

1–2 Tbsp oil
1 clove garlic
1 Tbsp water
1 lb new potatoes
sea salt, to taste
juice of $\frac{1}{2}$–1 lemon

[*picture on page 84*]

1 Choose a heavy-based saucepan into which the potatoes will fit in one layer. Put in just enough oil to line the base of the pan and set it over a low heat. Finely slice the garlic and add, along with a couple tablespoonfuls of water.
2 Wash the potatoes, scrubbing them well, and put them in the pan. Add the salt and lemon juice, put the lid on the pan and shake well to coat the potatoes. Cook, covered, over low heat until cooked; this may take as little as 1 0 minutes, but new potatoes are surprisingly variable. Check every 5 minutes or so to make sure that the liquid does not completely dry up before the potatoes are cooked. If necessary add a little more water, cover the pan and shake again.

OLD POTATOES can be cooked in the same way, but first cut them into chunks and half cover them with water.

SHREDDED CABBAGE

PREPARATION TIME
**1 0–1 5 minutes, including
    cooking**

1–2 Tbsp oil
1 Tbsp tomato purée
salt, to taste
2 Tbsp water
1 medium white or solid green
    cabbage, about 2 lb
1 Tbsp coriander seed

[*picture on page 84*]

1 Coat the bottom of a large heavy-based saucepan with oil. Stir in the tomato purée, salt and a couple of tablespoonfuls of water, and set over low heat.
2 Shred the cabbage thickly and add it to the saucepan in batches; each batch will soften a little and make room for the next when it is ready. Stir thoroughly to mix in the sauce. Cover the pan and simmer gently. Meanwhile dry roast the coriander seed, crush it roughly and add to the pan, stirring thoroughly. Continue simmering for a few minutes until the cabbage is cooked to your taste.

CABBAGE AND LAMB CASSEROLE Put alternate layers of shredded cabbage mixed with 1 grated medium onion and slices of lamb leg sirloin into an oven-proof casserole, finishing with a layer of cabbage. Preheat the oven to moderate, 350°F. Mix 2 tablespoonfuls of oil with salt and pepper in a bowl with a little boiling water. Barely cover the cabbage with this mixture. Cook for 1 hour. Just before serving, fry a little paprika in a tablespoonful of oil and pour over the top.

A Moroccan stall stacked with beautifully arranged vegetables. They include *kabak* (large zucchini), eggplant, artichokes and white radishes, as well as the more familiar carrots, cauliflower and spinach; a string of fennel bulbs hangs from the stall. The stall owner is sitting on a box of green chilis; by his side are large bunches of flat-leafed parsley.

VEGETABLE STEWS

As you can see from the poultry and meat chapters, Middle Eastern stews are often a combination of meat or poultry cooked with vegetables in varying proportions. Once again, the cooking of vegetable stews is fairly simple, and variety comes from the choice and proportions of ingredients and from the various flavorings and seasonings. All the stews with meat in this chapter are also often cooked without it.

GREEN BEAN STEW

PREPARATION TIME
25 minutes, including 15 minutes cooking

1 recipe Tomato Sauce or Meat and Tomato Sauce [see page 137]
1–2 lb green beans [see right]
salt and pepper, to taste

[*picture on page 85*]

I was a teenager before I reluctantly agreed to taste a vegetable stew for the first time. It was a heavily-peppered green bean dish. I had to concede – despite myself – that I liked it. Even now, green beans in tomato sauce are not quite right for me without a lot of pepper.

1 Start with a basic Tomato, or Meat and Tomato, Sauce [see page 137]. If you are using the Meat and Tomato Sauce, you need only 1 lb of beans. Cut the ends off the beans and add to the sauce with salt and lots of pepper, tasting to check that you have got the right amount. Barely cover the beans with water, bring to a boil, lower the heat and simmer, covered, for 10 minutes or until cooked to your liking.
2 If you like crisp vegetables, the beans will be ready while the sauce is still quite liquid. I like them when they just lose their bright green color. Remove and reserve the beans while you reduce the sauce to a good thick consistency, then return them to the pan, reheat if necessary and serve.

OKRA WITH VEAL

PREPARATION TIME
30 minutes soaking
1 hour, including 30 minutes cooking

1 lb okra
½ cup 2 Tbsp vinegar
about 2 Tbsp oil
1 small onion
½ lb veal, cut from the shoulder or knuckle
1 tsp coriander seed
2 Tbsp tomato purée
salt and pepper, to taste
juice of 1 lemon

[*picture on page 85*]

1 Wash and top the okra pods. Soak them in vinegar and water for 30 minutes [see below], rinse and leave to dry, or dry with paper towels, and set aside.
2 Coat the base of a medium saucepan with oil. Finely chop or grate the onion, add to the pan and cook on medium heat until soft and transparent. Cut the meat into 1 in. chunks, add to the pan, raise the heat and turn the meat to brown it. Meanwhile gently dry roast the coriander seed in a separate pan and crush it. When the meat is browned all over, add the tomato purée, salt, pepper, roasted coriander seed, lemon juice and enough water to just cover the meat. Bring to a boil, lower the heat to simmer, cover and leave to cook for about 15 minutes, or until the meat is very tender.
3 Cut each okra pod into two or three pieces and add to the pan. If the liquid is drying up, add a little water. Simmer for another 10 to 15 minutes, or until the okra is cooked. If the liquid is too watery, reduce it to a thick sauce. Taste, adjust the seasoning and serve. This dish is best served with rice.

Instead of lemon juice, you might like to add a teaspoonful of crushed dried limes.

Using a very sharp knife, peel off a thin layer of the stem, following its cone shape.

PREPARING OKRA
Larger okra tends to have a slimy texture when cooked, which some people find unpleasant. There are a couple of ways of avoiding this. The first is not to cut into the okra, which is why the stem should be peeled in a cone shape without removing it completely (see left). I have also recently discovered the following tip, which I find very effective. Peel the okra, soak it in vinegar (about 1 cup per 1 pound) and water to cover for about 30 minutes, then rinse and dry.

CAULIFLOWER IN TOMATO SAUCE

PREPARATION TIME
45 minutes, including 15
    minutes cooking

1 cauliflower, about 2 lb
very fine dry breadcrumbs
oil for generous shallow frying
1 recipe Tomato Sauce [see
    page 137]
1 cup water

Cauliflower, like green beans [see page 87], is delicious cooked in tomato sauce; but it needs a slightly different preparation.

1 Cut the cauliflower into small florets, blanch them in boiling water, or steam them for a minute or so, and refresh under cold water. Then roll them in very fine breadcrumbs, fry in the oil until golden and drain on paper towels.
2 Pour away most of the oil from the pan, leaving about a tablespoonful of oil and any remaining breadcrumbs. Pour in the Tomato Sauce, stirring well, and the water, then the cauliflower, gently turning it over to coat the pieces with the sauce. Taste and adjust the seasoning if necessary, bring to a boil and simmer until the sauce is rich and thickened.

SPICED CARROTS

PREPARATION TIME
30 minutes, including 15–20
    minutes cooking

1 Tbsp oil
2 lb carrots
2–3 cloves garlic
1 tsp crushed caraway seed
2 Tbsp vinegar
salt, to taste
a small dot Harissa [see page
    140] or other red pepper
    [chili] sauce

1 Line the base of a medium saucepan with a thin layer of oil. Scrub the carrots well, slice them and put in the pan to cook over medium heat.
2 Finely chop the garlic and add to the pan with the caraway seed and vinegar. Stir. Add salt, a small dot of Harissa if you like and enough water to barely cover the carrots. Cover and reduce the heat to simmer. Leave to cook until the carrots are tender, shaking the pan occasionally to prevent sticking. Check that the liquid does not completely dry up before the carrots are cooked. If necessary, add a little more water. Serve hot.

You can also mash the carrots to a purée and serve cold. Spiced puréed carrots make an excellent *mezze* (picture on page 27).

ZUCCHINI IN SAUCE

PREPARATION TIME
30–45 minutes, including
    15–30 minutes cooking

6 medium zucchini, about 1½ lb
    in all
½ tomato
1 Tbsp tomato purée
about 1¼ cups water
1 Tbsp oil
salt and pepper, to taste

TA'LEYA
2 cloves garlic
2 tsp crushed coriander seed
oil for shallow frying

Our cook in Cairo always served vegetables such as zucchini, okra or green beans arranged in a pretty pattern. She laid them in this pattern in the pan before cooking, then turned them out in one piece onto the serving dish. But in fact, this recipe is delightful no matter how it is presented.

1 Wash and dry the zucchini and cut off the ends. Cut them diagonally into $\frac{3}{8}$ in. slices. Choose a saucepan which will hold 2 or 3 layers and arrange the slices in tightly overlapping neat circles, leaving a small hole in the middle. Into this hole put half a tomato, skin side down.
2 Mix the tomato purée with the water and oil, add the salt and pepper and pour carefully over the zucchini. The liquid should barely cover them. Take a plate that will fit fairly closely inside the pan, wrap it in foil and invert it over the zucchini [the foil will act as a handle so that you can lift the plate out]. Press the plate down and put the lid on the pan. Bring the mixture to a gentle boil, reduce the heat to simmer and cook for 15 to 30 minutes or until the zucchini are tender.
3 Meanwhile, prepare the Ta'leya in a frying pan. Chop the garlic very finely and fry quickly in a little oil with the coriander seed until lightly colored.
4 Remove the lid and plate from the zucchini. Spoon a little of the liquid from the zucchini onto the Ta'leya, mix and return to the pan. If the sauce is too liquid, raise the heat and reduce to thicken it as much as possible. Cover the pan with a large round serving dish. Then, with gloved hands, very carefully but swiftly invert the pan so that its contents fall out onto the dish. With luck [and practice] there should be a pretty circle of zucchini slices with a domed red tomato center.

OPPOSITE Spiced Carrots (*top*),
Cauliflower in Tomato Sauce
(*center left*), Zucchini in Sauce
(*bottom*) and Rich Pilaf Rice
(*recipe on page 104*)

You can add a dash of Harissa [see page 140] or other red pepper [chili] sauce to the Ta'leya, and also a squeeze of lemon juice. Any leftovers should be saved. They are equally delicious if mashed with a fork and served as a cold *mezze* the following day.

MIXED VEGETABLE TAJINE

This belongs to the same tradition as French 'ratatouille'.

PREPARATION TIME
40–55 minutes, including
  25–30 minutes cooking

1 medium onion
1 lemon
2–3 carrots
about 1 cup each green beans,
  hulled peas and hulled fava
  beans, fresh or frozen
salt and pepper, to taste
1 tsp ground allspice
3 Tbsp chopped cilantro

1 Chop the onion finely and slice the lemon. Pour the oil into a large, heavy-based saucepan, add the onion and lemon and set over low heat. Add the rest of the vegetables as they are ready. Scrub and slice the carrots, cut the ends off the green beans and pod the fava beans and peas if using fresh ones. Frozen vegetables should be added straight from the freezer. Add the salt, pepper, allspice and most of the cilantro, keeping some back to garnish the finished dish.
2 Add enough water to barely cover the vegetables; if they are frozen, however, you will not need to add any. Bring to a boil, then lower the heat and simmer, uncovered, until the vegetables are just tender, about 20 minutes. Sprinkle with the rest of the cilantro and serve with rice.

Other combinations of vegetables are also very good cooked in this way. Peas, fava beans and artichoke hearts, for example, make a superb mixture. If you like, meat balls can be added before the second stage of cooking, or the flavor varied with a little cayenne pepper, powdered red chili or red pepper [chili] sauce, or a Ta'leya [see page 140]. You can also omit the lemon.

CELERY, ZUCCHINI AND GARBANZO BEANS

Mixtures of legumes and fresh vegetables are extremely popular in the Middle East. The balance of flavors, shapes, colors and textures also makes good nutritional sense to vegetarians.

PREPARATION TIME
8 hours soaking
1½–2½ hours, including 1 hour
  20 minutes–2 hours 20
  minutes cooking

¼ lb garbanzo beans
1 large onion
1 Tbsp oil
2 Tbsp tomato purée
4–5 sticks celery
salt and pepper, to taste
2 medium zucchini

[*picture on page 96*]

1 Wash the garbanzo beans and leave to soak at least 8 hours in plenty of water. Drain, reserving the soaking water and, if necessary, peel the garbanzo beans by rubbing them between your hands.
2 Grate the onion and cook slowly in the oil until transparent and soft. Add the tomato purée and cook a little longer, then add the garbanzo beans and their soaking water. Bring to a boil, lower the heat and simmer until cooked, 1 to 2 hours depending on the garbanzo beans. [If you use a pressure cooker, they will take about 20 minutes.]
3 Trim and wash the celery and cut into 1 in. pieces. When the garbanzo beans are tender, add the celery, salt and pepper and simmer for another 15 minutes or until the celery is just cooked; it should still be quite firm. Wash the zucchini, slice them thickly, add to the pan and cook for another 5 minutes.
4 If there is too much liquid left, move the vegetables to a serving bowl with a slotted spoon, reduce the liquid to a thickish sauce and pour it over them.

This dish can be varied by using different vegetables, such as spinach instead of zucchini: chop the spinach or tear it up roughly and add at the same stage.

    For a spicy flavor, add a little ground ginger, crushed garlic and a pinch of cayenne pepper or powdered red chili.

    Another very popular mixture cooked in the same way is lentils and spinach, which go particularly well together [omit the celery]. Just before serving, stir in a little natural yogurt.

    Non-vegetarians can also start by cooking pieces of meat with the onion, or by adding small meat balls before the celery.

SOAKING LEGUMES
The length of soaking time for legumes varies a great deal, and depends on how long the legumes have been stored since they were dried. Check that they are adequately soaked by biting a bean (or pea). It is ready to cook when it is soft enough to chew.

    If you are really pushed for time, you could use canned legumes instead of the dried variety, but I would not personally recommend it.

OPPOSITE Mixed Vegetable Tajine (*top*), Stuffed Vine Leaves (*right*) and Foul Medames (*recipe on page 100*)

STUFFING VINE LEAVES

1 Place a neat, sausage-shaped pile of stuffing on the leaf, just above the division at its base.

2 Fold each side of the leaf diagonally into the center so that they overlap over the stuffing.

3 Start rolling the leaf from the base to the tip, then fold the two sides into the center. Continue rolling and folding in this way until you have an even, sausage-shaped package.

4 Tightly pack the vine leaves, with the fold sides underneath, into the saucepan, with the larger packages in the center and the smaller ones in circles around them.

STUFFED VINE LEAVES

I always used to cook vine leaves with a meat stuffing until I tried this Persian-inspired herb, nut and fruit mixture. This dish should always be eaten cold so that the delicate flavors of the stuffing have a chance to blend.

PREPARATION TIME
10 minutes soaking
1½ hours, including 30 minutes cooking

½ lb fresh or preserved vine leaves [about 2 dozen]
2–3 Tbsp oil
1 Tbsp tomato purée
salt and pepper, to taste
juice of 2 lemons or limes
2 cloves garlic

STUFFING
½ cup uncooked short grain rice
⅓ cup raisins
5–6 medium dried apricots
2–3 green onions
4 Tbsp finely chopped parsley
3 Tbsp finely chopped cilantro
½ cup broken walnuts, roughly chopped
salt and pepper, to taste
2 Tbsp crushed dried dill weed
1 Tbsp crushed dried mint
1 tsp ground cinnamon
1 tsp ground allspice
2–3 Tbsp oil

[*picture on page 91*]

1 To make the stuffing, first wash and drain the rice. Pour boiling water over the raisins and apricots and leave to soak for 10 minutes.

2 Drain the apricots and raisins, reserving the soaking water, and chop the apricots finely. Chop the green onions, including the green tops, very finely. Put all these in a bowl with the rice, parsley, cilantro and walnuts. Mix together, then add the salt, pepper, dill weed, mint, cinnamon, allspice and 2 to 3 tablespoonfuls of oil. There should be just enough oil to make the mixture glisten when you have given it another thorough mixing.

3 If you are using fresh vine leaves, blanch them in boiling water for less than 1 minute, just long enough to soften them. If using preserved vine leaves, rinse them well and blanch for 3 to 4 minutes. In either case, blanching time depends on the age of the leaves: they should be tender enough to bite through, but they should not tear. Rinse the leaves well in cold water, drain on paper towels and sort them out by size.

4 Choose a wide saucepan with a tight-fitting lid, which will hold all the stuffed leaves in a single tight layer, or at most two layers. Line it with 3 or 4 of the thickest, largest leaves, and any unsuitably small or broken ones. Stuff all the other leaves with filling, folding and rolling them into small, neat packages as shown in the illustration above. Make sure that the filling will stay in a compact pile before you start rolling. Pack the pan tightly, with the larger leaves in the center and smaller ones arranged in circles around them. Beat together 2 to 3 tablespoonfuls of oil with the tomato purée, salt, pepper and lemon juice and pour all this over the leaves. Add some of the soaking water from the fruit until the leaves are barely covered. Finely slice the garlic and insert slices between the stuffed leaves.

5 Bring to a boil. Cover the top of the largest plate that will fit inside the pan with a sheet of foil. Put it in the pan upside down, so that the corners of the foil form a handle for lifting the plate out. Put the lid on, lower the heat and leave to simmer for about 1 hour, or until the largest packages in the center are cooked. The only way to tell if they are done is to taste one. Adjust the flavoring of the sauce: it may well need more lemon juice.

6 Serve cold. If you first try one hot and another one later, you will notice how the flavors have blended into full harmony.

Vine leaves can also be stuffed with a meat filling, such as the one used for stuffing leeks [opposite]. They are often served with a *mezze* spread, with Tahina Dip [see page 16]. and other dips.

STUFFED LEEKS

PREPARATION TIME
10 minutes soaking
1 hour, including 30–45
   minutes cooking

8–10 medium dried apricots
2 large leeks
2–3 Tbsp oil
salt and pepper, to taste
juice of 1 lemon

STUFFING
¼ cup uncooked short grain rice
1 medium onion
½ lb minced lamb
3 Tbsp chopped parsley
1 Tbsp crushed dried mint
salt and pepper, to taste

[*picture on page 95*]

1 Pour boiling water over the apricots and leave to soak for about 10 minutes.

2 To make the stuffing, first wash the rice thoroughly and drain it. Grate the onion. Mix the lamb with the rice, onion, parsley, mint, salt and pepper. Knead the mixture thoroughly until smooth and set aside.

3 Discard any discolored outer leaves from the leeks and cut off the untidy tops and solid bottoms. With a very sharp knife, cut each leek open lengthwise to the center, following the step-by-step instructions below. Open out the leaves and wash thoroughly in cold water.

4 Drain the apricots, reserving the soaking liquid, and chop them very finely. Chop the small, innermost leaves of the leeks very finely and mix in with the apricots. Add a couple of tablespoonfuls of this mixture to the stuffing and reserve the rest.

5 Choose a large, heavy-based saucepan that will hold all the stuffed leeks in a single layer, or two layers at most. Chop the coarse outer leaves of the leeks and line the pan with them. Cut the rest of the leaves into 2 in. lengths. Fill each leaf with a small, sausage-shaped roll of filling slightly shorter than the cut section of leaf, and wrap it up to make a roll [rather like cannelloni]. With those pieces of leaf too small to go around the filling, close one piece partly around the filling, then put another piece on the other side to completely cover it. The curl of the leaf will keep the package together. Gently fry the rolls of leek in the oil in a frying pan, taking care that they do not unravel – which is easier than you might think. When they are golden, transfer them to the saucepan, packing them closely and neatly with the larger rolls in the center.

6 Pour away any oil left in the frying pan, add the leek and apricot mixture, cook quickly over fairly high heat, stirring constantly, for a minute or so; then add the soaking water, salt, pepper and lemon juice. Pour this mixture over the leeks in the saucepan; they should be just covered. Set the pan on the stove, bring to a boil and lower the heat to simmer. Cover the leeks with an upturned plate wrapped in foil, put on a tight-fitting lid and leave to cook for 30 to 45 minutes. Check from time to time that the liquid is not drying up too quickly: it should have reduced to a thick sauce by the time the leeks and filling are cooked. If it isn't thick enough, reduce quickly with the lid off the pan. Serve warm or cold.

STUFFED ZUCCHINI The above recipe for leeks is actually an adaptation of a traditional one for zucchini, whose flavor also goes very well with the sweet and sour apricot filling. Make the stuffing as above. Cut each zucchini in half across the middle and hollow out each half with a cylindrical apple corer, reserving the scooped-out middle. Chop this and add to the apricots for the sauce, as above. Push the filling quite loosely into the hollow zucchini, leaving a little gap at each end to give the rice plenty of room to expand as it cooks.

STUFFING LEEKS

1 Cut off the top leaves and bases, then cut to the center of the leek all along its length.

2 Open out the leaves and wash thoroughly. Cut them into 2 in. lengths.

3 Stuff the larger leaves first. Put a roll of filling along the leaf which will naturally curl itself over to cover it.

4 To stuff the smaller leaves, put the filling along one leaf, then place another leaf on top to enclose the filling.

STUFFED LETTUCE LEAVES

PREPARATION TIME
2 hours, including 1 hour
  cooking

12 outer leaves of lettuce or
  romaine
3 large slices white bread made
  into soft crumbs
1 lb hamburger
2 eggs
salt and pepper, to taste
flour for coating
oil for shallow frying
1¼ cups meat broth
juice of ½–1 lemon, to taste

I had never thought cooked lettuce leaves could be nice until I was given this Sephardic recipe from Salonika by Mrs Bondi Attas.

1 Carefully remove a dozen large, sound leaves from the lettuce and blanch them for 5 minutes in lightly salted boiling water. Refresh under cold water and drain on paper towels.
2 To make the stuffing, mix the breadcrumbs with the hamburger and one of the eggs, season with salt and pepper and knead well.
3 Take an egg-sized ball of the stuffing and place it on the stem end of a leaf. Begin rolling it up towards the tip. Fold the sides in to make an envelope, then roll it up completely. Beat the remaining egg. Roll each stuffed leaf in flour, then dip in the egg.
4 Choose a wide pan with a tight-fitting lid large enough to hold all the stuffed leaves in one compact layer. Pour in enough oil to coat the bottom generously and set over high heat. When hot, put in the stuffed leaves and fry quickly, turning until brown all over. Lower the heat and add enough meat broth to just cover the stuffed leaves. Add a little lemon juice, cover and simmer for 1 hour.
5 Transfer the stuffed leaves to a serving dish, and keep them warm if necessary while you reduce the liquid in the pan to make a fairly thick sauce, adding more salt, pepper or lemon juice to taste. Pour the sauce over the leaves and serve hot or cold.

SARMA

PREPARATION TIME
3 hours, including 2¼ hours
  cooking

1 medium green cabbage,
  about 2 lb
1 lb smoked pork or ham
1 Tbsp oil

STUFFING
2 medium onions
2 oz bacon
1 lb minced pork and beef
1 Tbsp uncooked short grain
  rice
salt and pepper, to taste
1 egg, lightly beaten

The recipe for this Yugoslav stuffed cabbage dish was sent to me by Mrs Zagorka Cvejić. Any kind of green cabbage or spring greens is suitable, as long as the leaves can be separated without tearing. For an authentic flavor use smoked pork or ham with quite a strong smoked taste.

1 To make the stuffing, first finely chop the onions and bacon. Set a little of the onion aside. Use some of the bacon fat to grease a pan, and gently fry the rest of the onion and the bacon until the onion is soft. Add the minced meat, mix and fry until all is well combined. Add the rice, salt, pepper, egg, and the rest of the raw onion. Stir well for a minute or so. Remove from the heat and reserve.
2 Carefully dismantle the cabbage and select about 2 dozen sound, not too coarse leaves. Cut the larger leaves in halves down the middle, removing and reserving the midrib. With medium-sized leaves, pare away the thick part of the midrib, taking care not to cut through the leaf. Blanch the leaves in boiling water until slightly softened. Stuff each leaf by putting some filling in the middle, folding over the stem end, then the tip, and rolling the leaf up sideways to make a cylindrical package.
3 Cover the bottom of a heavy-based pan with the rest of the cabbage, including the bits of leaf rib, coarsely chopped. Put half the rolls in the pan, cover with half the smoked pork or ham, cut into thin strips, then add the rest of the rolls and a final layer of pork. Add a tablespoonful of oil and water to just cover, set the pan on the stove and simmer very slowly for about 2 hours. Check occasionally that the liquid is not drying up too quickly, and add a little water if needed. It should have thickened slightly by the end of the cooking. Serve hot or cold.
* This dish can be prepared in advance. It reheats very well; in fact, it can be reheated several times and, if anything, becomes tastier each time.

OTHER STUFFED VEGETABLES
All kinds of other, sometimes less expected, vegetables can also be stuffed: eggplant, peppers, tomatoes, potatoes or artichokes. They may be cooked on top of the stove or baked – in the Middle East they are sometimes cooked together in a large baking dish so that the flavors of the vegetables and stuffings blend. They are then served hot or cold, often with natural yogurt or an Egg and Lemon Sauce (see page 136).

Stuffed Leeks (*left*), Sarma (*top right*) and Stuffed Lettuce Leaves. Stuffed vegetables are often served with natural yogurt, or a sauce

STUFFED ONIONS

PREPARATION TIME
1 hour 20 minutes, including 1
   hour cooking

4 large, mild Spanish onions
1 recipe stuffing [see page 93]
1 Tbsp oil
juice of 1 lemon
salt and pepper, to taste
1 Tbsp sugar

[*picture on page 99*]

These caramelized stuffed onions are absolutely delicious. Large, mild Spanish onions are the best ones to use.

1 Open the onions out in the same way as leeks, by removing the top and bottom and slicing from one side to the center. Then blanch them until they soften enough to pull apart and fill each 'leaf', which will roll itself naturally around the stuffing. Again, use any stuffing you like. Of the several stuffings it would be possible to use, the one on page 93 is my favorite.
2 Pack the rolls in a pan and add the oil, lemon juice, salt, pepper and sugar. Cook slowly, covered, for at least 1 hour, allowing the liquid to reduce slowly until it caramelizes the onions. They will need to be turned over several times.
3 Transfer the onions carefully to a serving dish [they should be very soft] and spoon over the juices.

LEEK AND POTATO EGGAH

PREPARATION TIME
50 minutes, including 30 minutes cooking

½ lb leeks
¼ lb potatoes
2 Tbsp milk
6 large eggs
salt and pepper, to taste
¼ lb Emmenthal or Swiss cheese
about 2 Tbsp clarified butter

[*picture on page 66*]

I made up this recipe recently, thinking that leeks and potatoes go very well together, but so do leeks and eggs – a very traditional combination. Like most 'eggahs', this can be baked in a moderate oven for about 45 minutes [see pages 66–7] or fried as below.

1 Wash the leeks thoroughly, discarding any discolored parts, and dry them. Peel the potatoes, dry them and grate into a mixing bowl. Slice the white parts of the leeks finely and add them. [A food processor can be used for all the grating and cutting.] Pour in the milk, then stir in [but do not beat] the eggs one-by-one. Add salt and pepper, and grate in the cheese. Taste, and adjust the seasoning.

2 Heat a frying pan and add enough clarified butter to line it well, swirling it around to coat the sides. When the butter is hot, add the egg mixture. Cover the pan and cook on very low heat. After 10 or 15 minutes, check that it is not sticking, and slide a metal spatula around the edge. Replace the lid.

3 After about 20 to 25 minutes in all, depending on thickness, the *eggah* should be set, except for the surface. Remove the lid from the pan and put the *eggah* under a medium-hot broiler for 2 to 3 minutes, or until the top is set. There is no need to brown it. Serve warm or cold.

To bake the *eggah*, use a moderate oven, 350°F, and allow up to 45 minutes, depending on the depth of the mixture.

ABOVE Celery, Zucchini and Garbanzo Beans and Lentils and Rice; Spinach Eggah and Leek and Potato Eggah

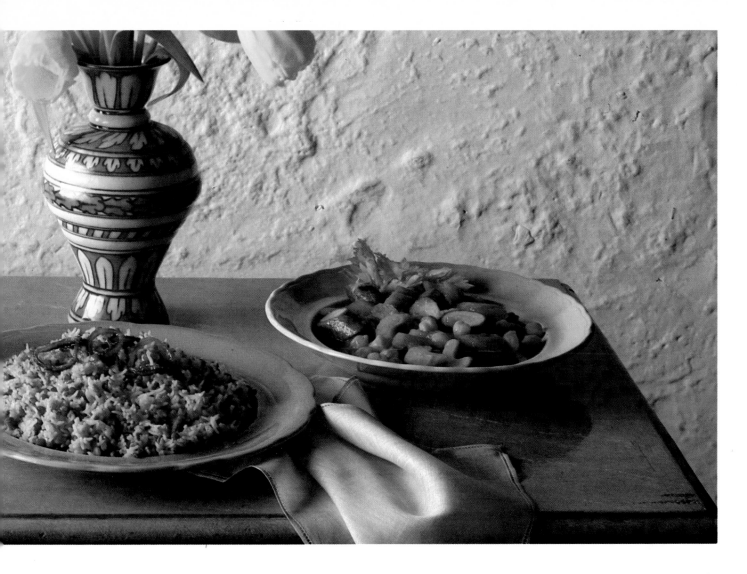

SPINACH EGGAH

PREPARATION TIME
1 hour 5 minutes, including 35
  minutes cooking

1 lb package frozen chopped
  spinach
4 Tbsp [½ stick] butter + more
  to grease dish or frying pan
1 rounded Tbsp flour
about ½ cup milk
⅔–1 cup grated cheese, to taste
breadcrumbs for coating dish
4–5 large eggs
salt, pepper, grated nutmeg and
  ground allspice, to taste

[*picture on page 66*]

1 Put the spinach and salt in a heavy-based pan over low heat to thaw slowly. Add the butter. When it has melted, raise the heat so that all the water evaporates from the spinach. Squash with a spoon, sprinkle in the flour and stir very thoroughly. The flour will absorb any extra moisture; make sure there are no lumps.
2 Stir in the milk a little at a time, thoroughly blending it in before you add more. As you stir, scrape the bottom and sides of the pan to prevent the mixture from sticking.
3 Add the grated cheese. The quantity of cheese will depend on its strength and your preference. Continue to cook gently until the mixture has the consistency of a dry purée, dropping but not runny. Leave to cool.
* The dish can be prepared in advance to this stage.
4 If you are baking the *eggah*, preheat the oven to moderate, 350°F. Heat a baking sheet in the oven. Choose a fairly shallow dish, such as a quiche dish or pie pan, which the mixture will about half fill; it must not come more than two-thirds of the way up. Butter the dish and coat it thoroughly with breadcrumbs, shaking off the excess.
5 Stir the eggs, one at a time, into the spinach mixture. Check the seasoning, and add salt, pepper, a little grated nutmeg or ground allspice, as you like. Pour the *eggah* into a baking dish.
6 Put the dish on the hot baking sheet in the oven and bake for 35 minutes. It is done when the center is firm to the touch, and may need another 5 or 10 minutes. Alternatively, pour the *eggah* mixture into a buttered, preheated frying pan and cook over low heat for 10 minutes or longer until it has risen and is firmly set all through. Brown the top under the broiler before serving, or turn it in the frying pan and leave to cook for 1 minute on the other side.

NAVY BEANS IN RICH MEAT STOCK

PREPARATION TIME
8 hours soaking and overnight
cooling
1 hour 10 minutes, including 1
hour cooking

1 lb navy beans
1 cow's foot or 2 calf's feet
2 large onions
2 Tbsp oil
4 eggs
salt, to taste

This was one of my favorite childhood dishes. The quantities are rather large for four people, but this dish reheats beautifully and can also be frozen. It can be time-consuming to make, but a large pressure cooker speeds things up. If you do not have one, you will need to quadruple the cooking times [multiply by 4]. Cow's feet are not always available, but it is worth while asking your butcher to order one. They are usually cut and split to fit into a saucepan: try to get your butcher to use an electric saw if possible, because a cleaver tends to produce bone splinters.

1 Wash the beans thoroughly, cover with plenty of water and leave to soak for at least 8 hours.

2 Wash the cow's foot and wipe with paper towels. Any bone splinters will stick to the towel. Put the foot in the pressure cooker and cover with cold water. Bring to a boil, uncovered, and skim off the scum several times. When you have got rid of all the scum, put the lid on, bring up the pressure and cook for 15 minutes. Strain and reserve the cooking liquid. When the pieces of foot are cool enough to handle, remove all the bones and return the meat [if any] to the cooking liquid. Refrigerate overnight and remove the fat which sets on the surface.

3 Chop the onions very finely and cook them gently in the oil in the bottom of the pressure cooker until well softened. Raise the heat and brown them, stirring, until dark brown. Add the meat, its liquid and the drained beans. The liquid should cover the beans by about 2 in. – but make sure you don't fill the pressure cooker above its recommended limit, which is usually half full. Add the eggs in their shells, nested into the beans. Attach the lid, bring up the pressure and cook for 15 minutes. The beans should now be cooked, but whether they are or not, the flavor will improve with extra simmering, half covered, for at least another 30 minutes.

4 When ready to serve, there should be no more than $\frac{3}{8}$ in. of broth above the beans, which should be tender. Add salt. Serve with Plain Pilaf Rice [see page 104]. The eggs are peeled and seasoned at the table. Although the combination of rice and beans is unexpectedly delicious, I like to add the contrasting texture of a green salad.

NAVY BEANS FOR VEGETARIANS Soak the beans as in step 1. Then cook from step 3, ignoring references to the meat, but doubling the amount of onions.

YUGOSLAV BAKED BEANS

PREPARATION TIME
8 hours soaking
2½ hours, including 2 hours
cooking

1 lb navy beans
3 large onions
4 Tbsp oil
2 fresh chili peppers
salt, to taste
1 Tbsp paprika

When I tasted this dish cooked by my Yugoslav friend Vera Janković, I was struck by the similarity of its flavor to one of my childhood favorites, the navy bean dish above; yet it is cooked in a completely different way.

1 Rinse the beans until the water runs clear, then cover with water and leave to soak for 8 hours.

2 Put the beans with their soaking liquid in a saucepan, and bring to a boil. Finely chop one onion. When the water boils, lower the heat, spoon off the scum, add the onion and half cover the pan. Simmer until the beans are cooked: if fresh, they will need about 1 hour; if older, up to 3 hours. From time to time, add more water as necessary to keep the beans just covered. [A pressure cooker will take about a quarter of the cooking time.]

3 Slice the other two onions into rings and gently fry them in the oil until soft and transparent. Add the whole chili peppers, paprika and plenty of salt – enough for the beans as well.

4 Preheat the oven to 375°F. When the beans are cooked, drain them, reserving the liquid. Put a layer of onions in a baking dish, then a layer of beans, then more onions, finishing with a layer of beans. Pour the cooking liquid in, and bake for about 1 hour, or until the beans are brown and gooey from the melting browned onions. Remove the chili peppers.

5 Serve hot or cold. Though very good as a hot vegetable dish with a main course, beans cooked in this way are more usually eaten cold as a first course. A small bowl of them makes an ideal addition to a *mezze* spread.

* This dish can be prepared in advance and will keep for up to a week in the refrigerator.

OPPOSITE (*left to right*)
Yugoslav Baked Beans, Stuffed
Onions and Navy Beans with
Eggs in Rich Meat Stock

LENTILS AND RICE

PREPARATION TIME
30 minutes soaking
35 minutes–1 hour 5 minutes,
 including cooking

¼ lb brown lentils
½ lb uncooked long grain rice
salt and pepper, to taste
1–2 Tbsp oil
1 large onion
2 Tbsp clarified butter or oil

TO SERVE [optional]
1 Tbsp dry roasted sesame seeds
small carton natural yogurt
1 tsp crushed dried mint
a pinch cayenne pepper or
 powdered red chili

[*picture on page 96*]

Legumes – dried peas and beans of all kinds, lentils and garbanzo beans – are the staple diet of an enormous number of people in the Middle East. They are eaten in a great variety of ways, and these dishes are a rich source of ideas for Western vegetarians.

1 Pick over the lentils and remove any small stones and debris. Wash them thoroughly until the water runs clear. Wash the rice well and leave to soak for at least 30 minutes. If you suspect that the lentils are old and tough, soak them too.
2 Choose a heavy-based saucepan which the lentils and rice will no more than half fill. Put in the lentils, cover them with water to a depth of at least 1 in., bring to a boil, lower the heat, cover and simmer until they are tender. This could take from 15 minutes to 1 hour, depending on the age of the lentils, so check from time to time. Add more water if necessary.
3 When the lentils are cooked, strain the rice and add to the lentils. Add the salt, pepper, oil and enough water to cover the mixture to the top joint of your thumb. Bring to a boil, lower the heat to simmer, cover and cook for about 15 minutes without lifting the lid. Check to see if the rice is cooked; if not, replace the lid and cook for a few more minutes.
4 Meanwhile, slice the onion in rings and fry in very hot clarified butter or oil until brown and crisp. Drain on paper towels. Serve the rice and lentils in a large dish topped with the onion rings. If you like, sprinkle with dry roasted sesame seeds and accompany with a side bowl of natural yogurt, either on its own or seasoned with crushed dried mint and a pinch of cayenne pepper or powdered red chili.

FOUL MEDAMES

PREPARATION TIME
8 hours soaking
1½ hours, including cooking

½ lb foul
4 eggs
brown outer skin of 1 onion

[*picture on page 91*]

OPPOSITE Legumes commonly
used in the Middle East:
1 Red lentils 2 Garbanzo
beans 3 Kidney beans
4 Flaked dried fava beans
5 Unpeeled dried fava beans
6 Foul 7 Brown lentils
8 Peeled dried fava beans
9 Green lentils

This is the national dish of Egypt, eaten by kings [when such creatures existed] and peasants alike, and pronounced 'fool medamess', with the accent on the last syllable.. It is consumed at all times of the day: breakfast, lunch and dinner, and between meals, enclosed in Arabic bread as a snack, either cooked at home or bought from street stalls. Many families always have some foul in the kitchen and will offer some whatever the menu. It is a very simply cooked, substantial and nourishing dish. Like all legumes, the flavor of these small brown beans improves the longer they are cooked, so a pressure cooker or a slow cooker is particularly suitable. Whichever you use, it should be a fairly large one which the beans and water do not more than half fill.

1 Pick over the beans and remove any stones or debris. Wash and rinse well. Soak in plenty of water for at least 8 hours.
2 Put the beans in a saucepan or pressure cooker and cover with about 2 in. of water. Add the whole eggs in their shells, nested into the beans, and the washed brown outer skin of an onion, which will help to give the eggs an attractive color. Cover and simmer for 1½ hours. [If using a pressure cooker, attach the lid, bring up the pressure and cook for 15 minutes.]
3 Remove the lid and allow the beans to simmer uncovered until the water is only ¾ in. above the beans. The liquid that is left will resemble a rather thin soup. Remove the onion skin and serve in any of the following ways.

At a meal, the foul is served in a tureen and ladled into soup bowls. All seasoning is done at the table according to individual taste. Salt, pepper, ground cumin, cayenne pepper, oil and lemon juice, and sometimes butter [which some people prefer to oil and lemon] will always be on the table, together with a bowl of Tahina Dip [see page 16], an Egyptian Salad [see page 25] and sometimes some Falafel [see page 18]. Each person seasons the foul to their own taste, peels the egg [which has acquired an interesting color and texture] and, if they like, mashes it into the beans.

For breakfast or as a snack it is seasoned and eaten as a sandwich in Arabic bread.

Leftover foul can be transformed by adding two or three skinned, chopped tomatoes to a Ta'leya [see page 140]. While simmering the foul, fry the mixture briefly and add to the foul. Add salt to taste and simmer for at least 15 minutes to let the flavors blend.

RICE, GRAINS & PASTA

Rice, grains and pasta all form a significant part of Middle Eastern fare, though rice is the most universally used. Wheat is also important, not only for bread-making; it is often cooked and eaten in the same way as rice. Couscous, a special type of semolina especially associated with North Africa, is enjoyed in other Arab countries as well. Pasta is also much appreciated in most of its forms, and an Italian influence is to be seen in many Middle Eastern dishes.

Rice is part of the staple diet in many countries of the Middle East. It is cooked on its own or with meats and vegetables; combined with legumes and pasta; and goes into stuffings for fish, poultry and vegetables.

For most of my rice cooking I use basmati, Patna or any long grain rice. The grains remain whole and separate if properly cooked. However, I prefer short grain rice for use in stuffings for exactly the opposite reason – because it clings together. Its softness makes it absorb the flavors of other ingredients very well.

Although I do recommend soaking rice for a couple of hours before cooking, this is not absolutely essential, but washing the rice should never be omitted.

Clockwise from top left Rice and Fava Beans, Persian Rice with a Crust, Sirloin of Lamb Cooked with Rice and Milk and Bulgar Wheat Pilaf with Eggplant and Cheese

PLAIN PILAF RICE

PREPARATION TIME
2 hours soaking [optional]
30 minutes, including 20
    minutes cooking

1½ cups long grain rice
2 Tbsp [¼ stick] butter or oil
1½ cups water
salt, to taste

There are several recipes for 'perfect' rice. Although some are far from perfect, others do work for some cooks. For instance, I have eaten very good rice made with double the amount of water I use, or cooked uncovered for part of the time; but whenever I have tried these methods, they have failed. So I stick to the methods which are foolproof for me, one of which is given here and the other on page 106.

It is important to note that in the pilaf method below the proportion of water to rice increases with the quantity of rice being cooked; for example, 3 cups of rice require 4 cups of water. For this reason I tend to use the Persian method [p. 106] when I am cooking large amounts of rice since the water does not have to be measured at all.

1 Wash the rice well until the water runs clear, then leave to soak for a couple of hours. The soaking is not essential, but the washing is.
2 Drain the rice. Heat the butter or oil in a saucepan, then add the water and bring it to a boil. As soon as it boils, tip in the rice, add some salt, give it a good stir, and lower the heat to very low; a heat diffuser is advisable. Cover the pan and leave to cook, without lifting the lid, for 20 minutes.
3 Check the rice. It should have absorbed all the water; if so, there will be little holes all over its surface. Take a few grains from the top center and chew them; they should be tender. If not, replace the lid and cook for a few minutes more. When the rice is ready, let it rest off the heat, covered, for a couple of minutes, then transfer it to a serving dish with a large metal spoon.

The rice can be cooked in stock instead of water, in which case you should omit the butter or oil.

Another method is to gently fry the rice before adding the water. This second method is the one to use for more elaborate pilafs: just before you fry the rice, fry a finely chopped onion with a handful vermicelli and tomato purée [for pink rice] or turmeric [for yellow rice]. You can also make a plain brown and white rice by first frying a small quantity until it starts to brown, then adding the rest of the rice with the water and proceeding as in the main method.

RICE FOR FISH Measure, wash and soak the rice as above. Heat the oil in a heavy-based saucepan while you finely chop a small onion and fry until it is dark brown. Add the water, bring to a boil, then add the drained rice and salt, lower the heat, cover and cook until the rice is done. It should be a nice brown with little black specks; the flavor goes particularly well with fish [*picture on page 51*].

RICH PILAF RICE

PREPARATION TIME
2 hours soaking [optional]
40 minutes, including 30
    minutes cooking

2½ cups long grain rice
1 medium onion
1 Tbsp oil
½ lb chicken liver and heart
¾ cup 2 Tbsp pine nuts
½ cup raisins
about 12 cracked cardamom
    pods
salt and pepper, to taste
2 tsp ground cinnamon
3 cups 2 Tbsp water

[*picture on page 89*]

Because of all the additions, it is not worth making a small quantity of this pilaf. The quantities given here would feed 6 people, or 4 with very healthy appetites.

1 Measure the rice, wash it until the water runs clear, then leave to soak in plenty of water for a couple of hours or longer. [The soaking is not essential.]
2 Chop the onion and fry it in the oil in a heavy-based saucepan over medium heat until soft and brown. Chop the liver and heart into small pieces, add to the pan and fry until brown. Add the pine nuts, raisins, cardamom pods and rice, and stir well. Add the salt, pepper, cinnamon and water. Bring to a boil, lower the heat to a gentle simmer and cover the pan. Cook for about 20 minutes without lifting the lid.
3 Check to see if the rice is cooked. If it is, all the water will have been absorbed and there will be little holes all over the surface. Leave to rest, covered, for a few minutes off the heat before serving.

For a delicious vegetarian dish, simply omit the chicken liver and heart.

Rice dishes form the basis of Iranian cuisine. ABOVE Rice fields in the foothills of the Elborn mountains.

RICE AND FAVA BEANS

PREPARATION TIME
50 minutes, including 10–15
   minutes soaking and 35
   minutes cooking

3–4 green onions
1 Tbsp oil
3 Tbsp chopped cilantro
$\frac{1}{2}$–$\frac{5}{8}$ lb frozen fava beans
salt and pepper, to taste
1 tsp ground allspice [optional]
1$\frac{1}{2}$ cups long grain rice
3 cups water

[*picture on page 102*]

I usually keep a package of fava beans in the freezer. Since they are young, unlike most fresh ones, they need neither thawing nor peeling and are handy for a variety of quick dishes.

1 Cut the green onions into 1 in. lengths and put them in a heavy-based pan with the oil and half the cilantro. Set over medium heat. Add the fava beans straight from the freezer, and the salt, pepper and allspice if you like. Cover and cook for 10 to 15 minutes, shaking the pan from time to time. Meanwhile, wash the rice and leave it to soak.
2 When the beans are cooked there should be hardly any liquid left. Drain the rice and add to the pan. Add the rest of the cilantro and the water, which should cover the ingredients to a depth of about 1 in. Bring to a boil, then lower the heat and simmer, covered, for 20 minutes without lifting the lid. When the rice is cooked, let it rest for a few minutes before serving.

> FINDING SPECIAL INGREDIENTS
> Unusual ingredients can be hard to find because they are known under different names. If you can't find fava beans, ask for 'broad beans'; cilantro is sometimes sold as 'Chinese parsley'; and garbanzo beans can be called 'chickpeas'.

PERSIAN RICE WITH A CRUST

PREPARATION TIME
2 hours soaking [optional]
45 minutes, including 35
  minutes cooking

1¼ cups basmati [or long grain]
  rice
salt, to taste
4–6 Tbsp [½–¾ stick] butter
1 egg yolk [optional]

[picture on page 103]

This is the second method of cooking rice that I find successful; one advantage is that there is no need to measure the water. However, the first few times you cook this rice, you might not succeed in getting a whole crust. At least you will get loose crusty grains, and the rice will be delicious anyway. It is possible to make a crust without using an egg yolk [see below].

1 Wash the rice until the water runs clear and leave to soak for a couple of hours, if you have the time.
2 Put plenty of water in a large, heavy-based, preferably non-stick or Teflon saucepan and bring to a boil. Drain the rice and tip it into the boiling water, add salt, and boil, uncovered, for about 4 minutes or until the grains are cooked through, but not soft or soggy. Drain the rice, reserving a couple of tablespoonfuls of water in the pan.
3 Chop half the butter into small pieces and add to the pan along with the egg yolk. Return just enough of the rice to cover the base. Mix all thoroughly and spread the rice out evenly by tapping the sides of the pan. Then add the rest of the rice and dot with the remaining butter. Tap again to level the rice, then cover the pan with a clean cloth and replace the lid tightly over it. If you don't have time to wait for a crust to form, rice cooked in this way is actually ready to eat a few minutes after returning it to the pan. Set the pan over medium heat, on a heat diffuser if you have one, making sure that the cloth is folded up so that it does not catch fire. After about 15 minutes, turn the heat down to low and cook for another 15 minutes, or until the crust is formed.
4 Plunge the pan into cold water and remove the lid for a few seconds or until the crust is free from the bottom of the pan. Immediately spoon out the rice from above the crust onto the serving dish, then lift out the crust and pull or cut it into pieces. Serve these on a separate plate, or arrange around the rest of the rice, to munch on throughout the meal.

Other cooked ingredients – meat, poultry or vegetables – are often incorporated with rice cooked this way. They are added at step 3, sandwiched between 2 layers of rice.

You can have a different, but equally delicious, crust by omitting the egg yolk. Simply mix half the butter [or, if you prefer, a mixture of butter and oil] with enough of the rice to just cover the base of the pan and continue as above.

A non-stick or Teflon cake pan, generously buttered, can also be used. Put the pan, well-covered with foil so that it does not dry out, in a hot oven, about 425°F, for 30–45 minutes. You should be able to turn it out on a plate like a cake with a crusty surface.

LAMB SIRLOIN COOKED WITH RICE AND MILK

PREPARATION TIME
2 hours soaking [optional]
1 hour 15 minutes, including 1
  hour cooking

1¾ cups 2 Tbsp short grain rice
1 lb lamb leg sirloin
6 Tbsp [¾ stick] butter
5–6 cracked cardamom pods
¼ tsp crushed mastic
1 tsp salt
2 cups 2 Tbsp milk

[picture on page 103]

Years after I left Egypt I was introduced to this unusual but very simple dish from the countryside. The ingredients should be measured using a 2-quart soufflé dish. The dish should be only two-thirds filled by the rice, lamb and milk, to allow for rising. This way of measuring is also most useful if you want to vary the quantity.

To me, this dish owes its success to the special, delicate aroma of the cardamom and mastic, blended with the rice, milk and lamb.

1 Take a soufflé dish and pour in dry, unwashed rice until it just covers the top joint of your thumb – make sure it is evenly spread. Remove the rice, wash it and soak in plenty of water for at least 2 hours.
2 Preheat the oven to 350°F. Cut the meat into slices about ⅜ in. thick. Use some of the butter to grease the soufflé dish generously, not forgetting the sides.
3 Drain the rice and put half of it into the dish. Tap the dish to make sure that the rice is evenly distributed. Spread the pieces of meat over it, dot with the rest of the butter, sprinkle with the cardamom and mastic, and top with the rest of the rice. Sprinkle with the salt and pour the milk on slowly until it covers the rice to the depth of the top joint of your thumb. Put the dish in the oven for 1 hour or until it is puffed up with a beautiful golden crust.

POURGOURI PILAFI [BULGAR WHEAT PILAF]

PREPARATION TIME
30 minutes, including 20 minutes cooking

1¼ cups bulgar wheat
about 2 Tbsp olive oil
2 oz vermicelli
1¾ cups 2 Tbsp stock or water
salt, to taste

[*picture on page 76*]

1 Rinse the bulgar wheat in a bowl of water, removing any chaff which floats to the surface. Tip into a clean cloth and squeeze hard to remove most of the water.
2 Line the bottom of a heavy-based saucepan with olive oil and set over medium heat. Crush the vermicelli and fry it, stirring frequently, until golden brown. Take care not to burn it. Add the bulgar wheat and mix well. Add the stock or water and salt. Bring to a boil, then lower the heat to simmer. Cover the pan and cook for about 20 minutes. When the pilaf is done, there will be little holes all over the surface.
3 Stretch a cloth over the top of the pan, replace the lid and leave off the heat for a few minutes before serving in the same way as rice.

VERMICELLI can be cooked in the same way on its own. Just brown it in oil or clarified butter, barely cover with water or stock and bring to a boil. Lower the heat and simmer, covered, for 4 or 5 minutes.

Rice can also be cooked in the same way.

BULGAR WHEAT PILAF WITH EGGPLANT AND CHEESE

PREPARATION TIME
30 minutes salting
20 minutes, including cooking

1 medium eggplant
salt
1¼ cups bulgar wheat
2 Tbsp oil
1¼ cups water
¼ lb halumi, mozzarella or Monterey Jack cheese

[*picture on page 102*]

One of the best cooks I know, Mrs Lucie Farhi, taught me this unexpectedly delightful dish.

1 Cut the eggplant into 1 in. cubes. Put them in a colander, sprinkle with salt and leave to drain for at least 30 minutes. Meanwhile, wash the bulgar wheat and drain immediately.
2 Pat the eggplant dry with paper towels and fry it for a few minutes in the oil. With a slotted spoon, transfer the cubes into a sieve to let the oil run off. If you are using the same pan to cook the bulgar wheat, pour away the oil.
3 Tip the bulgar into the pan, add the water, and simmer, covered, for about 5 minutes. Then add the eggplant, mix in gently with a metal spoon, cover and return to the heat for a few more minutes. Then rest to see if the bulgar wheat is tender.
4 When the bulgar wheat is done, cut the cheese into small cubes and add. Leave the pan covered, off the heat, until ready to serve.

RIGHT The summer wheat harvest in North Yemen. Bulgar, or cracked, wheat is made by washing and picking over the grain, then allowing it to dry and harden before it is stone ground to the required size.

COUSCOUS

PREPARATION TIME
1 hour 15 minutes, including
    1 hour 10 minutes cooking

SERVES 6

1 lb or 1 lb 3 oz package
    couscous
salt

[picture on page 83]

This traditional North African food is basically semolina. It is cooked in a couscousière, a special two-part steamer with very small perforations in the base of the upper part. You can also use an ordinary steamer with a layer of cheesecloth in the top to stop the grains of couscous falling through the larger holes. Preparation is simplicity itself, thanks to modern pre-processed couscous. Before this product was introduced, preparing couscous was a long and tricky business. Even pre-processed couscous is normally cooked in two stages, the first of which can be conveniently done in advance. Here is a successful and easy method for one standard-sized package, either 1 lb or 1 lb 3 oz, which feeds about 6. I usually make more than I need and store the couscous and the stew to go with it in the freezer. They can both be reheated by steaming straight from the freezer.

1 Empty the couscous into a large bowl. Cover with cold water and immediately drain through a sieve. Turn the couscous out onto a large tray, spreading it out with the palms of your hands and rubbing it to keep it from forming lumps. Leave for about 20 minutes, sprinkling it with water and rubbing it from time to time.

2 Fill the bottom part of the steamer with water and set the top in place, making sure that it fits tightly. Bring the water to a boil: no steam should escape around the join. Put a shallow layer of couscous in the top of the steamer over boiling water. When steam rises through the couscous, add the rest of the grains and sprinkle with salt. Steam uncovered for about 30 minutes.

3 Remove the steamer from the heat, carefully take off the top and turn the couscous out onto the tray. Again rub out the lumps. Sprinkle the couscous with about $2\frac{1}{2}$ cups of cold water, rub out the lumps again and leave until you need it.

4 The second steaming is done the same way, except that you steam the couscous over the stew with which it is to be eaten, and only 20 minutes' steaming is needed. Before you put the couscous in the steamer, rub out the lumps again. Fluff the couscous up with a fork from time to time. It can then be tipped straight from the detached top of the steamer into the serving dish.

QUICK COUSCOUS

PREPARATION TIME
35 minutes, including 25
    minutes cooking

1 small onion
2 Tbsp oil
1¼ cups couscous
1¼ cups water
salt, to taste

Some people – though certainly not North Africans – cook couscous like the rice for pilaf. It is a quick and simple method, but it does not give the lightness that real connoisseurs demand.

1 Finely chop the onion and gently sauté in the oil until transparent, then add the couscous, water and salt and stir well. Bring to a boil, lower the heat and simmer, covered, without disturbing, for 15 minutes.

2 Uncover the pan to see if the couscous is done. If it is, it will have absorbed all the water and the surface will be pitted with holes. Cook, covered, for a couple more minutes if necessary. Then remove from the heat, stir, put a cloth over the pan, replace the lid and leave to sit for 10 minutes. Serve as you would rice.

The various kinds of rice, grains and pasta commonly used in Middle Eastern cooking: 1 Brown rice 2 White rice 3 Whole wheat 4 Orzo ('birds' tongues': small pasta grains) 5 Coarse bulgar wheat 6 Penne 7 Tiny pasta for soups 8 Couscous 9 Fine bulgar wheat 10 Pasta shells 11 Pasta bows 12 Rigatoni 13 Macaroni 14 Vermicelli

KIBBEH

PREPARATION TIME FOR BAKED
  KIBBEH
3 hours 10–40 minutes,
  including 1 hour resting and
  1 hour 10 minutes–1 hour
  40 minutes cooking

PREPARATION TIME FOR FRIED
  KIBBEH
3 hours 15–35 minutes,
  including 2 hours resting
  and 35–55 minutes cooking

SHELL
1 cup fine or medium bulgar
  wheat
1 small onion
¼ lb lean lamb
1 Tbsp flour [optional]
salt and pepper, to taste
1 tsp ground allspice

FILLING
1 medium onion
¾ lb minced lamb or beef, or a
  mixture of the two
1 Tbsp oil
⅔ cup water
salt and pepper, to taste
1 tsp ground allspice
1 tsp ground cinnamon
3 Tbsp chopped parsley
2 Tbsp pine nuts or coarsely
  chopped walnuts

2 Tbsp [¼ stick] butter [for
  baked kibbeh] or oil for deep
  frying [for fried kibbeh]

I only started making this bulgar wheat-based Lebanese and Syrian delicacy [which, incidentally, is also found in Cyprus] when I acquired a food processor. Traditionally, the bulgar wheat was pounded into a paste after soaking. Even using a meat grinder with a fine disk, this is a tedious job – a food processor keeps the work to a minimum.

Kibbeh come in two forms, either baked on a tray or deep fried. The first is the simpler to make: the filling is sandwiched between two layers of shell dough, then cut into rectangles or diamonds after baking. The second consists of meat-filled shells of varying shapes.

Shell

1 Wash the bulgar wheat and soak for 15 minutes in a bowl of water. Meanwhile, grate the onion in the food processor, add the meat in pieces and reduce to a smooth paste.

2 Drain the bulgar wheat in cheesecloth and squeeze dry. Add it, a little at a time, to the running processor. Then add the flour if you are using it [though not essential, it does help to bind the dough] and the salt, pepper and allspice. Leave the dough in the refrigerator, uncovered, for about 1 hour before using.

Filling

3 Grate the onion and put it in a heavy-based frying pan with the minced meat, oil, water, salt, pepper, allspice and cinnamon. Set over medium heat, break the meat up and turn it over, mix in the parsley and leave to cook, half covered, for 15 to 30 minutes.

4 When the meat is cooked and the whole mixture soft, add the nuts and raise the heat to brown it. Transfer to a bowl, leave to cool, then taste and adjust the seasoning.

Baked Kibbeh

5 If baking the dish, knead the shell dough with your hands [see page 77]. Dampen your hands with cold water whenever the dough begins to stick to them. Preheat the oven to 350°F.

6 Butter an 8in. square baking pan [not non-stick or Teflon, which would get scratched] and line it with half the shell dough about ½in. thick, pressing down to achieve an even surface. Spread the filling mixture over it, then spread the rest of the shell dough over the top. To avoid disturbing the filling when you even out this top layer, add it layer a little at a time and smooth the pieces together with dampened hands. Use a sharp knife with a wet blade to cut it clear through to the bottom into 2in. diamonds or rectangles. Pour melted butter over the top. Bake for 45 minutes or longer, or until brown. Serve warm or cold.

SHAPING AND FILLING KIBBEH FOR DEEP FRYING

Always keep a bowl of cold water handy, and moisten your hands whenever necessary.

1 Take an egg-sized piece of shell mixture, knead thoroughly and form into a smooth round ball, then shape it into an oval.

2 With your wet forefinger, gradually bore a hole in the center of the oval, turning the kibbeh as you work the shell up your finger, pressing against your other hand. The shell should be as thin as possible.

3 Fill the shell with the meat mixture, and pinch with wet fingers to seal the end. If any cracks appear, smooth them out with wet fingers.

4 Roll the finished kibbeh in the palms of your hands to perfect the shape.

There are two ways of cooking Kibbeh: frying (*left*) and baking on a tray

Fried Kibbeh

7 If frying the kibbeh, have the shell dough, filling mixture and a bowl of iced water ready on your work surface.

8 Dampen your hands slightly with the iced water. Follow the step-by-step directions opposite. Take an egg-sized piece of shell dough and knead it well to make a round, even ball. Re-dampen your hands whenever the dough starts to stick. Shape the ball into an oval. Wet your forefinger and bore it gradually into the oval from one end, pressing against the palm of your other hand while turning and squeezing it with your fingers. Work the dough up your forefinger to make a long, hollow 'torpedo' shape, squeezing the shell as thin as you can. [The more experience you have, the thinner the result will be.] Spoon in the filling mixture and seal the end, smoothing any cracks closed with wetted fingers. Put each completed kibbeh on a plate. Leave them in the refrigerator or a cool dry place for about 1 hour before frying.

9 Deep fry until golden brown. They are delicious with Tahina Dip [see page 16].

Kibbeh shells can also be made with very lean beef, without meat at all, or with any proportion of meat to bulgar wheat; with experience, you can vary the quantities as you like. However, it is advisable for beginners to follow the recipe given above, especially if the dough is to be formed into 'torpedoes', filled and fried.

MATZO MEAL AND RICE FLOUR SHELL This meatless, very light and crisp shell for fried kibbeh was made for me by Sonia Cohen. Use $\frac{3}{4}$ cup matzo meal and $\frac{1}{4}$ cup rice flour, seasoned with salt, pepper and 1 tsp ground allspice. Mix to a firm dough by gradually adding cold water: a food processor, though useful, is not necessary for this. Fill and fry by the method given above.

KIBBEH NAYE Literally, 'raw kibbeh', this dish is rather like *steak tartare*. It is made with a mixture of high grade, very lean lamb and a small amount of bulgar wheat [about 6 parts lamb to 1 part bulgar wheat]. Process together with a small onion and season with salt, pepper and allspice. Flatten the mixture on a small tray and serve with a little olive oil dribbled over the top.

Baked Macaroni and Ferik

BAKED MACARONI

PREPARATION TIME
1 hour 10–25 minutes,
    including 50 minutes–1
    hour 5 minutes cooking

1 lb long, thick macaroni
salt
1 recipe Meat and Tomato
    Sauce [see page 137]
5 cups Béchamel Sauce [see
    page 138]
2 eggs
1 cup grated cheese, a mixture
    of Emmenthal or Swiss with
    Cheddar or Parmesan

Pasta of many different shapes and forms, both fresh and dried, is popular all over the Middle East. The small kinds are added to soups. Others are cooked in broth, or boiled in plain water, and served with sauces made from the cooking liquid from braised chicken or meat. Baked macaroni dishes are particular favorites, made at home or bought from fast-food shops or street stalls. This was one of my mother's specialties.

1 Cook the macaroni in a large pan with plenty of fast-boiling, salted water. The pan should be large enough for the macaroni to swim freely: this is one of the secrets of good pasta cooking. After about 15 minutes test by biting a piece. It should be just tender. Drain it and put in a large bowl with the Meat and Tomato Sauce and a couple tablespoonfuls of the Béchamel Sauce. Mix well.

2 Preheat the oven to 400°F. Transfer the mixture to an oven-proof dish. Beat the eggs into the rest of the Béchamel Sauce, which should be allowed to cool a little if just made, or the eggs will curdle. Pour over the macaroni and top with the grated cheese. Bake for 30 to 45 minutes, until golden on top. Cut into squares to serve.

BAKED MACARONI WITH EGGPLANT Slices of fried eggplant, some added to the macaroni and others laid on top before pouring on the Béchamel Sauce, make a delicious addition to this dish. Before frying, sprinkle the eggplant slices with salt and leave overnight [see page 21] to reduce the amount of oil they take up.

MOUSSAKA I make Moussaka, the classic Greek dish, in the same way, using more fried eggplant slices – instead of the macaroni – layered with the meat and Béchamel Sauce, finishing with Béchamel Sauce.

FERIK

PREPARATION TIME
10 minutes soaking
45 minutes [or 2 hours 15 minutes], including 30 minutes in a pressure cooker [or 2 hours cooking in a saucepan]

2 cups whole wheat
1 large onion
1 lb veal shank [weight without bone]
2 Tbsp oil
4 eggs
salt and pepper, to taste

TO SERVE
salt, pepper and ground cumin

Wheat, man's oldest cultivated crop, was first domesticated in the Middle East. Much of the grain is ground into flour, but the whole grain is also cooked (*see right and page 122*) or boiled whole with sour milk and dried to make *kishk* or *trahanas* (*see pages 43, 60 and 136*). BELOW Sacks of grain being loaded onto an oxen-drawn cart during the Turkish wheat harvest.

This hearty dish is usually made in the Middle East with green, not quite ripe wheat; but ordinary, dry whole wheat is perfectly adequate. Use a pressure cooker, as described here, to save time. If you don't have one, a large, heavy-based saucepan will do. Simply quadruple the cooking times given for the pressure cooker [multiply by 4]. The pressure cooker should be a fairly large one, which the ingredients only half fill, since the wheat will swell quite a bit. Alternatively, you could take the opposite course and cook the dish in an electric slow cooker, which will take several hours. Veal knuckle is ideal for slow cooking dishes of this type. Ask your butcher to bone it and give you a couple of pieces of marrow bone for extra flavor.

1 Wash the wheat well and soak it in water for at least 10 minutes.
2 Finely chop the onion and cut the meat into chunks. You can remove the bone if you like, but will achieve better flavor if you leave it in. Pour enough oil into the base of the pressure cooker to coat it, and set over medium heat. Brown the meat, remove and set aside; then lower the heat, add the onion and cook until soft. Increase the heat to brown the onion, then return the meat to the pan, and the bones, if you have them.
3 Drain the wheat and add to the pan along with enough water to cover the wheat by 2 in. Add the eggs in their shells. Close the lid, bring up the pressure and cook for 20 minutes. At the end of this time the meat should be tender enough to cut with a fork, and the wheat swollen and burst. Add salt and pepper.
4 Serve in a deep bowl or tureen, leaving the eggs unpeeled and providing dishes of salt, pepper and ground cumin. Each person peels an egg and dips it in the condiments. The whites will have turned brown and the yolks a creamy ocher, and they will have a special, delicate flavor.

Ferik is also often cooked with beef foreshank or cow's or calf's feet, in the same way as the navy beans on page 98.

For a vegetarian dish, cook as above but without the meat, and add another medium onion. Fry the onions until soft, then increase the heat and cook until dark brown. This gives the dish a delicious flavor, and the eggs make it a rich and nutritious meal.

For added flavor, Ta'leya [see page 140] made by frying thin slices of onion and crushed coriander seed can be added just before serving.

DESSERTS & BREADS

The most common dessert in the Middle East is fruit, which the region produces in abundance: grapes, melons and watermelons, citrus fruits, apricots, figs, dates, mangoes and guavas, among others. The best dried fruits come from this area, and form the basis of both desserts and savory dishes. Dried dates and figs served after a meal with a mixture of nuts are nibbled throughout the evening, much the way we might eat them at Christmas time.

Puddings made with rice or rice flour and milk or water, flavored with rose or orange flower water and sometimes mastic, are popular throughout the region, and usually served cold. Such puddings are often eaten for breakfast and as well as at the end of a meal. Ice cream, sherbets and ices are Middle Eastern favorites, and it is hardly surprising that you find an enormous variety of seasonal fruit ices. The recipes I have given can be produced either in an ice cream maker or by more laborious, but equally satisfactory, hand beating. Perhaps the chief glory of the region is its pastries. Baklava is but one of several small delicacies stuffed with nuts and dried fruits, which are enjoyed with coffee at any time of the day.

Three delicious fruit desserts (*left to right*) Pomegranates in Lime and Rosewater Syrup, Date and Banana Dessert and Guavas in Lime Juice

GUAVAS IN LIME JUICE

PREPARATION TIME
10 minutes
30 minutes refrigeration

juice of 1–2 limes
2–3 Tbsp sugar, or to taste
4 guavas

[picture on page 115]

The fragrance of guavas marinating in lime juice and sugar always reminds me of childhood. When I came home from school at lunch time it wafted over me the minute I opened the door. My mother used to prepare guavas this way as soon as they were in season.

1 Mix the lime juice and sugar in a bowl, stirring until the sugar dissolves. Guavas, like bananas or pears, turn brown as soon as they are peeled, so prepare them one at a time and add the flesh to the lime juice right away. Peel each guava, cut in half, scoop out and reserve the soft center with its seeds, then slice the rest and turn it over in the lime juice until well coated. When all the guavas are prepared, put the bowl in the refrigerator.

2 Press the remaining guava centers through a plastic sieve to separate the pulp from the seeds [or use a food processor], and add to the bowl. Taste and adjust the flavoring. Refrigerate for at least 30 minutes until serving time.

POMEGRANATES IN LIME AND ROSEWATER SYRUP

PREPARATION TIME
10 minutes
2–3 hours refrigeration

2 pomegranates
½ cup sugar, or to taste
1 cup water
juice of 1 lime
1 Tbsp rose water

[picture on page 114]

The pretty, transparent ruby pulp enclosing pomegranate seeds makes a very refreshing dessert. Pomegranate seeds are delicious to eat or suck fresh from the fruit, but removing them can be time-consuming and messy, since the flesh is quite juicy. This dish is a good way of presenting this otherwise popular food as a formal dessert.

1 Cut the fruit in half and carefully remove the seeds in their transparent coats, discarding the white membrane to which they are attached. This can be tricky, so take care not to squash them.

2 Dissolve the sugar completely in the water, and mix the resulting syrup with the pomegranate seeds and lime juice in a bowl. Add the rose water and refrigerate for a few hours. Before serving, taste and add more rose water if needed. Serve in individual bowls.

Dried pomegranate seeds also have their place in Middle Eastern cooking, and are one of several ingredients used to add a sour or lemony flavor to any dish which requires it. Use dried pomegranate seeds as a substitute for lemon juice, lime juice or tamarind.

DATE AND BANANA DESSERT

PREPARATION TIME
30 minutes
2 hours refrigeration

2½ cups pitted fresh or dried
    dates
3–4 medium bananas
1¼ cups heavy cream

[picture on page 114]

When I first returned to Egypt in the mid 1950s, six years after my family had emigrated, I was everywhere offered this 'new' dessert, which I loved. So did my Egyptian friends in London when later I made it for them after my return. Use fresh dates if you can: they are quite easy to find these days. Dried dates are a good substitute so long as they aren't old and withered.

1 Dried dates don't require washing or peeling, but fresh ones should be washed one by one in a large bowl of water, then peeled. To peel fresh dates, cut off each end with a sharp knife, then make a shallow cut barely piercing the skin around the middle. Hold the date with the thumb and two fingers of each hand on either side of the cut, and twist the two halves of the skin. It should come off quite easily if the date is ripe. Split the date open lengthwise to remove the pit, but don't completely halve it. You will need to keep your hands and the knife blade wet while peeling and pitting the dates. Cover the bottom of a serving bowl with a single layer of dates and reserve the rest.

2 Peel and slice enough bananas to make a single layer on top of the dates, and pour on some of the cream to keep them from turning black. Then add more dates, more bananas and cream and so on, finishing with a layer of dates, and pour the last of the cream over to coat the dates evenly. Leave in the refrigerator at least two hours before serving.

To make an even richer dessert you can add a few roughly chopped walnuts or roasted almonds.

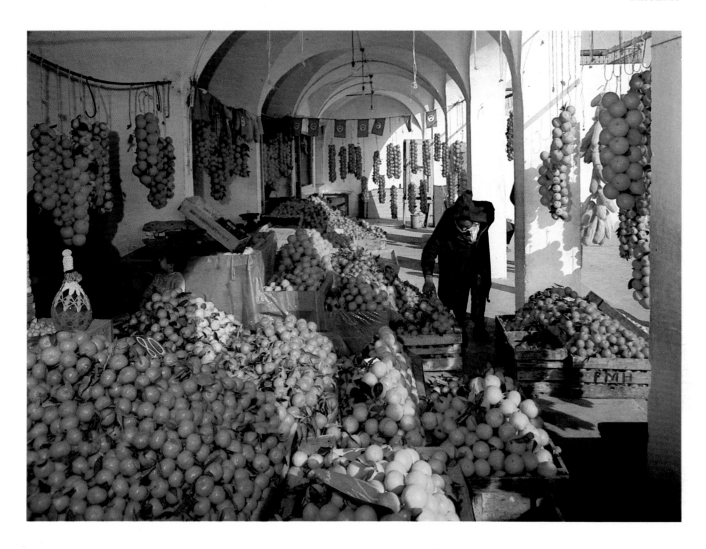

Oranges, lemons and limes on sale in the orange market at Hammamet in eastern Tunisia

KHOCHAF

PREPARATION TIME
15 minutes
3 days soaking

SERVINGS FOR SEVERAL DAYS

$\frac{2}{3}$ **cup raisins**
$\frac{2}{3}$ **cup sultanas**
$\frac{3}{4}$ **cup dried peaches**
$1\frac{1}{2}$ **cups dried apricots**
a piece *amardine*, about 4 in.
  square [optional]

TO SERVE [optional]
a few roasted almonds,
  walnuts, pistachios or
  hazelnuts, coarsely chopped
rose or orange flower water

[*picture on page 119*]

This recipe makes quite a large amount of dried fruit salad because it requires such a variety of dried fruits, which swell as they soak up water. Fortunately, it keeps well in the refrigerator and will improve with soaking longer than the three days recommended here. A vegetarian friend has even adopted Khochaf as his favorite breakfast. Nuts and flavoring are added just before serving. The inclusion of 'amardine' [an apricot paste available in Middle Eastern grocery stores, camping supply stores, and health food stores] in the salad improves it tremendously. It is well worth looking for, but if you can't find some, add more dried apricots instead.

1 Cut any of the fruit larger than a small prune into a few pieces, but leave the rest whole. Cut the *amardine* into $\frac{3}{8}$ in. squares with scissors, wetting the blades if they stick. Put this with the fruit into the largest bowl that will fit into your refrigerator, to allow the contents to swell. Cover with water to a depth of at least 2 in.
2 Referigerate for 3 days. Stir well from time to time and add more water as necessary to keep the fruit covered. It is superb served just as it is, or with one of the following additions sprinkled on top just before serving.

Roasted, coarsely chopped almonds, walnuts, pistachios or hazelnuts, or a mixture, provide a crunchy contrast of texture in as well as flavor. A sprinkling of rose or orange flower water lends a light freshness to this rather rich dessert.

FRUITS

In the Middle East, fresh fruit is so varied, plentiful and cheap that it not only features regularly at the end of every meal, but is also eaten at all times of the day. Freshly squeezed fruit juices of every kind – from mango and orange to guava, apricot and sugar cane juice – are sold on street corners everywhere.

Fruit is often part of a light evening meal on a hot summer evening: one of my favorite combinations is iced watermelon and feta cheese. Oranges and grapes also go very well with feta cheese, and bananas are nice with *kashkaval*, a goat's cheese similar in texture to a good mature Cheddar – which, incidentally, also goes surprisingly well with bananas.

A fresh fruit salad has always been my favorite dessert. In my family, it was usually a simple combination of oranges, bananas and strawberries with orange or lime juice. In the following recipe, substitute any fruit you like.

FRESH FRUIT SALAD

A good range of tropical and subtropical fruit is now sold year round, and I often make fruit salad with whatever is available, supplemented by good local fruit – fresh, never canned – such as apples, pears and strawberries, if a large quantity is required. To serve 8 to 10 people, peel and slice some or all of the following: a medium-sized ripe melon, a mango, a small papaya, $\frac{1}{2}$ pineapple, 2 or 3 guavas, and mix in a bowl with the juice of a lime [or lemon] and 1 or 2 oranges [or cup of mixed tropical fruit juice]. I never add sugar, as I find the sweetness of the fruit adequate. [* The salad may be prepared in advance to this stage and refrigerated.] Peel, slice and add 2 bananas at the very last moment, mix in well and serve.

The richly varied fruits of the Middle East:
1 Mangoes **2** Limes
3 Papayas **4** Fresh Fruit Salad
5 Kumquats **6** Khochaf, a rich dried fruit salad **7** Persimmons
8 Figs **9** Pomegranates

ICES

Anyone who lived or served in Egypt during the Second World War will have fond memories of Groppi's, which we proudly called the best *patisserie* in the world. This Swiss firm excelled in ices. As soon as the mango season started, we would rush from school to Groppi's for a daily mango sherbet, and their strawberry, apricot and pistachio ices were just as tempting. Eventually, I came to consider that by far the best ice cream was served in a popular café whose Yugoslav owner specialized in *dondurma kaymak* – simply Turkish for 'ice cream'. It was snow-white, with a most distinctive flavor of mastic and an astonishingly elastic texture – almost like melted Gruyère cheese! The essential ingredients for this delicacy were milk, cream, sugar, mastic and a thickener called *sahleb* [see page 141], made from the root of an orchid.

As you can see from the following recipes, you don't have to own an ice cream maker to enjoy home-made ices.

DONDURMA KAYMAK

PREPARATION TIME
30–34 minutes, including cooking
about 13 hours freezing

$1\frac{1}{2}$ tsp arrowroot
$4\frac{1}{3}$ cups milk
$\frac{3}{4}$ cup vanilla sugar
$\frac{1}{4}$ tsp crushed mastic
1 cup 2 Tbsp heavy cream

In the early 1950s, during my family's first years in Britain, my aunt sent me a recipe for this much-loved ice cream, giving cornstarch as a substitute for 'sahleb', which she was sure would be unobtainable in Britain. Little did she realize that with postwar rationing in Britain, cream was almost as scarce! Although you might find 'sahleb' under its Greek name, 'salep', at some Greek grocery stores, I find that arrowroot is a much better substitute than cornstarch.

1 Dissolve the arrowroot in a cupful of the milk in a heavy-based saucepan. Begin to cook over low heat, stirring continuously. Remove from the heat when it begins to thicken and beat vigorously into a smooth paste. Add another $\frac{1}{2}$ cupful milk, stir until even, return to the heat and continue stirring and adding milk until you have used most of it, which should take about 20 minutes. Then add the vanilla sugar and the last of the milk, stir to dissolve the sugar completely and continue to cook over low heat, stirring continuously.

2 Add the crushed mastic and the cream, and begin stirring again as you raise the heat to medium. Bring the mixture to a boil, making sure that your spoon reaches every part of the bottom and sides of the pan to prevent sticking. Boil for about 1 minute, stirring continuously, then pour into a heat-proof bowl and let cool.

3 When completely cool, taste and adjust the flavoring if necessary. Place in ice cream maker, if you have one, and churn according to manufacturer's directions. Otherwise, place in the freezer for about 1 hour, until it becomes slushy, then remove and beat vigorously [using a food processor or blender if you have one].

4 Return to the freezer for 30 minutes, then and remove and beat vigorously. Repeat this freezing and beating process 3 or 4 times at 30 minute intervals. After the last beating, pour into a mold, cover and freeze for about 10 hours. Transfer from the freezer to the refrigerator about 20 minutes before serving.

Huge bunches of dates drying in the sun on a fruit stall in Jericho. Dates, figs and apricots are often dried together in Middle Eastern homes, hanging in bunches from the ceiling. In Islamic countries, dates are one of the holy foods with which Moslems may break their daylight fast during the month of Ramadan.

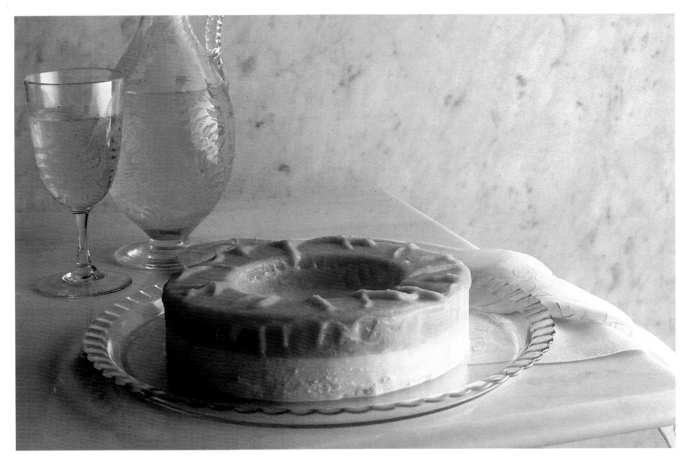

The contrasting flavors and textures of creamy Dondurma Kaymak and Mango Ice combine to make a deliciously refreshing dessert

MANGO ICE

PREPARATION TIME
**10 minutes, including cooking
about 15 hours freezing**

**14 oz can mangoes or mango
   pulp
1 Tbsp sugar [optional]
juice of 1 lime or lemon**

Generally, I make fresh fruit ices using $\frac{1}{2}$ lb fruit, a syrup made with $\frac{1}{2}$ cup sugar and 1 cup 2 Tbsp water and the juice of a lime or lemon. For dried fruit, I use water in which the fruit has soaked instead of syrup. However, since the canned fruit used for this Mango Ice is already sweetened, you will only need to add a little sugar, if any, and no water. The canned mangoes should be either Indian or Egyptian. A food processor or blender is more or less essential for this recipe.

1 Liquidize the mangoes and their juice if necessary. Place in a pan with the sugar [if used] and lime juice, bring to a boil and stir for 3 or 4 minutes. Transfer to a heat-proof bowl and leave until completely cold. Beat for 1 minute in a food processor or blender. Place in ice cream maker, if you have one, and churn according to manufacturer's directions. Otherwise, place in the freezer for 1 hour.

2 Remove from the freezer, beat for 1 minute in a food processor or blender and return to the freezer for another 30 minutes. Repeat 3 or 4 times at 30 minute intervals. The more times you do this, the creamier the ice will be. Transfer to a mold, cover and freeze for 12 hours. Move from the freezer to the refrigerator 20 minutes before serving.

COMBINED ICES Not only are Dondurma Kayak and this Mango Ice my favorites, but they make an unbeatable combination. Use a mold which will take both. Make the Mango Ice first, and begin making the Dondurma Kayak as soon as the first has been placed in the freezer. After 3 or 4 beatings of the Dondurma Kayak, pour it into the final mold. After 30 minutes, beat the Mango Ice for the 4th or 5th time and pour on top. The Dondurma Kayak should be stiff enough to keep the two separate. Freeze for 12 hours. To serve, plunge the mold almost to its rim in hot water for a few seconds and turn out onto a serving plate.

Alternatively, you could make the two separately, one in a ring mold and the other in a round bowl small enough to fit inside the ring, and unmold them so that one surrounds the other.

MEHALABEYA

PREPARATION TIME
40–50 minutes, including
   25–35 minutes cooking
1 hour cooling

Servings for several days

5 Tbsp cornstarch
6¼ cups milk
3 Tbsp sugar
1–2 Tbsp orange flower water
⅛ tsp crushed mastic

TO GARNISH
ground cinnamon or nuts

The wide range of Middle Eastern milk or milk and water puddings thickened with cornstarch [or ground or whole rice] are usually flavored with rose or orange flower water and cinnamon, mastic or vanilla, variously combined, and often enriched by the addition of pistachios, almonds or hazelnuts, and dried fruits such as raisins.

1 Choose a large, heavy-based pan or a large double boiler and in it dissolve the cornstarch in just enough of the cold milk to make a smooth, thin paste. Set the pan over very low heat, or medium heat for a double boiler, and stir continuously. As soon as the paste thickens, begin to stir vigorously, not neglecting the edges of the pan, while gradually adding all but a cup of the milk.

2 Add the sugar, stir well and taste. If you can detect the taste of uncooked cornstarch, continue adding milk gradually and stirring, but if the uncooked taste has gone, you can add the milk more quickly. When all the milk has been added and the taste is satisfactory, raise the heat to medium – or high for a double boiler – and stir while it comes to a boil, making sure it doesn't stick. When it achieves a thick, creamy consistency, remove from the heat and add the orange flower water and crushed mastic. Taste, bearing in mind that the flavoring will be stronger after it has had time to infuse and the mixture has cooled.

3 Pour the mixture into individual bowls and leave in a cool place to set. It should have a pleasant, gelatin consistency, neither liquid nor rubbery. Refrigerate until ready to serve, then sprinkle with ground cinnamon or chopped nuts.

For a lighter, less rich pudding, replace some of the milk with water or use skimmed milk.

BALOUZA A version of this pudding made entirely with water, is a beautifully delicate, translucent gelatin.

Both Mehalabeya and Balouza can be made with ground or whole rice instead of cornstarch. Many different flavorings and additions can be stirred into the mixture before it sets. A few drops of vanilla extract [or use vanilla sugar] instead of mastic gives an equally delicious, and somewhat more familiar flavor. You can mix in shelled, whole or half pistachios, pieces of roasted almonds, raisins or other nuts or fruit. I like adding chopped dried apricots, which contrast sharply with the creamy flavor. A usual Egyptian addition is a tablespoonful of a wheat pudding, Ashoura [see below], which gives an interesting texture.

ASHOURA

PREPARATION TIME
10 minutes soaking
2 hours, including cooking
1 hour cooling

SERVINGS FOR SEVERAL DAYS

about 2½ cups whole wheat or
   barley

TO SERVE
milk
sugar
orange flower water
ground cinnamon

Ashoura is made with either wheat or barley, whose whole grains are simply boiled until they burst and eaten with milk and various flavorings. This surprisingly light but nourishing dish is equally good as a dessert or for breakfast. It is worth making a large quantity, since it takes a long time to cook and keeps extremely well in the refrigerator for about a week. Using a pressure cooker can save a lot of time.

1 Wash and rinse the wheat or barley thoroughly and leave to soak in plenty of water for about 10 minutes. Drain, rinse again and place in a pan or pressure cooker. Add enough water to cover to a depth of 1 in. and cook for at least 2 hours [or 20 minutes in a pressure cooker], until the grain has swollen and burst. Transfer the grain to a bowl and leave to cool completely. When thoroughly chilled, the liquid should be the consistency of gelatin.

2 Cover the bowl with saran wrap and refrigerate. Dip in whenever you need it, and eat in one of the ways described below.

Take a bowlful of Ashoura and add hot or cold milk and some sugar, according to taste. Then sprinkle on some additional flavoring, such as ground cinnamon or a few drops orange flower water. [If you overdo the flavoring, mix in more Ashoura and milk.] A tablespoonful of Ashoura is often added to Mehalabeya or Balouza [see above].

Ashoura (*left*), served for breakfast or dessert with milk, sugar and perhaps cinnamon, Mehalabeya (*front right*) and Sutlach

SUTLACH

PREPARATION TIME
$2\frac{1}{2}$–$3\frac{1}{2}$ hours, including cooking

SERVES 8

3 Tbsp ground rice
2 quarts milk
1 Tbsp sugar

CARAMEL
1 cup sugar
$1\frac{1}{2}$ cups water
a little lemon juice

Of all the puddings my mother used to make, this beautiful, brown-marbled dish was the most appreciated by the constant flow of my father's army colleagues who came to our table in Cairo during the Second World War. Essentially it is a rice pudding, much enlivened by a caramel topping.

1 First make a ground rice pudding using the method described for Mehalabeya [see opposite] with the ingredients listed at left. While the mixture is still hot, pour into an oven-proof, preferably glass, dish to a depth of no more than $1\frac{1}{2}$ in. Preheat the oven to cool, 300°F.
2 Make a caramel by dissolving the sugar in the water over low heat. When the mixture is transparent, add a squeeze of lemon juice. Increase the heat and cook until the syrup turns golden. Remove from the heat and add the water carefully, to avoid scalding splashes of the very hot syrup. Stir well, then trail over the rice pudding.
3 Place the dish on the bottom shelf of the oven, reduce the heat to very cool, 250°F, and cook for 2 to 3 hours, until the topping bubbles and seeps down into the rice pudding. [If using a glass dish, you will be able to see that this has happened.] Allow to cool, then refrigerate until ready to serve. This pudding requires no flavoring other than the caramel.

GHORAYEBA

PREPARATION TIME
30 minutes, including 20
minutes cooking

$\frac{1}{3}$ cup hazelnuts
$1\frac{2}{3}$ cups flour + more for
baking tray
1 cup [2 sticks] butter + more
for baking tray
$\frac{1}{2}$ cup sugar
confectioner's sugar

Also called 'ghorabi', this is at its simplest a rich shortbread made with flour, butter and sugar roughly in the proportions 5:4:2. Each of the numerous variations in ingredients and flavorings has a distinctive character. My favorite is the one with hazelnuts. I prefer to roast the nuts in a dry frying pan rather than blanch them, because it is then easy to rub off most of the peel.

1 Roast the hazelnuts, peel and grind them as finely as possible, but not so much that they become an oily paste. [If using a food processor, add a couple tablespoonfuls of the flour with the hazelnuts.] Sift the ground nuts together with the flour. Cream the butter and sugar together, then add the flour and ground nuts, mix well and knead until smooth. Leave in a cool place for at least 30 minutes while you prepare a baking sheet by buttering it, sprinkling with flour and shaking off the excess. Preheat the oven to moderate, 350°F.

2 Dampen your hands slightly with cold water [see page 77], take walnut-sized pieces of dough, knead very well and form into smooth balls, moistening your hands at the slightest sign of sticking. Lay the balls on the baking tray leaving plenty of space between them, damp your thumb and gently press the center of each ball to make a small dent.

3 Bake for about 20 minutes. The shortbread cookies should remain fairly white, and will be quite fragile, so leave on the tray for an hour or so, until completely cool. Leave them for an hour or so to dry out a little. Sprinkle them with confectioner's sugar and store in a cookie jar.

Ghorayeba are sometimes oblong, and sometimes the dough is bound with an egg. Whatever shape or ingredients you choose, the final result may be unexpected until you have baked them often enough in the same oven. Sometimes they spread and flatten, which is why they should be well-spaced on the tray; sometimes the shape changes very little. Some factors you can control, such as the way you knead and roll the dough – thorough kneading helps make them firm – and some you can't, such as temperature variations between different ovens, or differences in the flour, sugar or nuts. Whatever the shape, the taste is delicious. For different flavors, use ground almonds instead of hazelnuts, or moisten your hands with rose or orange flower water instead of plain water when handling the dough.

RIGHT A street-vendor in Aleppo, Syria, selling honey-sweet cakes and pastries made from the huge round trays in which they are baked. The cakes may be made from farina, flour or ground nuts: one of the most popular is an anise-flavored bread sweetened with rosewater syrup.

Walnut Cookies (*front*) and Ghorayeba, rich shortcake biscuits

WALNUT COOKIES

PREPARATION TIME
25–30 minutes, including
    15–20 minutes cooking

MAKES 2 DOZEN COOKIES

2 cups broken walnuts
$\frac{1}{4}$ cup sugar
2 egg whites

These cookies are made without flour.

1 Reserve about $\frac{1}{2}$ cup of the largest walnut pieces for decoration. Grind the rest to the consistency of coarse sand and mix with the sugar. Beat the egg whites, and mix the ground nuts and sugar in thoroughly.
2 Preheat the oven to moderate, 350°F. Lightly grease a baking tray. Knead the dough well [see page 77], moistening you hands with cold water as often as necessary to keep it from sticking to them, and roll into walnut-sized balls. Place onto the baking tray in well-spaced rows, and top each with a piece of walnut. Bake for 15 to 20 minutes, until they are a nice dark golden color.

MARONCHINOS are similar to Walnut Cookies. My grandmother used to make them using very finely ground almonds instead of coarsely chopped walnuts.

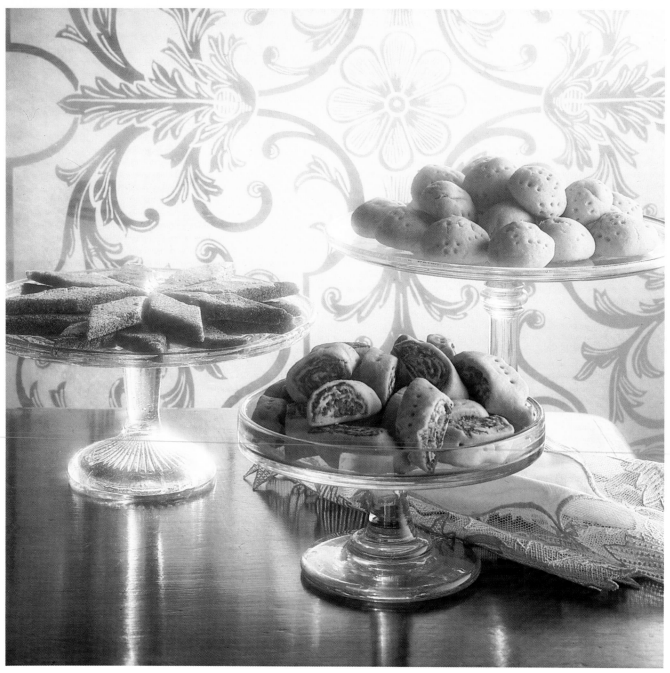

Farina and Date Bars, Date Menenas and Pistachio Menenas

FARINA AND DATE BARS

PREPARATION TIME
10 minutes, including 2–3
   minutes cooking
1 day drying

MAKES 2 DOZEN COOKIES

1¼ cups pitted dates
¼ cup [½ stick] butter
⅔ cups coarse farina

These delicious treats are extremely easy to make.

1 Finely chop the dates, mix with the butter and work into a paste using a damp knife or a food processor, if you have one.
2 Dry roast the farina in a heavy-based frying pan, preferably non-stick or Teflon, stirring constantly. As soon as it begins to color and smell roasted, remove from the heat, continuing to stir for a while. The pan can be returned to very low heat to achieve even color, but take care, as the farina burns easily.
3 Mix the farina and date paste thoroughly and spread ½ in. thick over a sheet of foil or waxed paper. Use a sharp knife with a wetted blade to cut into diamond shapes 1 in. wide. Separate them, peel off from the foil and leave to dry out in a cool place. The crunchy roasted farina contrasts pleasantly with the smoothness of the dates.

MENENAS

Also called *ma'oul*, this rich pastry is one of many filled with fruit pastes or nuts. It can be made in two ways: either the pastry and filling are rolled up together and cut into slices, or the pastry is formed into a hollow ball and stuffed with the filling. Of the many versions I've cooked, the two given here are my favorites. The first is by Angèle Argi, a great friend of my late aunt, with whom she always exchanged recipes and who comes to my rescue whenever I want to recreate any of my aunt's favorite desserts. Follow the step-by-step instructions below.

DATE MENENAS

PREPARATION TIME
2 hours softening butter
2 hours, including 30 minutes cooling and 1 hour cooking

MAKES 2 DOZEN PIECES

PASTRY
1¾ cups flour
7 Tbsp [⅞ stick] butter
1 Tbsp confectioner's sugar
1 Tbsp oil
2 Tbsp water

FILLING
1⅓ cups pitted dates
1 Tbsp [⅛ stick] butter
2 Tbsp water

confectioner's sugar

1 Leave the butter out of the refrigerator for a couple of hours, until it is completely soft.
2 Cut the butter into small pieces and work into the flour to make fine even crumbs using a pair of knives, a pastry cutter or a food processor. Add the confectioner's sugar and mix in thoroughly. Make a well in the center and pour in the oil and milk. Gradually mix it in until the dough comes cleanly away from the sides of the bowl. Knead well for a good 10 minutes, then wrap in saran wrap and place in the refrigerator.
3 To make the filling, first chop the dates finely, taking care to remove any pits which may remain. [If using a food processor, cut the block of dates into fairly small pieces first to locate any pits.] Place in a heavy-based frying pan with the butter and water, set over low heat and let the mixture melt gently into a paste, stirring and pressing from time to time. Leave to cool.
4 Grease and flour a baking sheet, shaking off the excess flour. Preheat the oven to moderate, 350°F. Remove the pastry from the refrigerator and cut into three pieces. Knead each well and roll out as thinly as possible into a rectangle. Spread ⅓ of the filling onto each rectangle, leaving a ⅜ in. border of uncovered pastry all around, and roll it up from one end. Once each roll is formed, continue rolling it backwards and forwards, pressing down lightly to lengthen it. Slightly flatten each roll and slice diagonally into pieces about ¾ in. thick. Place the slices on a baking sheet and prick the tops lightly with a fork.
5 Bake for 20 to 30 minutes. The menenas should be white on top and slightly browned underneath. Let cool, then sprinkle with confectioner's sugar.

SHAPING DATE MENENAS

1 Spread the date paste mixture thinly all over the rectangle of pastry, leaving a border of uncovered pastry all round the edge.

2 Roll up the pastry into a fairly thick sausage shape. Continue rolling it backwards and forwards, pressing down gently at the same time to make it thinner and longer.

3 Flatten the roll slightly, then cut it diagonally into slices about ¾ in. thick.

4 Separate the slices and place them on a greased and floured baking sheet.

PISTACHIO MENENAS

PREPARATION TIME
2 hours softening butter
1 hour 15 minutes, including
30 minutes cooling and 30
minutes cooking

MAKES 2 DOZEN PIECES

PASTRY
1¾ cups flour
6 Tbsp [¾ stick] butter
¼ cup confectioner's sugar
1 tsp skimmed milk powder
½ tsp single-acting baking
powder
3 Tbsp oil
3 Tbsp orange flower water

FILLING
1 cup pistachio nuts, shelled
2 Tbsp sugar
a little orange flower water

confectioner's sugar

[picture on page 126]

This specialty from Sonia Cohen's repertoire uses dried skimmed milk powder – a most unexpected ingredient from someone who insists that Baklava can only be made with pistachios or almonds, and never hazelnuts or walnuts as I make it. But I must admit that her Menenas are the best I have ever tasted.

1 Soften the butter at room temperature for a couple of hours.
2 Make the pastry dough [in a food processor, if you have one] as directed for the Date Menenas (see page 127), using the ingredients listed here – but reserve half the orange flower water for a later stage. Refrigerate the dough. Meanwhile, gently roast and shell the pistachios, chop fairly coarsely – not too large, or the stuffing will be difficult – mix with the sugar and lightly moisten with the orange flower water.
3 Lightly grease and flour a baking sheet, shaking off the excess flour. Preheat the oven to moderate, 350°F. Knead walnut-sized pieces of dough into smooth balls, moistening your hands when necessary with orange flower water to keep it from sticking. Moisten the tip of your index finger and make a hole in each ball. Insert a little filling, close up each ball, roll on your palm to restore a round shape, prick lightly all over with a fork and place on the baking sheet.
4 Bake for 20 minutes. The Menenas should not color. Let cool, and sprinkle with confectioner's sugar. They keep well in a cookie jar, but must be quite cold before you put them in.

The recipe for the following filling was given to me by Emily Arnel, a lifelong family friend now living in Canada.

PUMPKIN FILLING To make another delectable filling for Menenas, mix 1⅓ cups diced pumpkin with ½ cup sugar and the juice of ½ lemon. Cook, uncovered, over low heat until the liquid which exudes from the pumpkin has dried out. Flavor with cinnamon or, better still, a dash of crushed mastic.

APRICOT PETITS FOURS

PREPARATION TIME
2 hours 20 minutes, including
20 minutes cooking and 1½
hours cooling
2–3 days drying

MAKES 2 DOZEN PETITS FOURS

1⅓ cups dried apricots
½ cup sugar + more for rolling
2 Tbsp [¼ stick] butter
1 Tbsp orange flower water +
more for rolling
2 Tbsp water

These delectable fruit pastes are one of Sonia Cohen's specialties. They must be made a few days before they are needed, to allow time for drying out.

1 Chop the apricots very finely. Place in a heavy-based frying pan with the sugar, butter, orange flower water and water, set over medium heat and cook, stirring from time to time, until the mixture becomes a thick purée. Continue cooking until it no longer sticks to the pan. Transfer to a bowl and mix, pressing all over with a fork or the back of a spoon to ensure an even consistency. Leave to cool and refrigerate for a good hour.
2 Spread sugar over a pastry board, take marble-sized pieces of dough, form into smooth balls, dampening your hands with orange flower water to prevent it from sticking to them, and roll each ball in sugar. Put each ball into a paper *petit four* baking case or small cup cake case as soon as it is made.
3 Refrigerate, uncovered, for 2 to 3 days until dry.

As an alternative, roll the balls in roughly chopped roasted almonds instead of in the sugar.

SERVING BISCUITS, COOKIES AND PETITS FOURS AS SWEETMEATS
All the above, which can be defined as biscuits, cookies or *petits fours*, are usually offered to guests with Turkish coffee and a glass of cold water, not usually as a dessert, but at any time of the day. Each family will have a selection stored in separate cans in a cool place.

Left to right Basbousa, Baklava, Apricot Petit Fours and Konafa baked in a dish

BASBOUSA

PREPARATION TIME
1 hour, including cooking

MAKES 2 DOZEN PIECES

SYRUP
½ cup sugar
juice of ½ lemon
1 Tbsp orange flower water

2 cups farina
⅓ cup dried coconut
½ cup vanilla sugar
2 tsp single-acting baking
   powder
1 cup 2 Tbsp natural yogurt
2 Tbsp milk
1 large egg
1 cup [2 sticks] butter
about ½ cup whole peeled
   almonds

There are a thousand and one variants of these farina bars. This is my latest version, made with natural yogurt and flavored coconut.

1 Boil the ingredients for the syrup together with 1½ cupfuls of water until the consistency is just sticky.
2 Mix the farina, coconut, vanilla sugar and baking powder in a bowl. Separate the egg, reserving the white. Beat the yolk lightly. Make a well in the center of the bowl of dry ingredients and pour in the yogurt, milk, egg yolk and most of the melted butter [reserving enough to generously butter a dish]. Mix well and beat until smooth. Beat the egg white until not quite stiff and fold into the mixture.
3 Preheat the oven to fairly hot, 375°F. Butter a 2 in. deep square or rectangular oven-proof pan and pour in enough mixture to half fill it, spreading out evenly with a damp spatula. Gently tap the side to level it. Bake for 30 minutes.
4 Use a sharp, wetted knife to score the surface of the mixture with lengthwise and diagonal lines 1¼ to 1½ in. apart to divide it into diamonds. Slowly pour half the syrup over the mixture and stick an almond, pointed end down, into each diamond. Return to the oven for another 30 minutes.
5 Remove from the oven, pour on the rest of the syrup and leave to cool. Wet a knife and cut along the scored lines the whole way through. Transfer the pieces to a serving dish to cool.

BAKLAVA

PREPARATION TIME
$2\frac{3}{4}$ hours, including cooking
and 1 hour cooling

MAKES 2 DOZEN PIECES

SYRUP
1 cup sugar
$\frac{1}{2}$ cup water
a squeeze lime or lemon juice
1 Tbsp orange flower water

$\frac{1}{2}$ lb filo pastry
2 cups shelled pistachio nuts
$\frac{1}{4}$ cup sugar
1 Tbsp orange flower water
1 cup clarified butter, or half
butter and half oil

[picture on page 129]

This sumptuously rich pastry is the most universally popular of all Middle Eastern desserts. However some people consider it oversweet and soggy. I agree, but this happens because of the enormous amount of syrup or honey usually poured over it, and it is a problem which can be easily remedied. I make a crunchier, less sweet version. Baklava recipes vary, but all are based on layers of filo pastry filled with a nut mixture or thick cream and baked. Then a cold thick syrup is poured over and left to soak in. From the wide range of possible fillings, the following pistachio filling is my favorite, and also one of the most extravagant. Some people like to add a dollop of whipped cream when serving Baklava.

1 Make a thick syrup by boiling the sugar, water and lemon or lime juice together until it reaches the thread stage: that is, when you spoon a drop of syrup onto a plate and let it cool, then pick it up between your finger and thumb to separate it, it pulls out into a sticky thread. [If using a candy thermometer, cook to 230°F.] Add the orange flower water and let cool completely before using. The cooled syrup should be fairly thick, so that it will seep gradually into the finished Baklava.
2 Remove the filo pastry from its package and cover with a damp cloth to keep it pliable [see below]. Prepare the filling by gently roasting, shelling and coarsely grinding the nuts, and mixing with the sugar and orange flower water. Preheat the oven to moderate, 350°F.
3 Choose a high-sided baking pan, ideally $13 \times 8\frac{1}{2} \times 2\frac{1}{2}$ in. [Avoid non-stick or Teflon pans, which would be scratched when cutting the Baklava.] Melt the butter, add the oil if using both and brush over the pan, including the sides. Cover the bottom of the pan with half the filo pastry, laying it out one sheet at a time and brushing the whole of each sheet with butter before adding the next. [I prefer to do this with my fingers to ensure that I get the right amount.] If the size of the filo sheets doesn't correspond to that of your baking pan, you can cut, overlap and patch them as necessary.
4 Spread the nut mixture evenly over the filo, then add the rest of the filo sheets in the same way as before. Use a very sharp knife or razor blade to score through the top few layers of filo in a diamond pattern [about 2×1 in.]. Then sprinkle the top with water; I find a houseplant mister useful for this. Place the pan on a baking sheet, bake for about 30 minutes, then raise the oven temperature to hot, 425°F, and bake for another 30 minutes, or until golden brown. Pour the syrup slowly over the Baklava and leave to cool.
* Baklava can be prepared in advance to this stage and frozen either after the first half hour baking [thaw before continuing to bake] or when completely baked, but before adding the syrup.
5 Use a very sharp knife to cut through the Baklava along the scored lines, completely separating each piece. Transfer to a serving dish to cool.

Another filling I like is a mixture of roasted almonds, hazelnuts, walnuts and sugar flavored with the juice and grated rind of a small tangerine. This recipe can also be used to make individual finger-shaped pastries on the principle of borek [see pages 32–5], which can be baked or fried in the same way. If they are fried, use very little butter and don't brush the finished pastry with it.

KEEPING FILO PASTRY PLIABLE

Take the package of filo out of the refrigerator about 30 minutes before use. Open the package but do not unroll or separate the sheets. Cover them with a soaked and well wrung-out dish towel, draping this over two cups, one placed at each end of the roll of filo, so that the towel does not touch it. When you are ready to use the pastry, unroll just enough to cut off what you need. If you need whole sheets, take them out one at a time and roll up the rest again. Put it back under the towel straight away. If the pastry does dry up, you will still be able to use it flat in large pieces. Dried-up pieces of filo can also be used to make bases for tartlets (see page 28) or even for larger quiches and pies.

INDIVIDUAL KONAFA AND KONAFA BAKED IN A DISH

Individual Konafa

1 Unroll the defrosted konafa and take a thin layer about 12 in. long.

2 Spoon about half the melted butter thinly over the konafa, then spread a strip of nut filling along one long edge.

3 Gently roll the konafa over the filling to make a tight sausage shape.

4 Twist the roll from each end to give a rope effect and pour the rest of the melted butter over the top.

Konafa Baked in a Dish

1 Put the defrosted konafa in the largest mixing bowl you have and pour some of the melted butter over it.

2 Start pulling and tearing the konafa to mix it well with the melted butter. Keep turning it over and pulling and tearing, gradually adding more melted butter until it has all been added and the konafa is yellow and soft all over.

3 Line an oven-proof dish with half of the konafa. Spoon the custard evenly over it.

4 Cover the custard with the rest of the konafa in batches. Take as much as you can handle at one time and spread it out evenly on your hand before laying it on top of the custard. Repeat until the whole dish is covered with an even layer.

KONAFA

PREPARATION TIME
2–2¼ hours, including cooking and 1 hour cooling

SERVES 8

SYRUP
1 cup sugar
½ cup water
lime or lemon juice
1 Tbsp orange flower water

CUSTARD
3 Tbsp ground rice
4⅓ cups milk
½ cup 1 Tbsp heavy cream
1 Tbsp vanilla sugar
⅛ tsp crushed mastic

1 lb konafa pastry
1 cup [2 sticks] butter, or half butter and half oil

[picture on page 129]

Konafa or 'katafi' is the partner of filo, the other great Middle Eastern pastry. Like filo, it is made with flour and water, and needs to have butter added when it is made up. While filo looks like sheets of water, konafa looks like white shredded wheat. It is used in various ways, either as a pastry base and topping for a nut or cream filling with syrup poured over, or to make small, individual candies [follow the step-by-step instructions above].

1 Prepare a syrup as for Baklava [see opposite] and allow to cool. Make a custard following the method given for Mehalabeya [see page 122], but using the richer ingredients listed here and flavoring it with mastic or vanilla sugar. Let the custard cool completely; it should be firm enough to retain its shape when spooned.

2 Preheat the oven to moderate, 350°F. Prepare the konafa with melted butter or butter and oil, following the step-by-step instructions above, and use half to line a deep, oven-proof pan, either one suitable to use for serving or one with a removable bottom. Pour the custard evenly over the konafa, then spread the rest of the konafa on top and pour any remaining melted butter all over the surface. Bake for about 40 minutes, then increase the oven temperature to 400 to 425°F and bake for another 15 minutes, or until golden brown.

* Konafa can be prepared in advance to this stage and frozen. Thaw and warm for a few minutes in a hot oven to make it crisp again before pouring on the syrup.

3 Pour the cold syrup over the konafa. Sprinkle with chopped pistachio nuts and leave to cool before serving. Use a sharp knife to cut into slices.

Instead of the cream filling described here, you can use a nut filling like Baklava, both for this large dish and individual pastries.

BREADS

I have always been a bread addict, so the recent news form nutritionists that bread is no longer sinful delights me. In my youth in Egypt, my favorite bread was *eish baladi*, literally 'bread of my country'; in the recipe on page 134 I call it Arabic Bread. It is a flat, round, brown pita-like loaf. After much trial, error and perseverance, I have managed to reproduce it as closely as possible with different flours and ovens.

Of course, in Egypt many other breads were available: rings covered with sesame seeds, always fresh and crusty, which one bought in the street with a small package of Do'a [see page 140]; the plaited loaf decorated with colored eggs that our Greek baker used to present to us at Easter; Vienna and French loaves and bridge rolls. There was also a cylindrical brown loaf which my mother used to hollow out to insert a savory stuffing. She would place it in the refrigerator, then slice it into neat circles revealing exciting fillings of tuna, olives and pickles, or ham, eggs and cheese.

ALGERIAN BREAD

PREPARATION TIME
2 hours 20–50 minutes,
including 1–1½ hours rising
and 45 minutes cooking

MAKES 1 LARGE LOAF

1 envelope dried yeast
pinch sugar
1 cup 2 Tbsp lukewarm water
2 cups fine semolina
2 tsp ground cinnamon
1 Tbsp caraway seed
1 Tbsp sesame seed
1 Tbsp salt
2 Tbsp [¼ stick] butter + more
   to grease pan
1 egg
2 Tbsp oil

This is a spiced semolina loaf.

1 Dissolve the yeast in a cup with the sugar and some of the water, stirring well. Leave in a warm place.
2 Mix together the semolina, cinnamon, caraway seed, sesame seeds and salt, put on a board and make a well in the center. [If using a food processor or electric mixer, mix all the dry ingredients, turn the machine on and add the rest, leaving the water for last].
3 Melt the butter. Beat the egg, pour it into the well and add the oil, melted butter and yeast mixture. Mix to make a dough. Add water a little at a time, until the dough is a little stickier than ordinary bread dough, but still holding together. The quantity given here is a rough guide – use more or less depending on the absorbency of your flour.
4 Knead the dough well for at least 15 minutes.
5 Butter a large loaf pan and place the dough in. Cover with a plastic bag and leave in a warm place to rise for 1 to 1½ hours, until it has doubled in size. [This loaf does not need a second rising.] When it is nearly ready, preheat the oven to hot, 450°F.
6 Bake for about 45 minutes. Turn out the loaf, wait for a few seconds and tap the bottom, which will sound hollow if done. If it sounds dull, return to the oven upside-down for a few more minutes. Leave to cool before cutting.

OPPOSITE Home-baked breads surrounded by loaves, bread sticks and pita breads from the huge variety available in delicatessens and Middle Eastern shops. The Algerian Bread under the rack, Olive and Cheese Buns on the plate and flat rounds of Arabic Bread on their right are made from recipes in this chapter. *Left* Shaped loaves topped with sesame seeds, garbanzo beans and nuts in the window of an Israeli baker's shop.

ARABIC BREAD

PREPARATION TIME
3 hours, including 2 hours rising and 30 minutes cooking

MAKES ABOUT 7 ROUNDS

1 tsp sugar
1 cup 2 Tbsp lukewarm water
1 envelope dried yeast
2 cups graham [whole grain] flour
1 cup flour
¾ cup rye flour
1 Tbsp salt
½ tsp ground cumin seed
1 Tbsp oil
bran

[picture on page 133]

This glorious, mottled bread brings back vivid memories of my childhood. It has taken me a long time to get close to the 'eish baldi' of which I was so fond when I was young, but now I have nearly perfected it. I managed to learn in different stages: first by making wholemeal pita bread, then by adding the rye flour. Later I remembered the bran sticking to the bottom of the loaf. But the distinctive mottled brown patches were still missing. Then I hit upon the idea of cooking the bread under a preheated broiler instead of baking it in the oven. Yet I am still not quite there. There is another bread sold in Egypt, which is puffy, with a soft base and a crisp top that remains so even when the bread is cold. These I have not yet managed to achieve.

1 Dissolve the yeast and sugar in some of the water in a cup, leave in a warm place and warm a large mixing bowl.

2 Tip the flour into the bowl. Add the salt and cumin seed, and mix well. Pour in the dissolved yeast, then the rest of the water, using some to rinse out the yeast cup. Knead by hand for 10 to 15 minutes, until the dough is smooth and elastic and leaves your hands clean. [If using a food processor or electric mixer, put the dry ingredients in, start the machine, then gradually pour in first the yeast mixture, then the water. When the dough has come away from the sides and formed a mass around the dough hook or processor blade, take it out and knead by hand for a couple minutes to achieve a smooth, even ball of dough.]

3 Remove the dough and pour the oil into the mixing bowl. Roll the dough in the oil to cover it evenly, slip a large clear plastic bag over the bowl, folding it under the bottom so as to retain warmth and moisture, and leave in a warm place for about 2 hours, or until the dough has doubled in size.

4 Heat your broiler to maximum, remove the wire rack from the broiler pan and put the pan as close to the source of heat as possible. Spread some bran on a large tray and set it in a warm place. Knead the bread dough well and divide into about 7 equal portions. Take one piece at a time, knead in your hand and flatten into a tidy disk with your palm. Roll into a circle about 8 in. in diameter. Although this requires practice, the shape will improve with each piece you make and will taste delicious anyway. After shaping each round, place it on the tray of bran. By the time you have filled the tray, the first round will be ready to cook.

5 Cook one round at a time. Slip a spatula under a round and transfer to the hot broiler pan. If your broiler has a door or the oven door can be closed with the broiler pan in place, shut it. The round will take about 4 minutes to cook. [Meanwhile, roll another.] When it is puffy and moderately browned, remove and place on cooling rack.

* If you can keep yourself from eating all the bread at once, leave it to cool completely, stack in a plastic bag, seal and store in the refrigerator or freezer. When you want to eat it, turn the broiler on to maximum as before, remove the bread from its bag [no need to thaw] and broil with the pale side up for about 1 minute. With luck, it should puff up again to some extent; in any case, it will still be delicious.

PITA BREAD This is made in much the same way, but with all white flour or a mixture of white and graham flour. The small loaves are either round or oblong, and are usually baked on preheated baking sheets in a very hot oven for as little as 4 to 5 minutes.

Freshly baked bread from a *tanour*, or clay and brick oven. Villages often have a communal oven in which each family's bread, cakes and stews can be baked on a rotating basis.

OLIVE AND CHEESE BUNS

PREPARATION TIME
3 hours 45 minutes, including 2 hours rising, 1 hour proving and 15 minutes cooking

MAKES 6–7 BUNS

1 envelope active dried yeast
1 tsp sugar
1 cup 2 Tbsp lukewarm water
2 cups white flour
2 cups graham [whole grain] flour
1 Tbsp salt
2–4 Tbsp olive oil
about 12 pitted olives
6 oz halumi or Cheddar cheese

[picture on page 133]

In Cyprus they make loaves filled with olives or halumi cheese, which inspired me to make these smaller versions. I like to prepare the dough the evening before I need it and leave it to rise overnight. For faster rising in a warm place, use only 3 cups flour with the same amount of yeast, water, salt, etc.

1 Follow the method described in the recipe for Arabic Bread to the end of the rising [step 3], using the ingredients listed here.
2 Roughly chop the olives and cut the cheese into slices. Knead the dough well and divide into 6 or 7 portions. Oil your hands with the olive oil. Knead each piece thoroughly and form into a smooth ball. Flatten until it is about 4 in. in diameter and $\frac{3}{8}$ to $\frac{5}{8}$ in. thick. Use a very sharp knife to cut each bun in half horizontally, like a hamburger bun. Fill with olives and cheese. Close the halves around the filling pinching the edges. Leave in a warm place for about 1 hour.
3 Preheat the oven to hot, 450°F. Bake the buns for about 15 minutes, but check them after 10 minutes. They are delicious eaten as a warm snack, or can be left to cool before freezing and later reheated, wrapped in foil, straight from the freezer, or simply allowed to thaw without reheating.

SAUCES AND PRESERVES

The Middle East boasts a great number of sauces to accompany and enliven simply cooked dishes such as fried fish, grilled, broiled or roasted meats, pilaf and plain or stuffed vegetables. The simplest of these is a good thick natural yogurt, which may be flavored with garlic, onion or mint. Some, such as Tahina Dip, Hummus Dip and Babaghanoush [see pages 16 and 19] you will find in the mezze chapter. There is a further selection here below. In general, these sauces have the consistency of mayonnaise, even though most are not made with eggs.

This chapter also includes recipes for three basic sauces which form part of a number of dishes, both in this book and elsewhere.

EGG AND LEMON SAUCE

PREPARATION TIME
10–15 minutes
  cooking

1 cup stock or vegetable water
2 eggs
1 Tbsp cornstarch
juice of 1–2 lemons
salt if needed

[picture on page 138]

This sauce can be made with meat, chicken or fish stock, depending on the dish it is to accompany. It can also be poured over stuffed vegetables [see pages 92–95]; if so, make it with the cooking liquid from the vegetables.

1 Heat the stock in a saucepan. In a separate bowl, dissolve the cornstarch with a little stock. Whisk the eggs with the cornstarch mixture until frothy but not stiff, then gradually add the lemon juice. Beat 3 tablespoonfuls of hot stock into the mixture, one at a time.
2 Pour the mixture into the saucepan and keep whisking it until the sauce thickens. Be careful not to let it boil. Taste, and add salt or more lemon juice if needed. It should be the consistency of whipping cream. Serve hot or cold.

ZEMINO

PREPARATION TIME
20 minutes, including 10–15
  minutes cooking

2 cloves garlic
2 Tbsp dry breadcrumbs
1 small can anchovies in oil
1 Tbsp oil
1 Tbsp tomato purée
½ cup water
1–2 Tbsp vinegar, to taste
about 1 tsp sugar, to taste

We always had this anchovy and vinegar sauce with fried fish at home, but I am not sure of its origin. I've never had it anywhere else, either in Egypt or elsewhere. Even the name is a puzzle, for it does not seem to come from any language I know.

1 Crush the garlic with the breadcrumbs in a pestle and mortar [or a food processor], working them together until completely blended. Add the anchovies and keep blending to the consistency of a smooth purée.
2 Gently fry the purée in oil over low heat until you can smell the fragrance of cooked garlic. Stir in the tomato purée. Add the water, then the vinegar, stirring continuously. Taste, and add as much more vinegar as you judge right, and also a little sugar. Keep cooking over low heat, stirring constantly, until you have a thick sauce. Serve cold.

TRAHANAS SAUCE

PREPARATION TIME
2–3 hours soaking
10 minutes

4 oz trahanas
2 cloves garlic
salt, to taste
stock [optional]

[picture on page 138]

Since I discovered trahanas and found it so delicious, I have experimented with using it in all kinds of ways. I have devised this sauce, which makes a fine accompaniment to grilled meat or fish, or to stuffed vegetables. In fact, it can be used freely as an alternative to Egg and Lemon or Garlic Sauces.

1 Put the trahanas in a bowl, just cover with water and leave to soak for a few hours.
2 Squash it with a fork until it has the consistency of cooked oatmeal. Strain through a sieve and reserve the liquid. Crush the garlic with salt and mix well with a little of the trahanas paste. Add the remaining paste and mix well. This makes a splendid cold sauce just as it is.

For a hot, more liquid sauce, heat it gently, stirring all the time and adding some of the reserved soaking liquid [or any kind of stock, if you prefer] to give the right consistency; it should be like a rather grainy mayonnaise. Watch that it doesn't stick to the pan.

GARLIC SAUCE

PREPARATION TIME
30–40 minutes, including 25
minutes cooking

about ½ lb potatoes
2 cloves garlic
salt, to taste
juice of 1–2 limes or lemons
about ½ cup oil

[picture on page 138]

In our Sephardic family we called this sauce 'ajada' – from 'ajo', Spanish for garlic. In Spain itself you find a similar sauce called 'patatas al ajillo'; and the Skordalia paste [below] is another of the same type from Greece. Garlic sauces can be made with potatoes or bread. There must be as many versions as there are cooks who make them. Mine is inspired by the memory of one made by a neighbor in Cairo who originally came from Corfu.

1 Boil and peel the potatoes. Crush the garlic to a paste with a little salt.
2 If you are using a pestle and mortar [which must be large], add the potatoes a chunk at a time and blend well. Add more salt and a little lime or lemon juice gradually, then very slowly trickle in the oil, beating all the time. When the mixture has the right consistency, taste it and adjust the seasoning. If using a food processor or blender, blend the garlic with a bit of potato first, so that you start with a smooth, even mixture. Then add the remaining ingredients in the same order.

SKORDALIA Use about 2 cups soft breadcrumbs instead of potatoes. Vinegar is often used instead of lemon juice, and sometimes ground almonds are added. For obvious reasons, the final sauce is not as smooth as the one made with potatoes. It looks very similar to Trahanas Sauce [see opposite], but has a pungent sharpness rather than the milder bulgar wheat and yogurt flavor of trahanas.

MEAT AND TOMATO SAUCE

PREPARATION TIME
30–40 minutes cooking

olive oil
1 large onion
2 cloves garlic
3 Tbsp chopped parsley
½ lb lean beef or lamb, minced
    or cut into 1 in. cubes
1 large can tomatoes
1 Tbsp tomato purée
salt and pepper, to taste
a pinch thyme
1 bay leaf

1 Pour enough olive oil into a heavy-based saucepan to coat the bottom. Grate or finely chop the onion, add to the pan and set over medium heat. Cook until the onion is soft and transparent.
2 Finely chop the garlic. Increase the heat and stir until the onion begins to brown. Add the garlic, parsley and meat, and stir until the meat is evenly browned. Drain the tomatoes, reserving the liquid, and add, along with the tomato purée, salt, pepper, thyme and bay leaf. Bring to simmering point, half cover and cook over low heat for 20 to 30 minutes, stirring from time to time. If the sauce dries up or sticks, scrape the pan and add some of the reserved tomato liquid, or water. Taste and adjust the seasoning.

One of the traditional sauces of North Africa is a meat and tomato sauce like this one, with cubes of lamb and a handful of garbanzo beans cooked in it.

TOMATO SAUCE

PREPARATION TIME
30–40 minutes, including
    cooking

2 large onions
2 cloves garlic
2 Tbsp oil
3 Tbsp chopped parsley
6 or 7 tomatoes, or a large can
2 Tbsp tomato purée
a strip lemon peel
salt and pepper, to taste

The secret of a good sauce is to cook it until there is no taste of water; the ability to recognize this comes through experience. Taste after, say, 10 minutes cooking and again when the sauce is beginning to thicken. The difference will be obvious. When I ask students to do this, they often ask what I have added to improve the flavor so greatly. Canned tomato sauce may be used as a substitute for the sauce given here, but the flavor of the dish will not be as good.

1 Grate or finely chop the onions and garlic and place in a heavy-based pan with the oil. Cook over medium heat for about 10 minutes. Skin the tomatoes and discard any watery parts if using fresh ones, or drain canned tomatoes.
2 Add the parsley, tomatoes and tomato purée. Squash and mix with a wooden spoon. Add a strip of lemon peel, salt and pepper. Leave to cook, uncovered, over medium heat for 30 minutes, stirring occasionally, until the ingredients blend into a rich sauce.

The seasoning and flavor of this sauce can be endlessly varied. You can use one, two or more of the following: ginger, saffron or turmeric, cumin, coriander seed, cilantro, allspice, thyme, basil, mint, oregano ... the important thing is that no single flavor should be overpowering. You can also add some grated carrots or very finely chopped celery when the onions have cooked [end of step 1].
* This sauce is ideal for storing in the freezer. I usually omit any extra flavoring so that I can add whatever is appropriate when I come to use it.

Sauces and preserves (*left to right*) Egg and Lemon, Zemino, Trahanas and Garlic Sauces. In the jars: pink Pickled Turnips, Preserved Lemons and bought mixed vegetables.

BÉCHAMEL SAUCE

PREPARATION TIME
20 minutes cooking

2 Tbsp [¼ stick] butter
2 Tbsp flour
1 cup 2 Tbsp milk
salt and pepper, to taste

This white sauce, used in Middle Eastern as well as Western cooking, though one of the simplest basic sauces, often looks and tastes awful. It takes some patience to make it well: unctuous, free from lumps and, above all, fully cooked so that it does not taste of raw flour or cling to the palate. Whatever method you use, it will take a good 20 minutes to achieve a satisfactory result. I find that the following method is less boring than some, in which all the milk is added hot and you have to stir and wait patiently for the sauce to thicken.

1 Melt the butter over low heat in a heavy-based saucepan. As soon as it has all melted, add the flour and stir vigorously, keeping the heat low.
2 Add the milk very gradually – no more than a couple of tablespoonfuls at a time. Mix thoroughly, scraping the sides of the pan. As soon as each addition is blended smoothly, add a little more milk. As the sauce thickens, it is often necessary to take it off the heat as you add more milk. Eliminate any lumps as they form by vigorous stirring. Ensure that the heat is low enough to keep the mixture from coloring or sticking to the bottom of the pan. Continue until you have added about ¾ of the milk, stirring continuously.
3 Taste the sauce. If you can detect any taste of raw flour, don't increase the heat, but keep adding milk slowly. As soon as the sauce tastes properly cooked, stir in any remaining milk at once. Let the sauce cook until it reaches the required consistency, stirring frequently and making sure that it doesn't stick to the sides and bottom of the pan. Season with salt, pepper and whatever else you require.

PICKLED TURNIPS

PREPARATION TIME
14 days waiting

MAKES 2 LB PICKLES

1 lb turnips
1 raw beet
about 12 allspice berries
salt: 3 Tbsp ordinary salt or 2
    Tbsp sea salt per 1 cup [2
    Tbsp water]

All kinds of vegetables can be pickled. Cucumbers, turnips and cabbage are my favorites, and I like them in brine rather than in vinegar. It is cheaper and quicker to buy cucumbers already pickled: excellent ones pickled in brine are imported from Poland and Israel; the Israeli ones are especially small and delicate. Pickled turnips are not widely sold, but they are easy to make yourself. The turnips must be submerged all the time, but they tend to float in the brine. There are various ways of keeping them down. The first is to use a smooth, flat, well-scrubbed stone. An easier method is to clean and use a jar small enough to fit inside another jar.

1 Make sure your preserving jar [or jars] and utensils are all absolutely clean: use one of the preparations marketed for sterilizing babies' bottles or home wine-making equipment.
2 Wash and scrub the turnips, cut off the ends and halve them. If using large turnips, peel, slice and cut them into fingers. Wash, peel and slice the beet. Place the turnips in the jar, or jars, with slices of beet and whole allspice berries in between them.
3 Fill a pan with at least enough water to cover the vegetables: this will be over $1\frac{1}{2}$ cups for the quantities given here. Add the necessary amount of salt: because of its stronger flavor, you will need less sea salt than ordinary salt. Bring the brine to a boil, then let it cool for a minute or so and pour over the turnips. Press the turnips down with a smooth flat stone or a small jar of suitable size so that when the lid is on, they will be completely submerged.
4 Seal and leave in a warm place for about two weeks before using. Once opened, a jar should be refrigerated.

The beet is not necessary, but gives the pickled turnips a lovely pink color. Once you have mastered the technique described in this recipe for pickling turnips in brine, you might want to experiment with other vegetables you like.

PICKLED CAULIFLOWER Cut the cauliflower into florets and treat as above.

PICKLED CABBAGE Shred the cabbage thickly and treat as above, taking particular care to keep it all submerged.

All these pickled vegetables are very good without any further flavoring, but often a clove of garlic or a few celery leaves are added with the vegetables or brine [step 2 or 3].

PRESERVED LEMONS OR LIMES

PREPARATION TIME
2–3 minutes cooking
10–14 days waiting

8–10 lemons or limes
1 tsp salt for each fruit + one
    for the jar

Preserved lemons or limes add a sharp flavor and make a decorative addition to the 'mezze' table. Rinsed and cut into small strips, they may be added to an hors d'oeuvre dish with black olives and small cubes of feta cheese, and sprinkled with a little olive oil. They are added to a number of stews and salads, and can also be served as you would pickles or any pickled vegetable. Choose small, juicy, thin-skinned fruit. Use a large, wide-mouthed canning jar.

1 Wash and scrub the fruit thoroughly. Boil some water in a large saucepan. Use a little to rinse the preserving jar and its seal, and leave them to drain dry without wiping. Put the fruit into the boiling water for 2 to 3 minutes, then remove and plunge into cold water.
2 Sprinkle about a teaspoonful of salt over the bottom of the air-dried jar. Over a plate [to catch the juice], cut all but two of the fruit almost in quarters from one end, leaving the pieces just joined, and remove the seeds. Put a teaspoonful of salt into each fruit. Pack tightly into the jar, pressing each layer down hard before adding the next.
3 Slice one of the remaining fruits, place the slices in on top and sprinkle with a teaspoonful of salt. Squeeze the juice from the fruit and pour into the jar. Sprinkle the last teaspoonful of salt into the two squeezed halves and put them, peel upward, on top.
4 Push the jar contents down as hard as you can with a spoon to release more juice so that it covers the fruit. Then weight down to keep the fruits from floating up.
5 Set in a warm place for 10 to 14 days. The slices will be ready to use before the larger pieces. To test if they are ready, cut a piece off with a fork. If it cuts easily, rinse and taste: it should have no bitterness, but a refreshing sourness.

CONDIMENTS

Mixed condiments are often added to soups, stews and sauces. There are many different mixtures and ways of preparing them.

DO'A

Do'a is a general term which refers to various mixtures of nuts, seeds, spices or herbs, eaten with bread – either flat Arabic Bread [see page 134] or sesame-seed rings or sticks. Two recipes are given below.

Sesame Seed and Coriander Do'a This is by far my favorite. Take 1 cup 2 Tbsp sesame seeds and 4 tsp coriander seed and pick over both carefully, removing any stones or foreign bodies. Dry roast the sesame seeds, stirring constantly to avoid burning, until they are light brown, and set aside. Do the same with the coriander. In a food processor or blender, first pulverize the coriander, then add the sesame seeds. Stop as soon as the texture is sandy, or the sesame seeds will turn into paste. This would be fine if you were planning to use it right away – you could spread it on bread like peanut butter. But if you want it to keep, it must remain dry or it will go rancid. Tip the mixture into a bowl, add salt to taste, and mix well.

Every time I make this I get a slightly different result, depending mainly on the length of time I roast the ingredients. You can also add hazelnuts, or roasted peanuts, which are cheaper.

Herb Do'a This is a popular mixture: we used to buy little packages of it from street vendors to eat with sesame bread rings, and it is equally delicious with hard-boiled eggs. Simply mix salt, pepper and crushed dried mint in the proportions 1:2:3. *Za'atar* [wild thyme] is also used instead of mint; you could try it with any kind of thyme. A slice of good home-made bread moistened with olive oil and sprinkled with this *do'a* makes a splendid snack.

HARISSA

In its simplest form this hot preparation consists of chili peppers, salt and oil. You can buy Harissa canned or as a paste in tubes from Middle Eastern grocery stores, and the recipes in this book assume that you use ready-made Harissa. Any plain pepper or chili sauce can serve as an alternative. Look for these at Middle Eastern, Chinese or other ethnic food shops, or in the international section of your supermarket, but avoid using Mexican-style chili sauces containing tomatoes. It is easy to make your own Harissa, which allows you to make the flavor more interesting through the addition of extra ingredients. For plain Harissa, pound $1\frac{1}{2}$ cups dried red chili peppers with $1\frac{1}{2}$ tsp salt until reduced to a fine consistency, transfer to a jar and cover with oil. For a spicier mixture, use 1 cup 3 Tbsp dried red chili peppers, 2 cloves garlic, 1 Tbsp caraway seed and $1\frac{1}{2}$ tsp salt; pound and cover with oil as above.

TA'LEYA

This Egyptian favorite – absolutely essential for some dishes, such as Melokheya [see page 42] – is made from pounded or very finely chopped garlic fried with ground coriander and sometimes other additions. Crush 3 or 4 cloves of garlic with 1 Tbsp coriander seed. Fry gently in clarified butter or oil until the aroma develops, being careful not to burn it. Pour immediately into the dish to which it is to be added, and use a little liquid from the main dish to clean the remnants of Ta'leya from the frying pan.

T'ATBIL

This similar mixture comes from Tunisia, and invariably contains caraway seed and dried red chili peppers, as well as the other ingredients. Traditionally a large amount of T'atbil is made at once: the ingredients are pounded in a mortar, dried in the sun and sent a mill for grounding. For making small amounts of T'atbil, or any other spice mixture, at home, a spice grinder is very useful. For 3 cloves of garlic use 2 tsp each of coriander and caraway seed and 1 dried red chili pepper. The mixture can be fried, like Ta'leya, or used as it is.

A soft drink stall in Lebanon. The silver urns contain fruit syrups and juices, cold mint tea and perhaps pickle juices.

DRINKS

The Middle East produces some excellent wines, beer and a potent aniseed-flavored drink known as *ouzo, raki* or *arak*, which is usually diluted with water and served with food – olives, feta cheese or some other *mezze* dish. Since alcohol is forbidden in many areas, non-alcoholic drinks are usually served, either with or without meals. Fresh fruit juices of all kinds are among the most popular drinks. Here is a selection of my favorite non-alcoholic drinks.

COFFEE

Coffee prepared in the universal Middle Eastern way is known as Turkish coffee in the West, but exactly the same drink can be called Arabic or Greek coffee, depending on where it is served. Coffee beans are ground as fine as flour and brewed in a special, long-handled pot called *ibrik* in Turkish and *kanaka* in colloquial Egyptian. Traditionally, these were of copper or brass, often highly ornamental, but plain aluminium ones are now more usual. The size of pot to use will depend on the number of cups to be made, from one to four; it is not a good idea to make larger amounts of coffee in one pot. The quantities given here are for two tiny cupfuls of medium sweet coffee.

Turkish coffee is reputed to be over-sweet and full of muddy coffee grounds, but there is no reason why this must be the case. The coffee beans should be so finely pulverized that the powder sinks into a compact mass at the bottom of the cup. Since stirring would disturb and raise the grounds, the coffee is always sweetened to the required degree when it is made.

1 Place 2 tsp sugar with 2 coffee cupfuls water in a 2-cup *kanaka* or your narrowest small saucepan [this should almost fill it], and place on high heat to boil.
2 When the water boils, pour out about $\frac{1}{2}$ cupful and reserve. Add $3\frac{1}{2}$ tsp coffee, a spoonful at a time, stirring vigorously after addition until the spoon comes out clean. Put the pot back over medium heat and watch it closely.
3 The moment the water boils again, remove the pot from the heat and tap it gently against the side of the stove. The coffee will subside, and there will be room to pour back in the reserved $\frac{1}{2}$ cupful of water. Bring it back to a boil and tap again. By now there should be a good froth on top, and the coffee is ready to serve.

For an authentic touch, serve on a tray with the pot of coffee, two cups, two glasses of iced water and some small sweetmeats, or small saucers of jam to be eaten with a spoon. Pouring the coffee requires some care, though it gets easier with practice. First tip some of the froth into a cup with a single, quick movement, then pour the rest of the froth into another. Pour out the rest of the coffee slowly, so as to avoid spoiling the froth. The more coffee brewed at one time, the harder it is to produce enough of the hightly prized froth for everyone. Some people add a drop of cold water to the cup before drinking the coffee, which both cools it and ensures that the grounds are quite settled at the bottom. You should stop drinking before you reach them.

Spices, especially cardamom, are sometimes added to the cold water in the pot. Use a couple of cracked pods for 2 cupfuls. Arabic coffee with cardamom already added is available from Middle Eastern grocery stores.

DRIED LIME TEA

This is made with dried limes, crushed and steeped in boiling water for a few minutes. Use one dried lime per mug. I prefer it unsweetened, but most people do add sugar.

DRIED LIME AND GINGER TEA

I devised this marvelously warming drink one bitterly cold evening. Dried ginger root is better to use than ground or fresh ginger, though both these are adequate. For four mugfuls, use two dried limes and a piece of ginger root about 1 in. long, which will produce about 1 heaped teaspoonful of powder. [If using ground ginger, halve this quantity.] Mix the two in a teapot, pour in boiling water and allow to steep for a few minutes before serving. Alter the proportions to taste.

SAHLEB DRINK

This thick, cinnamon-spiced milk drink is correctly made with *sahleb* or *salep*, which can be hard to find. I have invented an acceptable alternative which I have offered to Egyptian friends who are fooled into thinking that it does contain *sahleb*. The quantities given here would make two mugfuls.

Measure out 2 mugfuls of milk, dissolve $1\frac{1}{2}$ tsp arrowroot in a couple tablespoonfuls of this milk and place in a heavy-based saucepan over medium heat. Add the rest of the milk gradually, stirring continuously. Stir in a good pinch ground cinnamon and crushed mastic. The mixture is ready when it thickens slightly. Pour into the mugs, add sugar to taste and sprinkle cinnamon and chopped hazelnuts or pistachios on top.

YOGURT DRINK

This is very refreshing and simple to prepare. Dilute natural yogurt with an equal amount of iced water [you can vary the proportion of water to taste], and add a pinch of crushed dried mint and salt to taste if you like.

ACKNOWLEDGMENTS

My first and greatest debt of gratitude is to the people who taught me to cook: my late mother and Aunt Mary; also to Ida Dolso who lived with us for some years and who first introduced me to soup with her superb minestrone (not so different from various lovely Middle Eastern soups), and who watched patiently as I took over her kitchen. I also wish to thank Lucie Farhi of Paris, who over the years acquainted me with the Syrian Jewish tradition in Egyptian cooking. She taught me to make different kinds of kibbeh, her way of using spices, and how to organize large buffet parties. Dalila and Nadja, two London friends from Algeria and Tunisia respectively, have not only introduced me to their own cuisines but have shown me how akin they are to my own. Fatima Ma'toughi, a Moroccan cook I met through friends in Paris, cooked with me for a week. She revealed all her secrets for making a perfect Pastilla and for blending herbs and spices in delicious *tajines*.

Many friends have generously provided or contributed to recipes in this book: Angèle Argi, Sonia Cohen, Vera Janković and Mireille Attas in London, Jacqueline Biancardi in Paris, Emily Amiel and Bondi Attas in Montreal, Vesna Karanović and Zagurka Cvejić in Belgrade.

I am also grateful to past students who have given me much insight into the way people read and use cookbooks, and who have shown by their enthusiasm that they appreciated my unorthodox way of teaching.

I thank Weidenfeld & Nicolson, my publishers, and Marks & Spencer for not only allowing, but even encouraging me to write this book in such a personal way.

My particular thanks go to Vicky Hayward at Weidenfeld who, from behind the scenes, encouraged, and coaxed me whenever I needed it; also to my copy editor, Ralph Hancock, whose academic knowledge and meticulousness did not deter him from accepting my idiosyncracies, and whose enthusiastic backing and advice sustained me through the most difficult periods. I also enjoy working with Lisa Collard, who cooked for the photographs. Last but not least, my grateful admiration goes to Celia Dodd, who as the editor was in the forefront of coordinating the work of many people, all pulling and pushing in different directions to produce what we all wanted to be a successful book.

American edition prepared by Debbie Loth

All food photography by Paul Bussell
Preparation of food for photography by Lisa Collard
Photographic stylist Penny Markham
Jacket, half title and black-and-white illustrations by Christopher Brown
Step-by-step illustrations by Edwina Keene
Design/Art Direction Sara Komar

Illustrations have been reproduced by kind permission of the following:

p.6 selling melons, Anne M. Holt/Sonia Halliday Photographs; p.7 nut harvest, Ingrid Rangnow/Zefa; p.8 Athenian Grocery, Jill Brown; p.9 market stall, Jill Brown; p.9 Samadi's Patisserie, Jill Brown; p.10 date harvest, G. Heil/Zefa; p.11 making coffee, Magnum; p.17 Yemenite market, Jane Taylor/Sonia Halliday Photographs; p.21 peppers drying, Robert Harding Picture Library; p.29 spice stall, Bernard Regent/Alan Hutchison Library; p.38 sacks of spices, Sybil Sasson/Robert Harding Picture Library; p.43 bread making, Liba Taylor/Alan Hutchison Library; p.46 fishing boats, Ian Berry/Magnum; p.56 vineyards and cone dwellings, Sonia Halliday Photographs; p.63 Berber market, Robert Harding Picture Library; p.70 butcher's shop, Jill Brown; p.80 legumes, nuts and seeds, Jane Taylor/Sonia Halliday Photographs; p.86 vegetable stall, Jill Brown/MEPhA; p.105 rice fields, Desmond Harvey/Robert Harding Picture Library; p.107 harvesting wheat, Middle East Pictures and Publicity; p.113 Turkish wheat harvest, Richard Ashworth/Robert Harding Picture Library; p.117 orange market, Sonia Halliday Photographs; p.120 market stall with dates, Gemma Levine; p.124 trays of cakes, Christina Gascoigne/Robert Harding Picture Library; p.132 baker's window, Jill Brown; p.135 village oven, Middle East Pictures and Publicity; p.143 fruit stall, Middle East Pictures and Publicity.

BIBLIOGRAPHY

Anthony, Dawn, Elaine and Lewis, *Lebanese Cookbook*, Lansdowne Press, Sydney, 1978

Bennani-Smires, Latifa, *La Cuisine marocaine*, Société d'Édition et de Diffusion al-Madariss, Casablanca, 1978

Bouayed, Fatima Zohra, *La Cuisine algérienne*, Société nationale d'Édition et de Diffusion, Algiers, n.d.

Bouksani, Mme, *Gastronomie algérienne*, Jefal, n.p., 1982

Boxer, Arabella, *Mediterranean Cook Book*, Biblio Distribution Centre, Totowa, NJ, 1982

Boxer, Arabella, *The Sunday Times Complete Cookbook*, Weidenfeld & Nicolson, London, 1983

Boxer, Arabella and Beck, Philippa, *The Herb Book*, Octopus, London, 1980

Corey, Helen, *The Art of Syrian Cookery*, Doubleday, New York, 1962

David, Elizabeth, *English Bread and Yeast Cookery*, Penguin Books, Inc., New York, 1982

David, Elizabeth, *Mediterranean Food*, (rev.ed.), Penguin Books, Inc., New York, 1965

David, Elizabeth, *Spices, Salt and Aromatics in the English Kitchen*, Penguin Books, Inc., New York, 1981

Davidson, Alan, *Mediterranean Seafood*, Louisiana State University Press, Baton Rouge, LA, 1981

Day, Irene F., *The Moroccan Cookbook*, The Putnam Publishing Group, New York, 1978

Grigson, Jane, *Fish Cookery*, Penguin, London, 1975

Howe, Robin, *Middle Eastern Cookery*, Eyre Methuen, London, 1978

Imy, Daisy, *The Best of Baghdad Cooking, with Treats from Teheran*, Saturday Review Press/Dutton, New York, 1976

Karsenty, Irène and Lucienne, *Cuisine pied-noir* (Cuisines du terrior series), Denoël, Paris, 1974

Kaak, Zeineb, *L'art de prépaper la véritable cuisine tunisienne*, Société tunisienne de Diffusion, Tunis, 1976

Khalil, Nagwa E., *Egyptian Cuisine*, Three Continents Press, Washington, D.C., 1980

Khawam, René R., *La Cuisine arabe*, Albin Michel, Paris, 1970

Kouki, Mohamed, *La Cuisine tunisienne*, Maison tunisienne de l'Édition, Tunis, 1971

Lamb, Venice, *The Home Book of Turkish Cookery*, Faber & Faber, London, 1973

Mallos, Tess, *The Complete Middle East Cookbook*, McGraw-Hill, Inc., New York, 1980

Mallos, Tess, *Fillo Pastry Cookbook*, Reed, Wellington, 1983

Mallos, Tess, *Greek Cookbook*, Lansdowne, Sydney, 1976

Macmiadhacháin, Anna; Reynolds, Mary; Roden, Claudia and Rubinstein, Helge, *The Mediterranean Cookbook*, Lyrics Books, London, 1979

Mark, Theonie, *Greek Islands Cooking*, Batsford, London, 1978

Mazda, Maideh, *In a Persian Kitchen*, Charles E. Tuttle, Company Inc., Rutland, VT. 1960

Nicalaou, Nearchos, *Cooking from Cyprus, the Island of Aphrodite*, published by author, Nicosia, 1979

Paradisis, Chrissa, *The Best Book of Greek Cookery*, International Publications Service, New York, 1981

Roden, Claudia, *A Book of Middle Eastern Food*, Alfred A. Knopf, Inc., New York, 1972

Salaman, Rena, *Greek Food*, Fontana, London, 1983

Sekelli, Z., *L'art culinaire à travers l'Algérie*, Société nationale d'Édition et de Diffusion, Algiers, n.d.

Shasheer, Jameela, *Arab World Cook Book*, International Bookshop, Dubai, 1973

Sitas, Amaranth, *Kopiaste*, published by author, Limassol, 1974

Sklavunu, Maria N., *Exciting Greek Dishes*, Artemis, Athens, 1976

Smouha, Patricia, *Middle Eastern Cooking*, André Deutsch, London, 1955

Stobart, Tom, *The Cook's Encyclopaedia*, Harper & Row, New York

Time-Life Books, Editors of, *Fish and Shellfish* (The Good Cook series), Time-Life Books, Inc., Alexandria, VA, 1979

Wolfert, Paula, *Couscous and Other Good Food from Morocco*, Harper & Row, New York, 1973

Wolfert, Paula, *Mediterranean Cooking*, Times Books, New York, 1982

INDEX

A Tunisian fruit stall: fresh fruit is varied and abundant in the Middle East